Postwar Japan

Postwar Japan

Growth, Security,
and Uncertainty since 1945

Editors
Michael J. Green
Zack Cooper

CSIS | CENTER FOR STRATEGIC &
INTERNATIONAL STUDIES

ROWMAN & LITTLEFIELD
Lanham • Boulder • New York • London

Center for Strategic & International Studies
1616 Rhode Island Avenue, NW
Washington, DC 20036
202-887-0200 | www.csis.org

Published by Rowman & Littlefield
A wholly owned subsidiary of The Rowman & Littlefield Publishing
Group, Inc.
4501 Forbes Boulevard, Suite 200, Lanham, MD 20706
www.rowman.com

Unit A, Whitacre Mews, 26-34 Stannary Street, London SE11 4AB

ISBN: 978-1-4422-7973-5 (cloth alk. paper)
ISBN: 978-1-4422-7974-2 (paperback)
ISBN: 978-1-4422-7975-9 (electronic)

The paper used in this publication meets the minimum requirements of
American National Standard for Information Sciences—Permanence of
Paper for Printed Library Materials, ANSI/NISO Z39.48-1992.

Printed in the United States of America

Contents

INTRODUCTION

Michael J. Green

The Japan Chair at the Center for Strategic and International Studies (CSIS) has identified the development of human capital in the U.S.-Japan alliance as a central goal for the Center as a whole. Under that aegis, and with the support of the government of Japan, CSIS has for the past three years invited leading scholars and policy analysts from Japan to spend two weeks in Washington, D.C., where each worked with Dr. Zack Cooper to develop a strategic paper in consultation with counterparts at CSIS and in the U.S. government, the Congress, and the academic community. The collected papers are then reviewed and edited as an annual volume that spotlights emerging Japanese thinking on key security and economic issues facing our alliance. For their dedication to this effort, Nick Szechenyi and Eri Hirano deserve great credit, as well as Jake Douglas, who spent countless hours reviewing the final product.

In 2015 and 2016, CSIS invited distinguished Japanese scholars to reflect on the evolution of Japanese foreign, defense, and economic policy in the 70 years since the end of World War II and to draw some lessons for the coming decade. Several broad themes knit their respective chapters together. First, the pillars of Japan's reentry into the international community since 1945 remain no less important seven decades later: alliance with the United States; engagement with Asia; leadership in the United Nations (UN) system and other multilateral institutions; reliance on economic strength over military might; and expanding contributions to economic development in other countries. Second, however, Japan must make harder decisions about choices and priorities in each of these areas as China's power grows and Japan's own economy and society enter a more mature phase. Japan's Cold War preference for avoiding risky entanglement in U.S. military strategy in Asia is now a liability as Japan itself has moved from the safer rear area to the front line of potential conflicts involving ballistic missiles and maritime threats to Japan's own home waters and islands. Japan's strategic relations across Asia are expanding, yet hampered in key countries like South Korea by continuing historical animosities. Multilateral diplomacy has become more complex as institutions and membership have grown and Beijing has learned to use proxies in Southeast Asia to block consensus on controversial issues, such as the South China Sea. Japan's economy has pockets of unique strength, but will not grow sufficiently until policies are implemented to unlock the potential of women, entrepreneurs, and foreign workers and investors. Japan's generous official development assistance must now compete with new Chinese institutions and alternate rules for transparency and governance. The six chapters in this volume demonstrate the continuing viability of Japan's postwar strategic choices but also the inevitability of adaption to challenging new circumstances.

Part I of this volume features two chapters on Japan's postwar security policies. In the first chapter, diplomatic historian Kazuya Sakamoto of Osaka University argues that a strengthened U.S.-Japan alliance must be the centerpiece of a more just and liberal world order. Professor Sakamoto is one of the leading protégés of Professor Masataka Kosaka of Kyoto University, who is Japan's most prominent postwar realist scholar of international relations. Kosaka had enormous influence with conservative pro-alliance politicians in the ruling Liberal Democratic Party (LDP), but his views were not openly embraced by the so-called mainstream factions of the LDP that preferred a more careful relationship with the United States in order to reduce risk of entrapment in U.S. Cold War strategies and give Japan greater freedom of maneuver in Asia. Professor Sakamoto's application of Kosaka's logic to the contemporary international security environment is compelling and reflects the current mainstream thinking in the LDP and the Japanese government. Sakamoto welcomes the evolution of the U.S.-Japan alliance toward accepting an explicit role in regional security (operationally and not just in terms of hosting U.S. bases in Japan). He focuses in particular on Prime Minister Shinzo Abe's decision to revise bilateral U.S-Japan defense guidelines and Japan's own postwar prohibition on the "exercise of collective self-defense" in order to make U.S. and Japanese forces more joint and interoperable—and inseparable in the event of regional crises. His argument is much broader than military strategy, however, focusing on the necessity for Japan to move beyond its earlier hesitance and clearly join what was once called the West in order to stand up for the very liberal international order that Japan itself benefited from over the past 70 years.

Professor Yoshihide Soeya of Keio University offers a rich history of Japan's postwar diplomatic recovery in East Asia and calls for a more balanced approach between great power realism and cooperative diplomacy within Asia. Where Professor Kosaka represents the intellectual tradition of realism in Japan, Professor Soeya is a leading strategic voice for liberal internationalism. Soeya does not refute the need for closer security cooperation with the United States, but worries that Japan's strategic competition with China has blinded Japanese policymakers to the importance of other relationships in Asia—particularly with the Republic of Korea, a like-minded democracy that remains highly sensitive to changes in Japanese security policy. One might read in the Sakamoto and Soeya chapters two divergent views of Japanese grand strategy, but in fact these two prominent scholars demonstrate the degree to which realism and liberal internationalism have converged in post–Cold War Japan. Few leading scholars in Japan posit a binary choice between the United States and Asia as was once fashionable in the halls of universities and Japan's Diet. The reality of security challenges in Asia has caused such a false dichotomy to ring hollow—as Prime Minister Yukio Hatoyama found in 2009 when he anachronistically called for the formation of a new East Asia Community without the United States. The most influential strategic minds in Japan, whether coming from liberal internationalist or conservative realist roots, are calling for a strong alliance with the United States *and* expanding relationships within the Indo-Pacific region. Indeed, the U.S. strategic debate about the alliance with Japan has narrowed in similar ways. Still, while consensus grows about the ends of alliance strategy, the Sakamoto and Soeya chapters demonstrate that there is still considerable room for debate about the *ways* and *means* of that strategy.

Part II focuses on Japan's postwar economic policies. Veteran economic official and scholar Jun Saito opens with an assessment of how Japan's economic policy and its relationship with the United States evolved in an historical and global context. He explains how Japan's postwar recovery depended on the United States and then increasingly on expansion within Asian markets, leading by the 1970s and 1980s to intense trade friction with Washington. With the subsequent collapse of Japan's bubble economy in the 1990s, however, Japan and the United States steadily converged because the steps Japan needed to take to restore growth were in precisely the areas that had been closed and caused friction with the United States in the past. These areas included greater opening to goods, services, and capital; accepting foreign workers; liberalizing through free trade agreements; and expanding economic partnership agreements.

Economist Yoko Takeda picks up the story by assessing the reasons for Japan's economic stagnation, including a declining population, lack of entrepreneurship, a decaying education system, rigid labor markets, underdeveloped secondary markets, and continuing obstacles to foreign direct investment. Takeda's chapter offers a harsher critique of Japan's economy than Saito's, but also suggests detailed steps that Japan can take to create a more liquid labor market, diverse society, and innovative private sector. As with the chapters on security policy, the economic chapters demonstrate growing consensus about what strategies are necessary for Japan, but in some respects the economic mission appears more daunting. Where external threats have sharpened the debate on changes necessary in a handful of defense bills and diplomatic policies, the stagnant economy requires reform across multiple jurisdictions with immediate repercussions for powerful interest groups. Abenomics, and particularly Japan's participation in the Trans-Pacific Partnership (TPP), represent an unprecedented level of reform and opening in Japan's postwar history—but the question remains whether these steps go far enough.

Part III of this volume examines Japan's growing leadership in multilateralism and development assistance in the postwar era. Professor Akiko Fukushima of Aoyama Gakuin University explains the powerful motivation for Japan to establish itself as a legitimate citizen of the international community after World War II, noting that in many respects liberal internationalists were seeking to return Japan to the prestige-driven multilateralism that had preceded Japan's precipitous descent into militarism. She explains how successful Japan was in returning to a central role in the United Nations system and in designing and supporting multilateral institution-building in Asia. Japan often exerted influence deferentially by leading from behind, as other states hosted meetings and established new forums. The challenge, as Fukushima notes, was once how to bridge aspirations for pan-Asianism within the region and the strategic necessity of a trans-Pacific architecture resting on the U.S.-Japan alliance and the U.S. economy. Now a new challenge has emerged: the tension *within* Asia between universalism, represented by Japan and other democracies, and pan-Asianism, which is championed by China. Rather than being discouraged about this growing contestation in Asia's crowded multilateral environment, Fukushima argues that Japan must recalibrate its approach to work more closely with like-minded states while continuing to build inclusive regional institutions.

Finally, Akiko Imai gives an example of how this new approach might work with respect to Japan's strategy for official development assistance. She considers the feasibility of active cooperation between Japan and the United States in the provision of development assistance in Asia, arguing that addressing social issues based on a horizontal division of labor, with the involvement of the business community and civil sector in both countries, could advance regional human dignity and quality growth. This broad-based, cross-sector approach would strengthen the Japan-U.S. alliance and enhance Japan's soft power projection in Asia. Imai's contribution is an example of how decreasing relative resources and growing competition from China are forcing Japan to think of smarter uses for foreign aid, including greater collaboration with other donors in the private sector and abroad.

It is our hope that these chapters will provide a unique scholarly take on Japan's postwar history; illuminate new thinking in Japanese foreign, economic, and security strategies; and enhance networks across the Pacific as the United States and Japan increasingly face these common challenges together.

Part I. JAPAN'S POSTWAR SECURITY POLICIES

1. WHAT IS THE STRENGTHENED JAPAN-U.S. ALLIANCE FOR? DEFENDING AND ADVANCING THE LIBERAL WORLD ORDER

Kazuya Sakamoto

INTRODUCTION

Since returning to office in December 2012, Prime Minister Shinzo Abe has made serious efforts to strengthen the Japan-U.S. alliance. His efforts include setting up a Japanese National Security Council to discuss security matters more closely with U.S. counterparts; introducing a stricter state secrets law, which is indispensable for the reliable exchange of military information with the United States and other strategic friends; revising Japan's military export controls, which had been too strict for the maintenance of a healthy defense industry; turning the tide of declining defense expenditure and actually starting to increase it, though still not by a great amount; and promoting a four-power "Security Diamond" framework in the Indo-Pacific by bolstering security relationships among the Japan-U.S. alliance, Australia, and India.

Most importantly, Prime Minister Abe and his administration in 2015 finally succeeded in revising the legal frameworks for Japan's security policies, making Japan legally more prepared than before to defend itself and to contribute to world peace. Coupled with the Guidelines for Japan-U.S. Defense Cooperation, also revised in 2015, the new frameworks will substantially enhance the mutuality of the

Japan-U.S. alliance, enabling much more solid and effective security cooperation.[1]

In this chapter I first examine the historical significance of the new legal frameworks for Japan's security policies with respect to the development of the Japan-U.S. alliance. Then I discuss how Japan and the United States should further develop the alliance, not only as regional but also as global partners. Regarding this point, I remind readers of the importance of Article 2 of the 1951 Security Treaty between Japan and the United States, commonly referred to simply as the Japan-U.S. security treaty.[2]

DEVELOPMENT OF MUTUALITY IN
JAPAN-U.S. SECURITY COOPERATION

> I'm told there's a phrase in Japanese culture that speaks to the spirit that brings us together today. It's an idea rooted in loyalty. It's an expression of mutuality, respect, and shared obligation. It transcends any specific moment or challenge. It's the foundation of a relationship that endures. It's what allows us to say that the United States and Japan stand together. Otagaino-tame-ni—with and for each other.[3]

President Barack Obama described the essence of the Japan-U.S. alliance at a joint press conference held at the White House after his summit conference with Japanese prime minister Shinzo Abe. The day before the press conference, Japan and the United States announced the introduction of the newly revised Guidelines for Japan-U.S. Defense Cooperation, which with Japan's new legal frameworks for security will substantially deepen and widen alliance cooperation. The Japanese phrase *otagaino-tame-ni* coming from the president of the United States symbolizes the evolution of the Japan-U.S. alliance and signals the beginning of a new stage in the relationship. Responding to the president, Prime Minister Abe declared, "Today, we turned a new page in the history of the Japan-U.S. alliance."[4]

For some 65 years, Japan-U.S. security cooperation has been moving in the direction of becoming more mutual, or *otagaino-*

tame-ni. When Japan made peace with the United States after World War II in the 1951 San Francisco Peace Treaty, Japanese prime minister Shigeru Yoshida believed that an alignment with the United States would bring peace and prosperity to postwar Japan. The U.S. government likewise judged that Japan would be a strategic asset of great value for the United States as it fought the Cold War to defend the liberal world and maintain its hegemonic position in the Pacific (the United States was fighting the Korean War at the time). Thus did the two nations begin their postwar security cooperation, lasting to the present day.

At the center of this alignment has been the Japan-U.S. security treaty, on which the alliance has been built. The treaty was signed just hours after the conclusion of the San Francisco Peace Treaty. Actually these two treaties were twin treaties for the United States' postwar settlement with Japan. With 48 nations, including the United States as signatories, the peace treaty gave Japan peace with honor. This treaty, for instance, did not have any clauses concerning war guilt or demands for heavy reparations. It was a generous peace treaty of "reconciliation and trust," as U.S. ambassador John Foster Dulles called it.[5]

The security treaty, on the other hand, gave Japan security but not much honor. The treaty was not formulated as a mutual treaty between sovereign equals. It was formulated as a treaty with which the United States would unilaterally protect a demilitarized and helpless Japan. It accorded the United States broad, unilateral basing rights in Japan for that purpose and also for "the maintenance of international peace and security in the Far East," but it did not formally oblige the United States to defend Japan. Japan had to rely on hope alone that the United States would actually use its forces in Japan for its defense.

As the preamble states, the security treaty was a "provisional arrangement" for Japan's defense, and it was considered from the outset to be a transitional treaty, which Japan would wish to revise under appropriate circumstances. In Japan, more and more criticism was heard against the treaty as Japan recovered politically and economically from the war, not just from socialists on the left but also from conservatives on the right. Meanwhile Japan created the Self-Defense Forces (SDF), which was an indispensable precondition for concluding a mutual defense arrangement with the United States.

In 1960, Prime Minister Nobusuke Kishi, grandfather of Shinzo Abe, worked with Ambassador Douglas MacArthur II, nephew of the famous General Douglas MacArthur, and succeeded in obtaining a treaty revision. The revision was meant to provide the security treaty with much needed mutuality to make it appropriate for sovereign equals and to put the alliance on a solid, long-term footing. To that end, the official name was changed from Security Treaty between Japan and the United States of America to Treaty of Mutual Cooperation and Security between Japan and the United States of America. The "mutual cooperation" phrase meant a lot for the bilateral security alignment. Prime Minister Kishi wanted to make Japan's security relations with the United States "close and equal." Ambassador MacArthur on the other hand wanted the United States' relations with Japan to be "reliable and sustainable." Both agreed that the mutuality of the security treaty must be developed for this purpose.[6]

The revised treaty was now formulated as Japan and the United States cooperating for the mutual purpose of maintaining "international peace and security in the Far East." Thus the revision gave the treaty two factors of mutuality: mutual purpose and mutual cooperation.[7]

It took some time, however, before a real sense of mutuality started to develop from this revision, though it was now clearer than before that the treaty is beneficial both to Japan and to the United States. For one thing, in the Cold War the defense of Japan itself had an aspect of mutuality—for example, the defense of Hokkaido would have the effect of checking the Soviet Pacific fleet from moving toward the United States. Therefore, the mutual purpose written into the new treaty did not need to be overly stressed.

More importantly, the forms of mutual cooperation in the treaty have their own limitations in cultivating a real sense of mutuality. There are two forms of mutual defense cooperation in the Japan-U.S.

security treaty. One is cooperation in which Japan rents military bases to the United States, and the United States stations U.S. troops in Japan. Article 6 of the security treaty states: "For the purpose of contributing to the security of Japan and the maintenance of international peace and security in the Far East, the United States of America is granted the use by its land, air and naval forces of facilities and areas in Japan."

The other is cooperation in which the SDF and U.S. armed forces in Japan jointly respond to armed attacks on Japan and the United States. The treaty prescribes in Article 5: "Each Party recognizes that an armed attack against either Party in the territories under the administration of Japan would be dangerous to its own peace and safety and declares that it would act to meet the common danger in accordance with its constitutional provisions and processes." We may call the former cooperation between goods and people (military bases and U.S. forces) and the latter cooperation between people and people (SDF and U.S. forces).

Both of these are reciprocal forms of cooperation. However, observers have long pointed out the shortcomings in terms of mutuality in both forms of cooperation. A shortcoming in the goods and people cooperation is a tendency for it to produce dissatisfaction for both Japan and the United States. Concerns rise to the surface periodically about whether the risks and burdens are fair because the mutuality is asymmetric. It may happen that the side providing people will not really respect the side that does not bear the risks, while the side supplying goods will not appreciate the side that does not really understand the inconvenience and other costs. Left untended, these shortcomings pose a risk to the psychological foundations of the alliance.

A different flaw found in the people and people cooperation is the extremely severe restrictions on what the SDF could do in terms of defense cooperation under the Japanese government's traditional interpretation of its constitution. According to this view, Japan's SDF could exercise the right of self-defense to the minimum amount necessary but could not exercise the right of collective self-defense to help the United States. Thus the area of mutual defense has been limited to only "the territories under the administration of Japan." So, in fact, Japan's contribution to the defense of the United States is just its contribution to the defense of U.S. armed forces in Japan. Moreover, up until 1972 this obligation did not include the defense of Okinawa, and until 1978 Japan and the United States had no official, well-coordinated plan for even the mutual defense of that narrow area. The Japanese and U.S. governments have tried hard to rectify these shortcomings through many efforts, including the return of Okinawa administrative rights to Japan in 1972. We may safely say that the history of the development of the Japan-U.S. alliance is the history of efforts to enhance the mutuality of the alliance by tackling these shortcomings in the security treaty.

The two governments have attempted to correct the former shortcomings mainly through the consolidation and downsizing of U.S. military bases in Japan; cooperation to relocate U.S. forces outside Japan in step with changes in the regional and global strategic environment; the improvement in the application of the Japan-U.S. status of forces agreement to various problems relating to U.S. bases; and the introduction of the so-called sympathy budget, which obliges the Japanese government to bear part of the expenses the United States requires for maintaining armed forces in Japan. Of the total cost of stationing U.S. forces in Japan (excluding U.S. military pay), about 70 percent is now paid by the Japanese government.

Regarding the latter form of shortcoming, Japan and the United States drew up the first Guidelines for Japan-U.S. Defense Cooperation in 1978 as a bilateral arrangement that supplemented the rights, obligations, and relations prescribed in the security treaty. The first guidelines gave substance to defense cooperation, setting basic rules for responses in the event of an armed attack against Japan (and against U.S. armed forces in Japan). According to the new rules, the SDF would serve as the shield for defensive operations, whereas U.S. forces would be the spear for counteroffensive operations in defending Japan and U.S. forces in Japan.

In the Cold War, when a total war between the United States and the Soviet Union was conceivable, the strategic value of cooperating to defend Japan and U.S. forces in Japan was obvious, and it was not difficult to see mutuality in the cooperation. The demise of the Soviet Union, however, made the alliance's mutual purpose less clear. It made both governments worry that the Japan-U.S. alliance might drift after losing its main enemy, even though there were a couple of security questions of Cold War origin left in the Far East (Korea and Taiwan). That is why the two governments issued a joint declaration in 1996 to reaffirm the essence of mutual purpose in alliance cooperation—namely, ensuring "peace and security in the Asia-Pacific region"—and also revised the guidelines in 1997.[8]

The 1997 guidelines widened the scope of defense cooperation to make the SDF and U.S. armed forces cooperate even outside Japan on the high seas and international airspace around Japan. They would now jointly cope with "situations in areas surrounding Japan" that if left unchecked could have a grave influence on Japan. Japan introduced a new national security law (Act on Measures to Ensure the Peace and Security of Japan in Perilous Situations in Areas Surrounding Japan) to deal with such contingencies. In these situations, the SDF was still not able to use force to help defend U.S. forces, but it was now able to perform some limited rear area support. It was a small but important step for Japan to enlarge people to people cooperation outside "the territories under the administration of Japan."

After the attacks of September 11, 2001, the Japanese government introduced a special temporary law emulating the national security law mentioned above and dispatched SDF vessels to the Indian Ocean to help refuel U.S. warships engaged in the War in Afghanistan. It was not Japan but the United States that had been attacked from outside the geographical scope of the security treaty. Japan did whatever it could legally do outside Japan (also outside the Far East) to help U.S. forces fight a war of self-defense. That clearly showed how much the efforts of both governments to enhance the mutuality of the alliance had been successful by the beginning of the twenty-first century and the 50th year anniversary of the original security treaty.

SIGNIFICANCE OF JAPAN'S NEW SECURITY LAWS
AND THE NEW GUIDELINES

Less than 10 years after 9/11, however, the rapid military rise of China and North Korea's nuclear development pushed Japan and the United States toward more efforts to strengthen defense cooperation. Japan's new security laws (Heiwa Anzen Hosei) and the 2015 Guidelines for Japan-U.S. Defense Cooperation are the results of several years of such efforts. Under these new frameworks, Japan and the United States can now significantly expand people and people cooperation.

First, the 2015 guidelines stress the global nature of Japan-U.S. security cooperation, stating that it can "provide a foundation for peace, security, stability, and economic prosperity in the Asia-Pacific region *and beyond* [emphasis added]." The 2015 guidelines expand the geographical scope of the alliance from the Asia Pacific to the world at large. This makes it clearer that the alliance is not only for the defense of Japan but also for the United States and its global strategy.

In step with this expanded perspective, Japan's new security laws replaced the security concept of "situations in areas surrounding Japan" with the new concept of "important influence situations." Both are situations that if left unchecked will have a serious influence on Japan's security, but the former are limited to those in the areas surrounding Japan. Now that this limit has been removed, the SDF may provide such rear area support to U.S. forces as was done in the war in Afghanistan without waiting for the enactment of any extraordinary law. Also the new laws increased the range of rear area support missions to include, for instance, the SDF providing U.S. forces with ammunition, which had been forbidden under previous law.

Second, under the 2015 guidelines and the new interpretation of Japan's constitution,[9] the SDF may use force to help defend U.S. armed forces outside Japan, albeit in a limited way. In the past, the Japanese government interpreted Article 9 of Japan's constitution as completely prohibiting Japan from exercising the right of collective self-defense, even though this right is enshrined in the UN

Charter and in fact is the legal basis of postwar alliances like the North Atlantic Treaty Organization (NATO) and the Japan-U.S. alliance. Thus in the past, the SDF was able to use force to defend U.S. armed forces only when actions took place inside Japan by appealing to the right of individual self-defense.

However, with the new interpretation and the new security laws, Japan can now use force

> not only when an armed attack against Japan has occurred, but also when an armed attack against a foreign country that is in a close relationship with Japan occurs and as a result threatens Japan's survival and poses a clear danger to fundamentally overturn people's right to life, liberty and pursuit of happiness.[10]

That Japan can now exercise the right of collective self-defense—long the desire of many experts who would like to make Japan a close and equal alliance partner with the United States—is a great change for the better regarding the mutuality of defense cooperation. In the previous government interpretation, this lack of mutuality was always a danger to the spiritual underpinnings of the alliance. For instance, the Japanese government, if asked, might have to make an absurd explanation about the interpretation, for example: if a U.S. naval vessel is attacked in service of the alliance within Japan's territorial waters, the SDF may use force to help the vessel by invoking the right of individual self-defense; if, however, the vessel is say 100 meters outside of Japan's territorial waters, the SDF may not be able to help because the Japanese government interprets Article 9 of the constitution as prohibiting the use of the right of collective self-defense in any circumstances, even if the U.S. vessel is defending Japan.

As is well known, Japan's use of the right of collective self-defense is still limited. Japan may use force to help defend U.S. armed forces outside Japan only when an attack against them "threatens Japan's survival and poses a clear danger to fundamentally overturn people's right to life, liberty, and pursuit of happiness." Moreover, the Japanese government still keeps its traditional interpretation of the constitution that Japan in general cannot send the SDF to the foreign territories for the purpose of using force. So in essence, Japan can use force only in Japan and on and above the high seas. This interpretation is in harmony with Japan's Upper House resolution of 1954, which forbids sending the SDF overseas.

We may argue that a limited use is far better than no use because the important point is deterrence, not the actual use of the right of the collective self-defense, which will only rarely be necessary. NATO has invoked the right only once in some 50 years. Still, it may not be enough for the daily activities of mutual defense in areas outside Japan.

Therefore, the 2015 guidelines introduced the idea of asset protection. The SDF will use weapons, not force per se, to protect U.S. assets like aircraft and naval vessels as if they were the SDF's own military assets. Use of weapons will be restricted to limited and proportional employment—not for armed conflict, but for lawful self-defense and lawful performance of one's duty. Firing warning shots against the violation of territorial airspace is an example. If the other side should start firing, the SDF may fire back proportionally. This asset protection will be done even if the situation does not threaten Japan's very survival or the fundamental rights of the Japanese people. Coupled with the possibility of using the right of collective self-defense, this idea of asset protection will enable the SDF and U.S. armed forces to perform security cooperation much more effectively outside Japan.

Third, the 2015 guidelines announced the establishment of a new standing alliance coordination mechanism for the Japan-U.S. alliance. This is an improvement over previous ad hoc arrangements. Close communications and consultations between the SDF and U.S. armed forces before something happens instead of after are essential for effective security cooperation. This mechanism is something the Japan-U.S. alliance should have had a long time ago.

Together, these changes have made significant progress in enhancing the mutuality of defense cooperation in the Japan-U.S. alliance. Turning "a new page in the history of the alliance" seems not to be an exaggeration.[11]

DEEPENING AND WIDENING THE PURPOSE
OF ALLIANCE COOPERATION

Japan and the United States must keep up their efforts to strengthen defense cooperation through enhancing mutuality, all the more so because the security environment in the Asia Pacific is increasingly precarious. North Korea's nuclear development and China's adventurism in the East and South China Seas are serious concerns. Japan, for example, needs to increase its defense expenditures, and the United States should give more substance to its rebalancing to the Asia Pacific. Japan should help the Philippines and Vietnam build up their maritime police forces. The United States should also continue conducting freedom of navigation (FON) operations in South China Sea.

The two allies should cooperate to put enough political and economic pressure on North Korea and should further their missile defense cooperation to counter the country's nuclear threat to the region. Regarding this point, the importance of close cooperation with South Korea is clear. The two allies also should not forget that one of their important strategic objectives is to encourage "the peaceful resolution of issues concerning the Taiwan Strait" through dialogue.[12] Chinese aggressive activities in the East and South China Seas make it essential for Japan and the United States to pay much more attention to this objective.[13]

Meanwhile, the two nations should also try to strengthen the alliance through enhancing the mutual purpose of the security treaty—namely, maintaining "the international peace and security of the Far East." There are two ways to do this.

One is to make it clearer what kind of Far East (or Asia Pacific) that Japan and the United States would like to see in the future. This is important because good security policy involves not only countering particular threats in given circumstances but also striving to build an environment that is non- or less threatening. Regarding this, we need to keep in mind Article 2 of the security treaty, which stipulates:

> The Parties will contribute toward the further development of peaceful and friendly international relations by strengthening their free institutions, by bringing about a better understanding of the principles upon which these institutions are founded, and by promoting conditions of stability and well-being. They will seek to eliminate conflict in their international economic policies and will encourage economic collaboration between them.

Coupled with the preface of the treaty, in which Japan and the United States express a mutual desire to "uphold the principles of democracy, individual liberty, and the rule of law," this article obligates the two nations to jointly contribute to "the further development of peaceful and friendly international relations" through the political and economic means of "free institutions." Neither nation should forget this obligation when they develop their security policies in the Asia-Pacific region. Their recent efforts to fashion a multilateral trade agreement in the region through the vehicle of the Trans-Pacific Partnership (TPP) may be better understood in terms of this alliance commitment.

Another way to enhance the mutual purpose of the alliance is to make sure that efforts to ensure security in the Asia Pacific are closely related to those to build security at a global level. The eventual success of the alliance depends on whether it can be a valuable asset not only for the region but also for the world. In this regard we should look at the current situation of the alliance from a broader perspective: the threats the Japan-U.S. alliance is facing are part and parcel of the threats facing the liberal world order, which is based on international law and universal values like freedom, democracy, rule of law, and basic human rights. Russian military adventurism in Ukraine and the Chinese military buildup in the South China Sea are cut from the same cloth in that they both threaten this order.

Those nations that support the liberal world order should unite and act cooperatively as much as possible to strengthen the order and counter threats to it. On this point it is important to note that Article 2 of the NATO treaty is almost identical to Article 2 of the Japan-U.S. security treaty. Through these commitments and as mutual allies of the United States, Japan and the major nations of Europe are partners in the defense and advancement of this order.

How helpful is the Japan-U.S. alliance for defending and advancing the liberal world order? Politically, the very existence of the alliance—an alliance between nations with different histories, cultures, and ethnic makeups—is proof that the values of the liberal world order are not just Western but can truly be universal. It helps make the order more appealing to people throughout the world. We should remember that an imperative for successfully defending and advancing the liberal world order is to include as many nations as possible within it.

Economically, the alliance is between nations with the first and third largest economies in the world. It thus cannot be unhelpful to the order. For example, Japan provided the International Monetary Fund (IMF), one of the economic pillars of the liberal world order, with a loan of $100 billion to bolster IMF's lending capacity in the middle of the Lehman Brothers shock in 2008.

Militarily, the alliance is one of the most important assets for the defense of the liberal world order. This very much depends on the control of the world seas, which occupy 70 percent of the globe and through which 90 percent of world trade passes. The area in which the Japan-U.S. alliance has security interests covers one of the most strategically important seas in the world, the South China Sea, which connects the Pacific and Indian Oceans. The alliance provides the U.S. Navy with essential naval bases from which to project power over the world seas, along with some 30 allied and friendly navies. In addition, Japan's new security laws and the 2015 guidelines heighten the capabilities of the alliance to cooperate on the high seas throughout the world, which is very important for a maritime alliance such as the one between Japan and the United States.

In sum, discussions on the Japan-U.S. security treaty will need to spend much more time than before on cooperating to defend and advance the liberal world order, in particular by paying appropriate attention to the stipulations of Article 2.[14]

CONCLUSION

At the April 2015 joint press conference, President Obama said that Japan and the United States are "not just allies" but also "true global partners." The president's words suggest how the two nations should develop the alliance in the future. For more than 60 years, both nations have made many efforts to enhance the mutuality of defense cooperation and become true allies in the Asia-Pacific region. The recent efforts embodied in Japan's new security laws and the 2015 guidelines will surely strengthen the bonds and effectiveness of the alliance to a level not previously experienced.

While continuing those efforts, Japan and United States should, from now on, make more effort to enhance the mutual purpose of the alliance. It should be deepened. This alliance cooperation must include efforts to make the Asia-Pacific region more favorable to such values as liberty, democracy, rule of law, and basic human rights. Security in the long term very much depends on those values. The alliance should also be widened. We must not forget that global peace and security are indivisible. Japan-U.S. alliance cooperation must be made to help the defense and advancement of the world order, which is based on both countries' shared values.

Only by enhancing the mutual purpose of the alliance in these ways do Japan and the United States deserve to be called true global partners as well as true allies in the Asia Pacific. In all, after turning this new page the Japan-U.S. alliance must work hard not just for the region but also the world, defending and advancing the liberal world order with all the means at its disposal.

NOTES

1. Japan Ministry of Defense, "The Guidelines for Japan-U.S. Defense Cooperation," April 27, 2015, http://www.mod.go.jp/e/d_act/anpo/shishin_20150427e.html. Also in 2015, Prime Minister Shinzo Abe had an important political achievement, which will indirectly but nevertheless substantially help the development of Japan's security policies including strengthening the Japan-U.S. alliance. His success in issuing a well-thought-out and largely popular government statement (called Abe Danwa) explains how the Japanese government has dealt and will deal with the history questions of World War II. Issued on the 70th year anniversary of the end of the war, the statement seems to have finally removed many questions from the

main arena of Japanese politics. For a long time, these questions had been in the way of Japan developing sound security policies by forcing Japanese government to be unnecessarily "history oriented." The statement is available at http://japan.kantei .go.jp/97_abe/statement/201508/0814statement.html.

2. The official title of the old security treaty is Security Treaty between Japan and United States. It was concluded in 1951. Full text is available at http://www.ioc.u -tokyo.ac.jp/~worldjpn/documents/texts/docs/19510908.T2E.html.

3. "Remarks by President Obama and Prime Minister Abe of Japan in Joint Press Conference" (speech, White House, Washington, D.C., April 28, 2015), https://www .whitehouse.gov/the-press-office/2015/04/28/remarks-president-obama-and-prime -minister-abe-japan-joint-press-confere.

4. Ibid.

5. See John Foster Dulles, "Peace in the Pacific" (speech, Whittier College, Los Angeles, CA, March 31, 1951), http://findingaids.princeton.edu/collections/MC016 /c9388.

6. On the revision of the Japan-U.S. security treaty, see Fumihiko Togo, *Nichibei Gaiko Sanju Nen: Anpo, Okinawa to SonoGo* [30 Years of Japan-U.S. Diplomacy: The Security Treaty, Okinawa, and After] (Tokyo: Chuou Koron sha, 1989); and Kazuya Sakamoto, *Nichibei Domei no Kizuna: Anpo-Joyaku to Sogo-sei no Mosaku* [The Bonds of the Japan-U.S.: The Security Treaty and the Search for Mutuality] (Tokyo: Yuhiaku, 2000).

7. If, for instance, the Japan-U.S. alliance is just for the defense of Japan, it does not have "mutuality in purpose." If only the United States works for the peace and security of the Far East, the alliance does not have "mutuality in cooperation."

8. Ministry of Foreign Affairs of Japan, "Japan-U.S. Joint Declaration on Security: Alliance for the 21st Century," press release, April 17, 1996, http://www.mofa .go.jp/region/n-america/us/security/security.html. For the 1997 guidelines, see Japanese Ministry of Defense, "Guidelines for Japan-U.S. Defense Cooperation," September 23, 1997, http://www.mod.go.jp/e/d_act/anpo/19970923.html.

9. In December 1959, the Supreme Court of Japan, in its ruling on the Sunagawa Incident case (relating to the constitutionality of the stationing of U.S. troops), decided that the Japanese government even under the Japanese (Peace) Constitution may resort to necessary measures of self-defense in order for Japan "to maintain peace and security, and to preserve its very existence." The Japanese government, with the help of this Sunagawa ruling, has held the position that the constitution allows Japan to use force (to the minimum extent necessary) to defend itself if an armed attack occurs against Japan. The government, however, had also held the position, up until July 1, 2014, that the constitution does not allow Japan to use force to help defend its ally even if it is essential to defend Japan, unless Japan is directly attacked. The government's new interpretation of the constitution, which was decided on July 1, 2014, makes Japan, with appropriate legislation, able to use force (to the minimum extent necessary) to help defend its attacked ally if it is essential to defend Japan's "survival" and the Japanese people's "right to life, liberty and the pursuit of happiness," even if Japan is not directly attacked. The government now explains that this use of force does not contradict the Supreme Court's interpretation of the constitution shown in the Sunagawa Incident and explains that such a use of force is allowed by international law, namely the exercise of the right of collective self-defense.

10.   Ministry of Foreign Affairs of Japan, "Cabinet Decision on Development of Seamless Security Legislation to Ensure Japan's Survival and Protect Its People," press release, July 1, 2014.

11.   "Remarks by President Obama and Prime Minister Abe of Japan in Joint Press Conference."

12.   Ministry of Foreign Affairs of Japan, "Joint Statement: U.S.-Japan Security Consultative Committee," press release, February 19, 2005.

13.   Japan and the United States must always keep in mind that the U.S. military commitment to Taiwan through the Taiwan Relation Act, as well as that to South Korea through the U.S.–South Korea alliance, is an indispensable asset for the Japan-U.S. alliance to cooperate for the maintenance of international peace and security in the Far East.

14.   In "defending" the liberal world order, there may be unavoidable cases in which the two allies might have to resort to the use of force in accordance with their own constitutional provisions and processes. However, "advancing" the order must always be done with peaceful means. The important point is to persuade, not force, as many nations as possible into accepting the basic principles of the order.

2. THE CASE FOR AN ALTERNATIVE STRATEGY FOR JAPAN: BEYOND THE ARTICLE 9-ALLIANCE REGIME

Yoshihide Soeya

INTRODUCTION

Will China rise peacefully? For major external actors such as the United States and Europe, the rise of China, if achieved peacefully, would entail acquiescence in Chinese power and/or peaceful coexistence with China on the global stage. Would this, however, be the same for its Asian neighbors, even if China rises peacefully? A Southeast Asian official attending the Shangri-La Dialogue in Singapore in May–June 2014 expressed the region's sentiment eloquently: "We do not think China wants to rule the world. China just wants to rule us."[1] Indeed, what China wants on the global stage, on the one hand, and in Asia, on the other, may not be the same.

Currently, the Japanese government, naturally and understandably, places a rising China at the center of its strategy. In a way, this is true of almost all the countries in China's neighborhood as well as the United States, which are all struggling to find an optimal strategy to cope with the shifting balance of power where the rise of China is the most critical factor. The current Japanese strategy, however, appears to be driven by a somewhat excessive sense of threat vis-à-vis China, and as a result tends to gravitate toward the alliance with the United States at the expense of another critical aspect of Japan's grand strategy, that is, security cooperation with its

Asian neighbors, including South Korea, Australia, and Association of Southeast Asian Nations (ASEAN) countries. This chapter argues for the case of substantiating security cooperation with these three East Asian actors as an alternative strategy of Japan, which as its backbone is to be sustained by the alliance with the United States. The analytical frame of reference, with which these arguments are made, is the postwar framework of Japanese security policy premised on Article 9 of the postwar constitution (A9) and the U.S.-Japan security treaty (alliance), which I dub the Article 9–Alliance regime, or A9A. I will argue that in order to fully substantiate security cooperation with Japan's Asian neighbors, Japan would need to go beyond the A9A regime, and that this would require a revision of Article 9 on the basis of liberal internationalism.[2]

A brief examination of the concept of a new model of major power relations with the United States, for which the current leadership of the Chinese Communist Party (CCP) under Xi Jinping appears to be aspiring as a long-term goal, is first in order.

THE RISE OF CHINA AND U.S.-CHINA RELATIONS

A New Model of Major Power Relations

In order to understand the Chinese leadership's strong urge for a new model of major power relations, it is useful to divide modern Chinese nationalism into two critical sentiments dominant among the Chinese people. One is strong awareness of victimization and humiliation during the modern history of China since the 1840–1842 Opium War, when Hong Kong became a colony of Great Britain. The other is a growing sense of confidence and pride, emanating from China's recent spectacular rise to great power status.

These sentiments combine to make up a unique brand of nationalism among the Chinese people.[3] As a result, many Chinese believe today that Asia with China at its center is the natural order for Asia, and that the time has come to bring Asia back to such normalcy. For many Chinese, a strong China reclaiming its core interests in Asia is still compatible with the country engaging in the liberal international order at the global level.

This unique role and status of a strong China is amply demonstrated by the idea of a new model of major power relations between the United States and China. The concept was proposed in February 2012 by Vice President Xi Jinping in Washington, D.C.[4] Xi said that such a relationship would be characterized by (1) "mutual understanding and strategic trust," (2) "respecting each other's core interests," (3) "mutually beneficial cooperation," and (4) "enhancing cooperation and coordination in international affairs and on global issues."[5] In June 2013, Xi Jinping, now general secretary of the CCP, reaffirmed the same four key elements at the summit meeting with President Barack Obama in California.

The four elements in Xi Jinping's formula of a new model of major power relations could be grouped into two categories: (1) strategic trust and (2) core interests, which are more relevant in the Asia-Pacific context, whereas (3) mutual benefits and (4) coordination on global issues are important for the U.S.-China relationship at the global level. Simply put, China wants to coexist with the United States peacefully in the Asia Pacific as well as at the global level, but one critical condition is for the United States to respect an Asian order with China as the primary architect. This message is explicit in the words of Xi Jinping that "the Pacific Ocean is wide enough to incorporate [the interests of] both China and the U.S."[6]

Implications for the Asian Neighbors

Hugh White, professor of strategic studies, recently presented a prescription to avoid an ultimate strategic clash between the United States and China, arguing for a power-sharing arrangement between the two great powers across the Pacific.[7] The premise of his argument points at the heart of the Chinese nationalism: China no longer accepts U.S. primacy as the basis of the Asian order, and alternatively views its own desire to have its dominant status accepted and respected as legitimate and necessary for stability in the Asia Pacific. A huge puzzle about this thesis, however, particularly for

China's immediate neighbors, is whether a strong China that rejects the U.S. primacy would be a benign hegemon in Asia. Many Chinese appear to believe or at least argue so. Yet China's behavior, particularly in its territorial disputes over the South China Sea and the Senkaku Islands, is convincing many of its neighbors otherwise.

In this realist exposition on the strategic relationship between the United States and China, what is often missing is the examination of the place and role of China's neighbors in Asia in the transformation of an Asian order. Obviously, Asian countries bear the direct impact of the behavior of a powerful China. Their coping strategies, or the lack thereof, will affect the reshaping of the Asian order in a significant way.

Such a strategy cannot be effectively constructed by any single country, including Japan. A truly equal partnership is the key to building cooperation among China's neighbors, with a view to consolidating effective infrastructure for an evolving regional order. Such an approach is a middle power strategy (elaborated below). Applying such a perspective to cooperation between Japan and other Asian countries has become increasingly important at a time when the rise of China has become an organizing principle in the transformation of an Asian order, and the role of the United States is being reexamined.

PITFALLS IN JAPAN'S RECENT APPROACH

Legislation for Peace and Security

Japan's new security legislation, passed in the National Diet on September 19, 2015, consists of revisions of 10 existing laws and the drafting of one new law. They could be categorized in three areas of Japanese security and defense policies: (1) situations threatening Japan's survival, (2) situations of important influence, and (3) international peace cooperation. The first category relates to the question of the right to collective self-defense, which will be discussed below.

The other two categories involve important changes from the previous typical Japanese self-restraint in the management of the

U.S.-Japan alliance, as outlined in the Guidelines for Japan-U.S. Defense Cooperation, and participation in international peacekeeping operations.[8] It can generally and reasonably be argued that options for the role of the Japan Self-Defense Forces (JSDF) in both of these areas are still quite modest compared to international standards, falling far short of those of Canada or Australia, for instance. The changes achieved in these areas by the new legislation for peace and security, therefore, are more than welcome.

The issue of the right to the collective self-defense, when situations threaten Japan's survival, gives rise to an interesting question as to the balance between continuity and change in Japanese security policy since the end of World War II. The evolution has occurred largely within the confines of the postwar framework, that is, the A9A regime. In brief, somewhat significant changes in Japanese security and defense policies have developed particularly since the end of the Cold War, but without a fundamental modification of the A9A regime per se. The new security legislation is also a case in point.

As a result of the legislation for peace and security, the revised "three conditions for the use of force for self-defense" now states:

> (1) When an armed attack against Japan occurs *or when an armed attack against a foreign country that is in a close relationship with Japan occurs and as a result threatens Japan's survival and poses a clear danger to fundamentally overturn people's right to life, liberty, and pursuit of happiness.* [emphasis added]
> (2) When there are no other appropriate means available to repel the attack and ensure Japan's survival and protects its people.
> (3) Use of force should be limited to the minimum extent.

The addition in the first condition (indicated by the added emphasis) gives room for the exercise of the right to collective self-defense, which Japanese governments had previously rejected due to the limitations arising from Article 9 of the Japanese constitution. Now, Prime Minister Shinzo Abe's administration has come to the new interpretation of Article 9, saying that self-defense allowed by

Article 9 consists of both self-defense and collective self-defense. Under the first condition stated, while the original reference pertains to self-defense in the strict sense of the term, the new addition makes collective self-defense part of self-defense in a broader sense of the term (reflecting the changing security environments, as explained by the government).

While many constitutional experts in Japan are shaking their heads about the new interpretation, as much about the substance of the right of collective self-defense as about the new security policies, the issue is not very straightforward. The opposition's argument that it is a war-making law is misplaced, and so is the case with neighbors' concerns about Japan's military expansion. This is so, primarily because the right to collective self-defense is a legitimate one for all sovereign states, which is justified by Article 51 of the UN Charter.

It can also be argued that these suspicions are groundless because the revised interpretation in the new law allows the exercise of the right for Japan basically only at a level that is 50 percent of what is allowed by the UN Charter, that is, only in situations where Japan's survival is directly threatened. In other words, the new legislation would not allow Japan to engage in military operations with the United States and other friendly nations if the case has no direct bearing on Japan's security. Preoccupation with Japan's own security alone is what I mean by 50 percent (at most, and perhaps even less in reality) of the stipulation of the UN Charter, which is in principle for the sake of international peace and order rather than a single country's security.

Legally, this incomplete nature of the new legislation is because of Article 9: as long as the Japanese government has to justify the right to collective self-defense without changing the constitution, this is perhaps the maximum interpretation possible within the confines of Article 9.

A twist, however, is that Prime Minister Abe originally wanted to change Article 9. The right to the collective self-defense was brought up as an extension of Abe's aspiration, but the new interpretation was made in the name of defending Article 9. All this was as if an invisible hand pushed Abe's agenda back into the box of the A9A regime, which is nothing other than the postwar regime from which he wanted to escape.

The process leading to the new legislation for peace and security and its successful passage also testify to the critical importance of the U.S.-Japan alliance for Japanese defense and security policy. With the new legislation, options for Japanese contributions to international peace cooperation activities and U.S. military operations in situations threatening Japan's survival and situations of important influence have expanded considerably within the confines of the A9A regime.

Despite the legal changes, an important question remains: Is Japan really ready to use them in a real world? To say that the new legislation would add to deterrence is one thing. Putting it into practice in actual situations is another. Without the preparedness and the determination for the latter, the former may turn out to be a paper tiger, as Chinese chairman Mao Zedong used to say. Also, if Prime Minister Abe still wants to change Article 9 in the years ahead, this should mean that he would step into the remaining 50 percent (i.e., beyond Japan's own security) of the right to the collective self-defense as stipulated by the UN Charter. Is he ready for this truly internationalist advance?

Déjà Vu?

Exploring a few cases in the postwar evolution of Japanese security policy can help highlight similar kinds of pitfalls, almost like déjà vu.

CASE 1

The first case involves the establishment of the JSDF in July 1954 and the new interpretation of Article 9 by the Ichiro Hatoyama administration, a strong advocate for revising Article 9, in December 1954.

Before this, it was almost common sense that in order for Japan to have a military, Article 9 would need to be changed. After actually establishing the JSDF, this logic quickly receded in the background and the argument as well as political moves to revise Article 9 subsided.

CASE 2

The second case involves the revision of the U.S.-Japan security treaty in 1960 by Prime Minister Nobusuke Kishi, grandfather of Shinzo Abe.

It was no secret that Prime Minister Kishi wanted to change the constitution if at all possible. However, as a result of the above development in Case 1, supported by the increasing power of the political left as well as a strong culture of antimilitarism among the general public, constitutional revision became a virtually taboo issue in domestic politics. Then, Kishi's aspiration for Japanese autonomy went toward the revision of the U.S.-Japan security treaty of 1951, which, in the eyes of Kishi as a nationalist, was too one-sided at the cost of Japan's self-esteem and independence. In the name of achieving an equal partnership with the United States, Kishi succeeded in regaining some autonomy on the Japanese side to the extent Japan moved toward an equal position with the United States in the revised security treaty in 1960. The outcome, however, was further institutionalization of the U.S.-Japan security relationship, with Article 9 remaining intact. Thus the A9A regime was further consolidated.

Is what Prime Minister Abe has just achieved with respect to the right to collective self-defense in the new security legislation almost like déjà vu of these two cases? The walls are being pushed out further, but the basic framework, that is, the A9A regime, still remains solid.

The Case for Going beyond the A9A Regime

Prime Minister Abe's renewed emphasis on Abenomics in the aftermath of domestic turmoil over the security legislation is somewhat reminiscent of former prime minister Hayato Ikeda's deliberate focus on economics after the political crisis caused by Kishi's handling of the revision of the U.S.-Japan security treaty. Still, Prime Minister Abe has not dropped constitutional revision from his agenda; the revision has been an important goal in itself for Abe for many years. An interesting development since the passage of the security legislation, however, is that he has stopped mentioning Article 9, and is now raising constitutional revision as a general issue, saying it needs to be debated nationally for years to come. This confirms the above point that Prime Minister Abe has perhaps achieved what he wanted to within the confines of Article 9.

Still, some frustration or a sense of trauma about the postwar regime still lingers on, and constitutional revision is still regarded as an important tool in order to escape from this framework. The political process over the security legislation as an Abe agenda has shown so far that the motive for the right to the collective self-defense originates from his dream of changing the constitution, even if only symbolically, which, however, has been pushed back into the A9A regime as if an invisible hand is at work.

This is in fact what happened with Ichiro Hatoyama and Nobusuke Kishi, the most prominent conservative politicians in the 1950s and the 1960s. My assumption for why this is the case is that, as long as one thinks of escaping from the postwar regime with a sense of trauma about the past, there is simply no way out. Any move in that direction is eventually drawn back into the A9A regime. This may once again breed frustration of one kind or another about the postwar regime, and so the same cycle is repeated.

This is a vicious cycle in the sense that Japanese security policy and its role in regional and global security will continue to be vague, causing misunderstanding and misperception particularly by Japan's neighbors, most notably China and Korea. It may not be so vicious as long as the outcome falls within the confines of the A9A regime. My prescription to avoid this vicious cycle is that although Japan eventually needs to change Article 9 and restructure the U.S.-Japan alliance, its cause and motive should be based on forward-looking liberal internationalism. This way, Japan should be able to move forward beyond the A9A regime.

The current state of this vicious cycle is particularly problematic in Japan's relations with China and South Korea. Chinese concerns about the new security legislation are simply out of touch with reality given the rather modest content stated above. Chinese perception and its reaction, however, are part of the complex realities with which Japan, as well as other countries including the United States and South Korea, need to cope. South Korean worries are equally not realistic, but its actual impact makes otherwise logical and reasonable security cooperation between Japan and South Korea quite difficult. These problems point to an alternative strategy of Japan, which should both lessen sources of unnecessary uncertainties in Japan-China relations and consolidate the basis of security cooperation with South Korea.

I still believe that, if Japan succeeds in forming a comfortable consensus domestically about its middle power strategy, it would ameliorate both Chinese and Korean suspicions in the direction just described above.[9] This would eventually make it possible for Japan to address the issue of revising Article 9 and thus to strengthen the U.S.-Japan alliance. This, however, is a loaded concept inviting all kinds of emotionally charged reactions, making rational strategic discussions virtually impossible. For the lack of a better term, however, I would still use this strategic concept in this chapter to point out pitfalls in the A9A regime and conceptualize an alternative strategy of Japan.

CONCEPTUALIZING AN ALTERNATIVE STRATEGY FOR JAPAN

Why Japan–South Korea Security Cooperation Is Important

Amid the shifting power balance between the United States and China, Japan and South Korea stand out as two countries whose levels of economic and political development, regional and global agendas, and even national interests are comparable.[10] Indeed, Japan and South Korea are similarly situated in the evolving East Asian regional order as important allies of the United States. This, however, does not necessarily mean they are united as a counterbalance against a rising China. Instead, the three countries will constantly adjust their views and agendas amid a shifting East Asian order where the roles of the United States and China are the most important factors shaping the future. Ideally, Japan and South Korea should lead this process of adjustment. In doing this, their standing between the United States and China is conceptually neutral, even if as U.S. allies they are closer to the United States in reality. Japan and South Korea must remain conceptually neutral because they must coexist in the region as close neighbors of China. At the same time, they continue to share concerns about the way China is using its growing power in attempting to consolidate a China-centered Asia that is somewhat reminiscent of traditional Sinocentricism, which is not a reassuring sign for China's neighbors.

Given this dynamic, Japan and South Korea need close relations with the United States in order to promote a liberal international order in East Asia and to socialize China into this order. Here there is a paradigm clash between the postwar liberal international order created by advanced democracies led by the United States, of which Japan and South Korea are key members in East Asia, on the one hand, and the Sinocentric order that China might be interested in reviving, on the other. Two basic factors, however, mean this clash is not necessarily preordained: China's spectacular economic rise is a result of the country entering the liberal international order, and there are liberal internationalists in Chinese society and the government. This, however, does not mean that China's liberal internationalists are entirely happy with the institutions and rules of the existing order. Thus, the danger always exists of power politics damaging China's relations with the liberal international order, despite the economic logic of China's participation in it.

Under this broad picture, from a Japanese perspective there are two dimensions in Japan–South Korea security cooperation. One is the domain of traditional security, most notably relating to the North Korea issue, where the Unites States, as an ally of Japan and South Korea, plays a key role. The other domain involves nontraditional security cooperation, where Japan and South Korea can and should promote substantial cooperation and involve other regional actors such as Australia and the ASEAN countries in efforts to consolidate political and nontraditional security cooperation among East Asian countries.

This chapter does not look at the history controversies that often prevail in the domestic politics of both Japan and South Korea, with negative effects on the management of the current bilateral relationship. While I am fully aware of the importance of these issues in reality, the management of the history problem, on the one hand, and the discussion of security cooperation between Japan and South Korea, on the other, should be compartmentalized and proceed side by side, without one interfering with or hindering discussion of the other. This chapter is concerned with the latter track. First, however, I will look into the recent security legislation passed in the Japanese Diet in September 2015 and discuss its implications for trilateral security cooperation.

A New Horizon of Traditional Security Cooperation between Japan and South Korea

As stated above, the legislation for peace and security, passed in the National Diet in September 2015, covers three areas of Japanese security and defense policies: (1) situations threatening Japan's survival, (2) situations of important influence, and (3) international peace cooperation. The first category of situations relates to the question of the right to collective self-defense (discussed above and also below in reference to South Korea), whereas categories two and three involve important changes from the typical Japanese exercise of self-restraint in the management of the U.S.-Japan alliance (the Guidelines for Japan-U.S. Defense Cooperation) and participation in international peacekeeping operations.

Revision of the existing laws in category two—situations of important influence—has opened up a new horizon for Japan's logistical support in the event of regional contingencies in two dimensions: expanding the activities of the Japan Self-Defense Forces in logistical support (short of the actual use of force) and enabling the provision of support activities to foreign countries' armed forces (beyond the United States).

This revision is an important change from the previous regional contingency legislation that limited Japan's logistical support to the United States. Now, at least legally and theoretically, Japan is able to work not only with the United States but also with South Korea, Australia, and ASEAN countries. Of critical importance is logistical cooperation between Japan and South Korea, or even trilaterally involving the United States, in case of a contingency on the Korean peninsula.

Category one, which pertains to the right to collective self-defense, gives rise to more complex issues. According to the revised "three conditions for the use of force for self-defense," as seen above, the first condition now allows Japan to exercise at most 50 percent of what is justified by the UN Charter—that is, situations where Japan's survival is directly threatened. Regarding a Korean peninsula contingency, such an event would clearly be interpreted as a threat to Japan's survival. With this new legislation, therefore, at least legally speaking, Japan would be able to fight side-by-side with the United States and South Korea in the unwanted event of a military conflict on the peninsula. In reality, politically and otherwise, however, it is hard to imagine that such military cooperation, involving Japan's actual use of force, would be realized even between Japan and the United States, let alone between Japan and South Korea or trilaterally.

It should be clear, therefore, that traditional security cooperation in a trilateral context—one that would involve the actual use of force by the Japan Self-Defense Forces—while now possible legally, will not happen in the foreseeable future. It is important, however, to recognize that in an actual crisis scenario this is an option that exists if indeed South Korea and the United States want assistance.

In reality, therefore, the task of trilateral cooperation involving category two of the new security legislation—situations of important influence—should be given more attention. Examples would include logistical support activities by Japanese Self-Defense Forces for U.S. and South Korean forces such as provision of food, fuel, and communications equipment. The United States and Japan have re-vised the Acquisition and Cross-Servicing Agreement (ACSA) on the basis of the new security legislation. Involving South Korea in this arrangement, however, seems politically unrealistic for some time to come, even though this is perfectly logical and rational from an operational perspective in the event of an emergency on the Korean peninsula. One should be aware, however, that in a real crisis situation Japan's unwillingness to use its full potential under the new security legislation would pose a bigger problem, quite contrary to typical South Korean concerns.

Security Cooperation among Japan, South Korea, and Australia

Category three of Japan's new security legislation concerns Japan's international peace cooperation activities, such as UN peacekeeping operations. In this area, too, the scope of Japanese activities and the range of cooperation with foreign countries engaging in the same missions are expanded by the new security legislation. In essence, this means that Japan has come closer to the international standard accepted and implemented by actors actively engaging in nontra-ditional security cooperation, such as Canada, Australia, and South Korea.

It then follows that the critical task for Japan now and ahead is to match its strategy explicitly with middle power internationalism amply demonstrated by its actual behavior throughout much of the postwar period.[11] The virtue of a middle power strategy is interna-tionalism, where cooperation with like-minded countries toward strengthening a liberal and open international order is the key to any aspect of strategy. Here, the three critical countries capable of developing such security cooperation are Japan, South Korea, and Australia.

The Japan-Australia Joint Declaration on Security Cooperation, signed in March 2007, is an embodiment of such nontraditional se-curity cooperation between middle powers. The agreed areas of security cooperation in the declaration are relevant primarily for human security, including law enforcement for combating transnational crime, counterterrorism, disarmament and nonproliferation, peace operations, humanitarian relief operations, and contingency planning for pandemics.[12] On the basis of this joint security declaration, Japan and Australia signed the Japan-Australia Acquisition and Cross-Servicing Agreement (ACSA) in May 2010, enabling the militaries of both countries to cooperate by reciprocally providing supplies and services. This was indeed a historic achievement in the postwar history of Japanese security policy, setting the legal framework for the JSDF to cooperate with a foreign country other than the United States for the first time.

South Korea and Australia also signed a similar, but much more comprehensive, agreement in 2009, titled Joint Statement on Enhanced Global and Security Cooperation between Australia and the Republic of Korea. There is no reason to believe that a similar agreement cannot be emulated between Tokyo and Seoul. In fact, at the end of the Lee Myungbak government in the first half of 2012, Tokyo and Seoul actually completed negotiations on the General Security of Military Information Act (GSOMIA), whose signing was postponed for political reasons. At that time, the bilateral ACSA was also almost complete. If Japan and South Korea should be able to revive negotiations over the bilateral ACSA and sign it, let alone the already completed GSOMIA, a new horizon for trilateralizing nontraditional security cooperation among Japan, South Korea, and Australia would be opened up.

Due to the importance of vested interests in the post–World War II liberal international order, as well as the magnitude of uncertainties associated with the rise of China, the choice for Japan, South Korea, and Australia has been and is likely to remain for the foreseeable future how to maintain a strong security relationship with the United States. The three countries, however, share interests in not destabilizing bilateral relations with China for two fundamental reasons.

First, an ultimate strategic clash between the United States and China, if it were to actually happen, would deprive the three countries of freedom of decision as well as action. In such an event, the choice for Japan, South Korea, and Australia should be nothing other than working closely with the United States as its allies. Second, there are many issues and areas where cooperation with China is important for the national interests of middle powers as well as for regional stability. These include maintaining a prosperous economic order and stable economic relations with China and involving China in regional institutions for trade, investment, financial, and other functional cooperation. In the short to medium term, middle power cooperation is the three countries' survival strategy, and in the long run it should strengthen the common ground on which Chinese neighbors coexist with a strong (or, alternatively, a disorderly) China.

A natural field for such nontraditional, middle power cooperation among Japan, South Korea, and Australia should be Southeast Asia.

Working with and Involving ASEAN

ASEAN is in the process of finalizing community building efforts in three areas: an economic community, a political-security community, and a social-cultural community. Although the limitations of the ASEAN way in constructing multilateral cooperation in East Asia have long been highlighted, the fact remains that ASEAN is still the sole case of successful institution building for the promotion of multilateral cooperation in the region. In conceptualizing the logic and the way with which to develop cooperation among Japan, South Korea, Australia, and ASEAN, Japan's experiences in developing functional and nontraditional security cooperation would provide rich grounds.

Indeed, ASEAN has marched a long way toward building regional institutions that can promote cooperation and a sense of community. This is all the more remarkable given the region's history of European colonial rule, Japanese military aggression, and a series of crises and conflict among its member states, mostly if not exclusively involving the CLMV countries of Cambodia, Laos, Myanmar, and Vietnam. Initially, the process of integration was largely top-down, initiated by the governments and elites of the member states. The process, however, has now reached the stage where further regional integration, to the extent of ASEAN aspiring for a regional community, should and could be conceptualized and led as a bottom-up process with the principle of a people-centered approach.[13]

ASEAN's regional role can be summarized as that of an initiator of regional integration with explicit emphasis on the importance of people-based agenda setting and integration processes. This focus should be important in order to highlight the strength of ASEAN, whose weakness is the inability or unsuitability of the past and present achievements of ASEAN to influence issues in the domain of traditional security and politics, involving shifting power balance between Japan and China in East Asia and between the United States and China in the broader Asia-Indo-Pacific context. Analytically, this means that we should explicitly be aware of differences between these two levels of analysis in assessing ASEAN's regional role and the implications of engagement by Japan, South Korea, and Australia.

As for the political-security community, ASEAN realizes that it cannot be a relevant pole in the traditional balance of power game. In the present context, worries about China's aggressive behavior are increasing, but ASEAN still cannot antagonize China explicitly. There remains some ambivalence among some ASEAN member states as to the roles of the United States and Japan, which could destabilize relations with China and by extension stability in Southeast Asia. The bottom line of Japan's cooperation with ASEAN, therefore, is to consolidate the foundation of a regional security order by strengthening internationally acceptable rules and norms, such as rule of law and non-use of force to settle political differences. A people-centered concept and approach is also critical for promoting human security, democracy, and human rights. Nontraditional security is a natural field of cooperation, including disaster relief, transnational crimes, counterterrorism, cybersecurity, peacekeeping, and preventive diplomacy. As to maritime security and defense cooperation, cooperation between Japan and ASEAN is evolving in specific cases, but not necessarily in a systematic way. Official dialogues involving and between military delegations are also expanding.

In sum, Japan stands in an effective position for engaging ASEAN to promote prosperity and stability in a wider regional context, where eventually cooperation among Japan, South Korea, and Australia should be developed. In the domain of traditional security Japan sustains the military presence of the United States through the alliance framework, which is the ultimate anchor of regional stability. In the recent security legislation, somewhat proactive participation by Japan in U.S. activities have also become at least legally feasible, while calculations of political will remains a separate issue in domestic politics.

Simultaneously, Japanese assistance in capacity-building for ASEAN countries has also been developing rapidly. This aspect of Japanese involvement may be politically motivated in Japanese domestic politics by a sense of rivalry vis-à-vis China, but it is important to recognize that Japanese engagement is more relevant for ASEAN's community building efforts rather than for countering Chinese influence. The same applies to the domains of economic and sociocultural communities. Ultimately, the goal in ASEAN-Japan cooperation is to strengthen ASEAN's resilience, which, after all, is an important asset in regional stability. There is no reason to believe that South Korea and Australia cannot join Japan in promoting truly region-wide security cooperation, which should help consolidate a robust infrastructure for a new regional order in East Asia.

CONCLUSION

Japan has had an image problem, particularly in Northeast Asia, that has prevented many observers from appreciating the real strengths of its de facto middle power strategy. In fact, Japan has been using its financial and diplomatic resources in many areas. This includes participation in various activities of the United Nations and other global institutions to address nuclear and conventional nonproliferation, economic governance, social welfare and education, poverty reduction, capacity-building, and more recently human security. These are natural and important areas of cooperation among Japan, South Korea, Australia, and ASEAN.

This liberal and internationalist aspect of Japanese strategy is a natural outcome of the A9A framework. The A9A regime constrains Japan's unilateral military options, rendering its regional military role, except in cases of immediate self-defense, relevant only under the framework of its alliance with the United States. At the same time, however, the A9A regime also places somewhat fundamental constraints on Japan's active participation in nontraditional security cooperation, such as international peacekeeping operations. This has been an actual limitation on security cooperation between Japan and Australia for several years. Japan's ability to deliver meaningful security cooperation with Australia has often fallen short of Australian expectations. In the domain of traditional security as well, Japan is likely to underperform relative to its newly allowed potential despite the recent security legislation. For example, this includes cooperation with the United States and South Korea in the event of a contingency on the Korean peninsula.

All of this makes the case for redefining the issue of revising Article 9 of the Japanese constitution on the grounds of future-oriented liberal internationalism, rather than a sense of trauma about the loss of autonomy in the postwar regime. In the A9A regime, Japan's history in World War II is closely and inseparably tied with Article 9 as two sides of the same coin. Without facing this history squarely in a way acceptable to the international community, let alone to the United States, changing Article 9 remains impossible. This is not because of the opposition of China or South Korea, nor Japanese liberals. This is an inherent logic of the A9A regime. In order to go beyond the postwar framework, liberal internationalism should therefore provide the key philosophy with which to redefine the issue of constitutional revision. For Japan to do this, an alternative, future-oriented strategy must be conceptualized and debated before anything else.

NOTES

1. Daniel Twining, "Is the 'Chinese Dream' Asia's Nightmare?," *Nikkei Asia Review*, June 11, 2014.

2. For a comprehensive analysis of this thesis in Japanese, see Yoshihide Soeya, *Anzen-hosho wo Toi-naosu: "Kyujo-Anpo Taisei" wo Koete* [Rethinking Security: Going beyond the "Article 9-Alliance Regime"] (Tokyo: NHK Books, 2016).

3. See Zhao Suisheng, *A Nation-State by Construction: Dynamics of Modern Chinese Nationalism* (Stanford, CA: Stanford University Press, 2004).

4. Xi Jinping, "Luncheon in Honor of Vice President Xi Jinping" (video transcript, National Committee on U.S.-China Relations, Washington, D.C., February 15, 2012).

5. David M. Lampton, "A New Type of Major-Power Relationship: Seeking a Durable Foundation for U.S.-China Ties," *Asia Policy* 16 (July 2013): 51–68.

6. Willy Lam, "Beijing's Aggressive New Foreign Policy and Implications for the South China Sea," *China Brief*, no. 13 (June 2013).

7. Hugh White, *The China Choice: Why We Should Share Power* (Oxford: Oxford University Press, 2013).

8. Japan Ministry of Defense, "The Guidelines for Japan-U.S. Defense Cooperation," April 27, 2015, http://www.mod.go.jp/e/d_act/anpo/shishin_20150427e.html.

9. Yoshihide Soeya, "A 'Normal' Middle Power: Interpreting Changes in Japanese Security Policy in the 1990s and After," in *Japan as a 'Normal Country'?: A Country in Search of its Place in the World*, ed. Yoshihide Soeya, Masayuki Tadokoro, and David Welch (Toronto: University of Toronto Press, 2011), 72–97.

10. Yoshihide Soeya and Geun Lee, "The Middle-Power Challenge in East Asia: An Opportunity for Co-operation between South Korea and Japan," *Global Asia* 9, no. 2 (Summer 2014).

11. Richard J. Samuels, *Securing Japan: Tokyo's Grand Strategy and the Future of East Asia* (Ithaca, NY: Cornell University Press, 2008), 128.

12. Ministry of Foreign Affairs of Japan, "Japan-Australia Joint Declaration on Security Cooperation," March 13, 2007.

13. Such was the key concept that emerged out of the ASEAN-Japan joint study group, initiated in 2010 and launched in 2012 by ASEAN's secretariat. It was comprised of scholars from ASEAN member states and Japan, who looked into the theme of "ASEAN-Japan Strategic Partnership in ASEAN Community Building." The study project, funded by the Japan-ASEAN Integration Fund (JAIF) and approved by all the governments of member states of ASEAN, was supervised by Jusuf Wanandi, cofounder of the Center for Strategic and International Studies (CSIS) in Jakarta, and Hitoshi Tanaka, senior fellow of the Japan Center for International Exchange (JCIE) in Tokyo. It was also coordinated by Rizal Sukma of CSIS and myself. The first phase of the study was conducted from September 2012 to July 2013, producing its results in 2013, and the second phase was convened in June 2013 to look into the ASEAN-Japan strategic partnership in East Asia and in global governance, for which the outcome came out in 2015. See Rizal Sukma and Yoshihide Soeya, eds., *Beyond 2015: ASEAN-Japan Strategic Partnership for Democracy, Peace, and Prosperity in Southeast Asia* (Tokyo: Japan Center for International Exchange, 2013); and Rizal Sukma and Yoshihide Soeya, eds., *Navigating Change: ASEAN-Japan Strategic Partnership in East Asia and in Global Governance* (Tokyo: Japan Center for International Exchange, 2015).

Part II. JAPAN'S POSTWAR ECONOMIC POLICIES

3. JAPAN'S ECONOMY AND POLICY IN A GLOBAL CONTEXT: POSTWAR EXPERIENCE AND PROSPECTS FOR THE TWENTY-FIRST CENTURY

Jun Saito

INTRODUCTION

The revival of the Japanese economy after World War II has often been referred to as an economic miracle. Having started from the ashes of destroyed factories and infrastructure as well as dwellings, the Japanese economy managed to develop to become one of the leading advanced economies in the world in less than a quarter of a century.

However, the economic miracle could not have been achieved by Japan alone. Interactions with the global economy were indispensable. If it were not for the exchanges of goods and services, capital, human resources, and technology with the rest of the world, the miracle would not have taken place. Participating in the global framework and helping to further develop the arrangement was vital for Japan, and the United States was always at the focal point in Japan's relationship with the rest of the world.

In fact, the close ties established between Japan and the United States after the war could likewise be called a political miracle. In contrast to the regrettable relationship seen before and during the war, in the postwar period the economic relationship between the two countries has been close and strong. It has become the single most important bilateral relationship for both countries.

The aim of this chapter is to review Japan's economic developments and policies in the 70 years after the war, shedding light particularly on the impact that Japan's economic relationship with the United States had on its path. Toward that end, focus will be given to the special features of the respective periods instead of going into the details of the historical events. It should bring out the basic momentum that operated behind the developments, which, in turn, would be useful in discussing the possible future scenario for the Japanese economy and its relationship with the Asia Pacific and the rest of the world. Suggestions on areas of possible contribution to the Asia-Pacific region and other parts of the global economy will be discussed before the concluding remarks, which will make some proposals.

ECONOMIC DEVELOPMENTS AND POLICIES IN POSTWAR JAPAN

Figure 3.1 shows how Japan's annual real gross domestic product (GDP) growth rate has evolved since 1956 (the first year for which Japan keeps data in its national account figures system is 1955). It shows that, during the past 60 years after World War II, there are a number of distinct periods that have different average growth rates, which, in turn, reflect the economic development and policy implementation specific to those periods.

The distinct periods that we focus on in this chapter are the reconstruction period (1945–1954); the high-growth period (1954–1970); the unstable external environment period (1970–1986); the bubble economy period (1986–1991); the burst of the bubble and the lost decade (1991–2002); the longest expansionary phase of the 2000s (2002–2008); the global financial and economic crisis and its aftermath (2008–2012); and the Abenomics period (2012–).[1] The features of each period will be discussed in turn below.

Figure 3.1   Real GDP Growth Rates

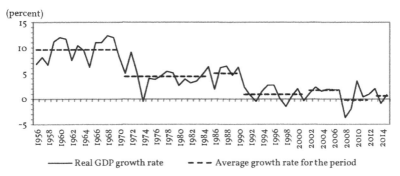

Data source: "Long-Term Data Series," Economic Research Bureau, Cabinet Office.

Reconstruction Period (1945–1954)

The most important task that had to be tackled immediately after the war was to restore the daily lives of Japanese citizens. Demand for food and other necessities exploded as people returned to their homeland from overseas. The supply of these goods, however, was far from enough because the devastation of farms, destruction of factories, and suspension of imports had reduced production levels to one-tenth of the prewar level (averaged across the 1934 to 1936 period). Accommodated by the ample liquidity that circulated as a result of deferred payments for the war, the wide gap between demand and supply resulted in hyperinflation.

During the early years, however, the focus of the policies directed by U.S. Army general Douglas MacArthur and his General Headquarters, Supreme Commander for the Allied Powers (denoted as GHQ hereafter) was the demilitarization and democratization of the Japanese economy. The goal was to completely transform the Japanese system so that it would no longer be able to challenge the new economic and political order put in place by the United States and its allies.

Rapid transformation of the legal and economic framework took place within about a year of the end of war. The new initiatives that were introduced include the establishment of trade unions (December 1945) and labor standards (April 1947), the dissolution of the *zaibatsu* (March 1946) as well as the introduction of an Anti-Monopoly Law (April 1947), and the creation of small agricultural land ownership (April and October 1946). These postwar reform measures, some of which had to be revised later, shaped the economic development of the following years. One of the important outcomes of the reforms was increased competition and market pressure. This proved to be essential in accomplishing reconstruction and preparing for the high-growth period that followed.

Meanwhile, the Japanese government tried to address the economic crisis by employing demand-side and supply-side measures, as well as price controls. Efforts to contain excess demand were made by freezing bank deposits and replacing old yen notes with new yen notes (February 1946). Supply was stimulated by funneling available resources into strategically important industries that had become bottlenecks for production in a wide range of other industries (December 1946). Prices of important goods and services were also directly controlled by the government (March 1946).

Real progress was not made, however, until the priorities of the GHQ shifted to restoring Japan as an ally. It was a response to the changes in the international political situation: the Cold War that broke out between the United States and the Soviet Union. Faced with the tense confrontation, the United States began to see Japan as a strategically important frontline state for the Western bloc to prevent penetration by the Eastern bloc into the Asia Pacific. While the United States provided military protection, Japan was encouraged to concentrate on restoring production and containing inflation and to become an independent partner.

The final stage of reconstruction was set by Joseph Dodge, chairman of the Detroit Bank, who was invited to make a set of recommendations to put an end to inflation and restore the economy. The most effective measure in his recommendations, called the

Dodge Line, was the immediate balancing of the budget, which had been running huge deficits (December 1949). While it exerted a severe deflationary pressure on the economy, its implementation made a dramatic contribution in calming down inflation.

Price stability and recovery of production paved the way for a more normal framework for economic activities. After fixing the exchange rate to 360 yen per U.S. dollar (April 1949), international trade managed by the government was liberalized to allow the private sector to engage in exports and imports once again (December 1949 and January 1950, respectively), and the authority for foreign exchange control was handed back to the Japanese government (January 1950).

The level of production at the beginning of 1950 was still below the prewar level. It was not until the surge in demand due to the outbreak of the Korean War in June 1950 that the economy finally took off. The Korean War was undoubtedly a surprise for the Japanese economy. Therefore, the recovery of the Japanese economy may look like an accident. Yet it should be noted that the Japanese economy would not have been able to take the opportunity if the economy was not prepared to respond to the surge in demand.

The production level surpassed the prewar level in the October 1950 and continued to increase. The *White Paper on the Japanese Economy for 1956* by the Economic Planning Agency of the Japanese government reported that "the Japanese economy can no longer be considered to be in a postwar reconstruction period."[2]

On the basis of these achievements, San Francisco Peace Treaty was signed (albeit only by Western bloc countries) in September 1951, and Japan was restored to independence in April 1952. Furthermore, Japan joined the International Monetary Fund (IMF) and the World Bank in August 1952 and the General Agreement on Tariffs and Trade (GATT) in September 1955. Japan's return to the international community was completed when it became a member of the United Nations (UN) in December 1956. The process of the return to the international community was not always a smooth one. In the case of GATT, for instance, Japanese membership faced strong opposition from the European countries. It was only because of the strong support provided by the United States that the accession made its way through.

High-Growth Period (1954–1970)

From late 1954, the Japanese economy entered a decade-and-a-half long period of high growth; real GDP growth recorded an average of about 10 percent during this period. The high-growth period, as it is now called, consisted of two distinctive phases.

The first half of the high-growth period that extended from 1954 to 1964 was characterized by domestic demand-driven growth. In particular, a rapid increase in private investment was the main factor of growth during the period. The *White Paper on the Japanese Economy for 1960* characterized the growth in this period as being driven by "investment which induced further investment."[3] It contributed to modernizing plant and equipment with new technology while expanding the production capacity of the economy.

Even though the momentum was still strong, booms during the period often had to be slowed down by a deliberate tightening of monetary policy. That was because the accompanying increase in trade account deficit led to the reduction of foreign reserves under the fixed exchange rate regime that was in place at that time. Since Japan's foreign reserves were very limited, its depletion had to be prevented by policy action.

The situation changed in the second half of the high-growth period that lasted from 1965 to 1970. The rise in the household savings rate gradually changed the macro-balance. The underlying balance of the current account shifted from deficit to surplus. The accumulation of foreign reserves that followed alleviated constraints on the economic expansion. Since there was no need to deliberately cool down the boom, the expansionary phase lasted from 1965 to 1970, making it the longest expansionary phase in the postwar period until more recent times (it was overtaken by the sustained expansion of the 2000s).

The preparation for an export-driven growth pattern had been made during the first half of the high-growth period when efforts to liberalize trade were initiated. An important initiative was the General Direction for Trade Liberalization announced in June 1960. The initial target of the initiative was to liberalize 80 percent of trade by April 1963. The efforts were accelerated (partly in response to a request by the United States) so that, by the target date, 89 percent liberalization was achieved.[4]

As a result of these efforts, Japan was able to accede to Article XI of GATT in February 1963. Further efforts were made under the GATT framework to reduce tariffs as well. Japan, whose economic growth relied heavily on increasing exports, is considered to be one of the nations that benefited the most from the tariff reductions of the Kennedy Round, which took place between 1964 and 1967.

Similar efforts were also made in the area of exchange controls, which included an arrangement called the foreign exchange budget system. It was an arrangement in which the government purchased all of the foreign exchange received by the exporters and allocated them to importers that met government policy objectives. It was in place until it was abolished in March 1964.

In fact, the year 1964 was an epoch-making year. Japan accepted Article VIII of the IMF agreement in April and celebrated the occasion by hosting the annual IMF–World Bank meetings in Tokyo in September. Japan also became a member of the Organization for Economic Cooperation and Development (OECD) in April and hosted the Olympic Games in Tokyo in October.[5] In view of these achievements, 1964 can be considered to be the year in which Japan formally became a member of the group of advanced industrial economies.

During the high-growth period, real gross national product (GNP) quadrupled, and nominal GNP became more than nine times larger. As a result, in 1968, Japan surpassed West Germany to become the second largest economy in the world (excluding the Eastern bloc), next only to the United States. It opened opportunities for Japan to participate in wider range of areas as one of the major economic powers.

However, the period was one that witnessed a widening of the trade imbalance. The U.S. trade account balance against Japan turned into a deficit in 1965, and the deficit continued to widen afterwards. It led to strong pressure from the United States and some tough negotiations, often involving the leaders of the two countries. In sectors such as textiles (wool and man-made), the issue was raised in the late 1960s, and Japanese firms finally agreed to engage in a voluntary export restraint (VER) in 1970–1971.[6]

Meanwhile, the economic relationship between Japan and other Asian countries deepened. In response to a request made by the United States, which had to bear a heavy burden because of the war in Vietnam and the widening of trade deficit, Japan became increasingly involved in the stability and the prosperity of the region. Japan started to provide official development assistance (ODA) in 1954, and increased its amount to the region after normalizing its relationship with South Korea in 1965. The Asian Development Bank (ADB) was also established in 1966 with Japan subscribing the most capital.

On the other hand, there were differences between the two countries in their attitude toward China. During the period, Japan was eager to strengthen ties with China through trade; the United States, however, expressed strong concern over such action in view of the military threat of China to the region.

Unstable External Environment Period (1971–1986)[7]

Obviously, the high-growth period could not have continued forever. As the catch-up had been made in late 1960s, a slowdown in the growth rate should have taken place. In the case of Japan, however, the completion of the catch-up coincided with an outbreak of a number of external shocks. The combined effect of the two overlapping events was to lower the average real GDP growth rate during the period to about 4 percent.

The first of these shocks was U.S. president Richard Nixon's surprise announcement in August 1971 that brought an end to the global fixed exchange rate system—the so-called Nixon shock.

President Nixon's announcement included the suspension of the convertibility of the U.S. dollar to gold and the introduction of an import surcharge of 10 percent, among others. It meant that the IMF system of global fixed exchange rates had collapsed. Efforts to reinstate the fixed exchange regime were made and led to a temporary agreement at the Smithsonian Institute in December 1971. The Japanese yen, which was one of the major currencies subject to realignment, was revalued to 308 yen from 360 yen per U.S. dollar.

However, the agreement proved to be short-lived, and the Japanese yen was finally floated in February 1973. Since the start of the floating, the yen has been subject to occasional rapid appreciation, which became the utmost concern for the government as well as the exporting sector. In that sense, the floating set the stage for economic policy implementation over the following 40 years.

The second shock was the steep rise in oil prices that followed the outbreak of the 1973 Arab-Israeli war. The first oil shock sent the Japanese economy into chaos. Oil prices shot up, and fear of shortages of oil-related goods led consumers into a panic. In response, direct price control was introduced. Macroeconomic policies were tightened to contain inflation.

However, as inflation peaked, the concern of the government turned to the recession that followed. Real GDP in 1974 showed its first negative growth rate in the postwar period. In order to counter the recession, the government's stance on macroeconomic policies was overturned. Fiscal stimulus measures were introduced, and in order to finance these measures, deficit-financing government bonds were issued for the first time since 1965 (and have continued to be issued to date except for a brief period in the early 1990s).

The trilemma (recession, inflation, and current account deficit) that followed the first oil shock was the main theme of the first economic summit between the leaders of the six advanced industrial countries (including the Japanese prime minister) held at Rambouillet, France, in November 1975. The economic influence that Japan had acquired by then was reflected in the agreements made in the following summit meetings, which called on Japan, together with the United States and West Germany, to expand its domestic demand in order to play the role of a locomotive pulling the rest of the world out of recession.

Compared to the first, the second oil shock in 1978 was dealt with more successfully, at least in Japan. With preventive monetary tightening in place, inflationary expectations were kept under control. The actual inflation rate turned out to be moderate, and the recession shallow.

The third shock was the trade friction with the United States, which intensified particularly in the early 1980s.[8] Having overcome the changes in the international monetary system and the two oil shocks successfully, Japan was able to sustain moderate growth with relatively low inflation. In such an environment, it was also able to improve productivity and international competitiveness. This was in stark contrast with the United States, which continued to suffer from stalled productivity growth and a high inflation rate. In order to improve the situation, expansionary fiscal policy and tight monetary policy were taken under President Ronald Reagan and Paul Volker, the Federal Reserve Board (FRB) chairman. The consequences of the policy mix were a high interest rate, strong dollar, and a large U.S. current account deficit.

Frustrated with the sustained and expanding current account deficit, the United States demanded that Japan improve market access and increase its imports. The two countries engaged in a series of difficult negotiations and agreements and reached agreements such as Japanese firms' voluntary export restraints on automobiles (1981–1994) and Japanese firms' import targets for semiconductors (1986–1992). Talks also took place on issues regarding the financial sector, where the report by the Yen-Dollar Committee in 1984 led to the liberalization and internationalization of the Japanese financial market. The discussions were expanded to include other sectors in the market oriented sector-specific (MOSS) talks (1985–1986), which covered telecommunications, medical equipment and pharmaceuticals, electronics, forestry products, and transportation machinery.

The fourth shock that characterized the period was the Plaza Accord in September 1985, which ignited a steep and significant appreciation of the yen. Seeing that its current account imbalance had not improved despite the trade agreements, the United States gradually leaned toward exchange rate realignment. At the meeting in the Plaza Hotel, New York, the finance ministers and central bank governors of the Group of Five (G5) nations announced that the Japanese yen needed to be revalued.[9] The exchange rate of the yen per U.S. dollar, which was 240 yen just before the Plaza Accord, appreciated to under 160 yen within 10 months.

The steep appreciation led the Japanese economy into a recession. The need to engage in structural reforms to transform the Japanese economy to a more domestic demand-oriented model was emphasized by the government-sponsored *Maekawa Report* published in April 1986. Meanwhile, the government introduced a series of economic stimulus packages to counter the decline in economic activities. The official discount rate, which was used by the Bank of Japan as the policy rate at the time, was successively cut; in response to the Louver Accord in February 1987, which aimed to stabilize the exchange rate, it was cut to a record low (at that time) of 2.5 percent.

Throughout the period, Japan sought closer relationships with its Asian neighbors. Building on the efforts made in the previous periods, and supported by the change in the environment as a result of the end of the war in Vietnam and President Nixon's new approach to China (the other Nixon shock for Japan), Japan agreed to open formal diplomatic relations with China in September 1972 and with North Vietnam in September 1973.

Efforts to further deepen the relationship with other Asian countries continued until a tour by Prime Minister Kakuei Tanaka was met by protestors in Thailand and Indonesia in January 1974. It did not, however, stop the commitment of Japan to the region. The overall approach of Japan to Asia was expressed in a speech made by Prime Minister Takeo Fukuda in August 1977. The speech, which is now known as the Fukuda Doctrine, declared that Japan would never become a military power again, would establish a heart-to-heart relationship with the Southeast Asian economies, and would make a contribution to peace and prosperity in the region as an equal partner.

The idea was further developed to include Australia and New Zealand as well as the United States and Canada when Prime

Minister Masayoshi Ohira proposed a Pacific Basin Cooperation initiative in 1979. The idea materialized in the form of the Pacific Economic Cooperation Council (PECC), which had its first meeting in September 1980.

Bubble Economy Period (1986–1991)

Improvement in the terms of trade brought about by the appreciation of the yen, and the impact of economic stimulus packages and monetary easing that were implemented in order to address the negative impact of the appreciation were successful in pulling the economy out of the recession. The real GDP growth rate rose to an average of about 5 percent between 1986 and 1991. In view of the favorable environment, a consumption tax was introduced for the first time in April 1989. The budgets in the early 1990s were also formulated without relying on deficit-financing bonds for the first time in nearly 15 years. However, it turned out that the achievements were based on unsustainable economic performance.

The problem with the economic expansion during the period was the fact that it was based on bubbles that were created in asset markets. The rapid increases in stock and land prices were founded, at first, on an expectation of a surge in real activity, that is, the expectation that Tokyo would become a global financial center. Ample liquidity provided by monetary easing, however, continued to pour into asset markets, accommodating the speculation of a further rise in prices. Monetary policy was left unchecked because of stable prices, due to the fall in import prices accompanying exchange rate appreciation. Prices in the stock and land markets—supported by self-fulfilling expectations—grew to be far in excess of the prices that could be justified by the economic fundamentals.

Discussions of the problem with the bubble during the period focused mainly on the widening inequality between asset holders and nonholders. In reality, a more serious problem was imbedded in the banking sector, that is, the damage that could be done by the nonperforming loans, but was not acknowledged during the period.

Its seriousness was not realized until it became apparent that the burst of the bubble had seriously affected banks' balance sheets.

Meanwhile, as the yen strengthened, the presence of Japan overseas increased. Japanese tourists became increasingly visible. In addition, increasing purchasing power allowed firms and individuals to purchase expensive real estate and valuable properties abroad, most notably in the United States.

Firms in the manufacturing sector, on the other hand, were distressed by a loss in competitiveness. In order to adapt to the new environment, their choice was to shift their production sites abroad, in particular to Asia, in order to benefit from the low labor cost. Foreign direct investment surged, raising anxiety over the possibility of a hollowing out of the Japanese industrial base. However, while assembling plants for final products shifted overseas, the production base for intermediate goods remained in Japan, and their exports increased in the medium term. It is during this period that a complex network of a global supply chain across the region began to be established.[10]

Trade discussions between the two nations entered a new stage when macroeconomic issues such as the savings/investment balance—not only that of Japan but also the United States—were taken up in the Structural Impediments Initiative (SII) (1989–1990). It provided an opportunity for Japan to express views about the U.S. macroeconomic balance, as well as to review its own regulations that prevented competitive pressure to play its full role. However, the talks were not enough to prevent Japan from being listed as an unfair trader under the 1988 Omnibus Foreign Trade and Competitiveness Act. Trade frictions during the period led to some tense moments between the two governments.

Burst of the Bubble and the Lost Decade (1991–2001)

The policy setting was finally reversed at the end of 1980s. The official discount rate was raised, legislation to limit the use of land was introduced, and bank lending to the real estate sector was restrained in 1989–1990. As a result, stock prices started to fall in the beginning of January 1990, and land prices started to decline after reaching a peak in September 1990.

The burst of the bubble economy had its consequences. Households were left with large debts backed by nominally valued financial and real assets, and firms suffered from excess capacity, excess employment, and excess debt. The most serious problem was the rapid increase of banks' nonperforming loans. Having to meet the capital adequacy ratio requirement, which was introduced in fiscal year (FY) 1992, banks engaged in a couple of apparently contradictory behaviors. On the one hand, they restrained lending to firms that had better balance sheets (credit crunch) in order to contain the growth of risk-weighted assets. On the other hand, banks continued forbearance lending to firms that were on the verge of collapsing in order to contain damage to their own capital. The former led to a fall in business investment, while the latter had an effect of preventing inefficient firms from exiting the market, and keeping the average productivity of the economy low. In order to address the weakening of the economy, a series of fiscal stimulus packages was introduced. The Bank of Japan assisted government actions by reducing the official discount rate to 0.5 percent by September 1995.

Mainly because of these policy efforts, the economy managed to enter an expansionary phase in 1996–1997, reaching a real GDP growth rate of almost 3 percent. This favorable performance led the government to go on with the planned consumption tax rate hike to 5 percent from 3 percent in April 1997. However, since the recovery at that time was policy driven, the economy was not strong enough to resist the deflationary effect of the consumption tax rate hike. Combined with the negative impact of the Asian financial crisis that broke out in July 1997, the economy quickly returned to a recession. The recession further worsened the balance sheet of banks and other financial institutions. The economy faced a financial crisis when a number of large financial institutions collapsed in late 1997 and in 1998. Japanese banks as a whole, which were perceived to be risky at that time, had to pay premiums to the foreign banks (called the Japan premium) for their borrowings.

The critical situation that erupted in the financial system was enough to wash out any optimism that the problem of nonperforming loans would be solved by the future economic recovery. Firms finally started to engage in severe restructuring. In addition to dismissals, early retirements were encouraged while new intake was virtually stopped. In the late 1990s the total number of employees started to fall. In order to put a stop to further deterioration of economic conditions, the government finally injected capital into the banks in 1998 and again in 1999. It also tried to support the economy by introducing more economic stimulus packages. The Bank of Japan responded by reducing the target for the collateralized overnight call rate to zero in February 1999 through August 2000.[11]

Because of the economic weakness that became apparent during this period, the 1990s is often called the lost decade for the Japanese economy. The average real GDP growth rate for the period actually fell to only 1 percent. Because of low growth in aggregate demand, the negative output gap with the potential GDP widened. Since the mid-1990s, price decline became chronic, and deflation started to torment the Japanese economy.[12]

While Japan was struggling with domestic economic difficulties, the global economy was facing one of the most significant turning points in the postwar period: the fall of the Berlin Wall in 1989 and the collapse of the Soviet Union in 1991. Former centrally planned economies started their transformation toward market-oriented economies. In addition, China had increased its presence in the global market with the reform and opening up policy initiated by Deng Xiaoping in 1979, and its commitment to these initiatives was renewed when Deng made his 1992 Southern Tour.

During this period, trade disputes between Japan and the United States continued. The two countries made efforts within the Japan–United States Framework for a New Economic Partnership (1993–1996). There were sharp disagreements as to the use of objective criteria, but the allies managed to reach agreements in areas such as automobiles and auto parts in 1995.

Meanwhile, Japan further increased foreign direct investment to the region, except for a short period in the late 1990s when a financial crisis broke out, in order to strengthen the global supply chain. Interdependence in the region was enhanced during this period. Japan took initiatives to establish a forum for the Asia-Pacific economies to discuss issues of mutual interest. In addition to the establishment of PECC mentioned earlier, Japan led the establishment of the Asia-Pacific Economic Cooperation (APEC) forum in November 1989.[13] APEC, for instance, agreed to achieve free trade and investment by 2010 for the developed economies, and by 2020 for developing economies (the Bogor Goals). In order to achieve this target, an action agenda was agreed upon in October 1995 when Japan hosted APEC meetings in Osaka.

When the Asian financial crisis broke out in July 1997, those economies facing difficulties asked for the IMF's support, which in turn collaborated with the World Bank, ADB, and other countries including Japan. In view of the need to have a regional arrangement to assist countries in need, Japan proposed the establishment of an Asian Monetary Fund (AMF)—an Asian version of the IMF—in 1997. However, due to the strong opposition from the United States, the proposal did not materialize as intended. The opposition seemed to come from the concern that the proposal overlapped with the functions of the IMF in the Asian region, and that it would provide less pressure on the borrower economies toward implementing reforms the United States considered essential.[14] A looser arrangement called the Chiang Mai Initiative (CMI) was established later in 2000.

Long Expansionary Phase of the 2000s (2002–2008)

As the global economy recovered from the aftermath of the burst of the information technology (IT) bubble in 2001, the Japanese economy also started to recover. The expansionary phase that started in January 2002 eventually lasted for more than six years, making it the longest expansionary phase since business cycles started to be recorded in the early 1950s.

With the help of favorable economic conditions, the new administration led by Prime Minister Junichiro Koizumi embarked on implementing bold structural reform measures that were considered essential to the improvement of long-term growth prospects. In line with his principles, no economic stimulus packages were introduced during the period.

On the other hand, the Bank of Japan was pressured to do more after the policy rate reached zero. The Bank of Japan became the first central bank to introduce an unconventional monetary policy called the quantitative easing policy (QEP). This switched the operational target from the policy rate to the current account balance of the financial institutions at the Bank of Japan, and gradually raised the target outstanding balance from 5 trillion yen (about 1 percent of GDP) in March 2001 to 30–35 trillion (about 6–7 percent of GDP) in January 2004. QEP was maintained until 2006, when the Bank of Japan judged that price levels had stabilized.

Among structural reform measures, Japan's highest priority was given to resolving the nonperforming loans problem. With a numerical target set by the government, banks were pressured to make considerable efforts to halve the volume of nonperforming loans that existed in FY 2001 (8.4 percent of total assets) by the end of FY 2004, a target that they managed to achieve (2.9 percent).

Other items on the reform agenda, including the privatization of the postal service and fiscal consolidation, were pursued with varying degrees of success. The privatization of the postal service faced strong political resistance, but it was overcome when the Liberal Democratic Party (LDP) gained a large majority in a snap election. Japan Post, a private company that started off with 100 percent of its stocks being held by the government, was established in October 2007.

Fiscal consolidation also faced strong headwinds due to its emphasis on spending cuts. In order to meet the target of achieving a primary surplus by FY 2011, the government decided to cut government expenditures by 11.4 percent to 14.3 trillion yen (about $185 billion). A ceiling was set for each of the spending categories, including social security expenditures, and was observed in the annual budget formulation. The target probably would have been achieved if not for the drastic change in Japan's economic environment brought about by the global financial and economic crisis in the late 2000s.

During this period, foreign direct investment to Asia continued, but a new trend emerged. A majority was still aimed at establishing or strengthening the global value chain across the region, but a greater portion of investment went to large economies, like China and India, and were aimed at capturing their fast-growing domestic markets. Also, because of rising labor costs, investments were diversified to new host economies like Vietnam.

In the area of international trade policy, Japan had been giving highest priority to achieving a multilateral agreement under a GATT/World Trade Organization (WTO) framework. However, difficulty in achieving agreement between developed and developing economies became increasingly evident and led many countries to engage in bilateral free trade agreements (FTAs) or economic partnership agreements (EPAs). Japan belatedly changed its stance in the 2000s and signed its first EPA with Singapore in 2002.

Global Financial and Economic Crisis and Its Aftermath (2008–2012)

Growth momentum of the Japanese economy gradually lost steam and entered a recessionary phase after a financial crisis broke out in the United States in the summer of 2007. The financial crisis almost brought financial activities in the United States to a standstill, and speculative money moved into government bonds (flight to quality) and to commodity markets (flight to simplicity).

The recession that Japan faced beginning in February 2008 was initially a mild one because Japanese financial institutions were not very exposed to subprime mortgage–related securities. The negative influence mainly came from the loss in terms of trade due to a steep rise in the price of oil and other primary goods. The situation suddenly worsened when Lehman Brothers collapsed in September 2008. A sharp drop in global demand for Japanese exports, automobiles in particular, resulted in large negative GDP growth, much bigger than that experienced by the country where the crisis originated, the United States.

In order to deal with the situation, the Group of Twenty (G20) members held a meeting in London in April 2009.[15] The G20 became the main forum for international policy coordination. It agreed to take concerted action to bring the global economies out of the crisis by introducing expansionary macroeconomic policies. The action helped Japan as well as other countries in recovering from the crisis. Economic recovery in Japan resumed after March 2009.

However, Japan's pace of recovery was more modest than that of the United States. Improvements in corporate profits were slow in benefiting the household sector, expansion of employment was mainly in nonregular workers, and the increase in wages was limited. Weak household consumption kept private demand fragile. Since the recovery was not full-fledged, it was susceptible to the shocks that periodically occurred in the early 2010s—namely, the European sovereign debt crisis that broke out in October 2010, the Great East Japan Earthquake that took place in March 2011, and the great flood in Thailand in the summer of 2011. As a result, deflation, which was temporarily alleviated during the period between 2006 and 2008, returned to the Japanese economy in 2009.

Low growth and a fall in prices limited the nominal growth of Japanese GDP relative to other countries. In 2010, Japan surrendered the seat for the second largest economy in the world to China.[16]

Abenomics (2012–)

Prime Minister Shinzo Abe, who came to office in December 2012, introduced Abenomics as his economic policy package. Abenomics gives highest priority to strengthening the growth potential of the Japanese economy and overcoming deflation. To achieve its objective, three arrows of economic policy were introduced: bold monetary policy, flexible fiscal policy, and a growth strategy to promote private investment.

Monetary policy took a major step forward when the Bank of Japan introduced quantitative and qualitative easing (QQE) in

April 2013, which included a commitment to achieve an inflation rate of 2 percent within two years by doubling the monetary base. Fiscal policy reversed the past trend of government expenditure cuts in order to provide short-term stimulus until monetary policy could start to show its impact. At the same time, the government maintained its commitment toward fiscal consolidation. The medium-term fiscal consolidation program of achieving primary surplus by FY 2020 and the plan to raise the consumption tax rate twice was reconfirmed. Finally, concrete measures for the growth strategy were listed in the Japan Revitalization Program, published in June 2013 and revised every year.[17]

In response to the announcement of new policy initiatives, stock prices soared, and private consumption strengthened in anticipation of the improvement in employment and wages. Depreciation of the yen also took place, relieving exporting firms that had been suffering from the appreciation that had continued since 2008. The economy showed recovery and reduced the negative output gap. The inflation rate started to rise toward the 2 percent target by early 2014.

Improvement in corporate profits led to an increase in employment. However, the tightening of the labor market led to only a very limited rise in wages. Improvement in household income proved to be insufficient to absorb the impact of the consumption rate hike that took place in April 2014. Private consumption dropped after the consumption tax rate hike, and the economy weakened. Judging that the economy was too weak to absorb the second consumption tax rate hike scheduled to take place in October 2015, the government postponed it to April 2017.[18] The Bank of Japan also expanded QQE by raising the pace of increase in the monetary base.

Even though the fall in oil prices improved the terms of trade, the slowdown of the global economy, most significantly in China, also delivered a negative influence on growth. As a result, real growth remained weak, and the inflation rate fell back to almost zero by early 2016. In order to address the increase in uncertainty, the Bank of Japan further reinforced QQE by introducing a negative interest rate for part of the current account balance held at the Bank of Japan by financial institutions in January 2016.[19]

In September 2015, Prime Minister Abe declared that Abenomics had entered the second stage. As an agenda for Abenomics II, he proposed a new set of three arrows: creating a strong economy to open up a new future, providing child care support to foster family dreams, and establishing a social security system that leads to a strong sense of reassurance. More than the details of the new three arrows, what should be noted is the fact that the government for the first time committed itself in setting a target for the size of the population; it aims to maintain a population of 100 million in 50 years' time. This reflects the problems that a shrinking population is expected to cause for the Japanese economy, an issue to be touched upon later.

JAPAN-U.S. ECONOMIC RELATIONS IN THE POSTWAR PERIOD

Basis of the Relationship

As the brief economic history indicates, Japan's relationship with the United States has been the most important and successful bilateral economic relationship that Japan has had in the postwar period.

The basis of the close ties between the two countries is their shared values. Both Japan and the United States believe in the importance of respecting the will of the individual and securing free choice. The political system is thus based on democracy, and the economic system on the market. The two countries not only base their systems on these values individually, but also cooperate in protecting and expanding these values. The cooperation of the two countries has been very important particularly in view of the challenges they faced from opposing powers who have had different set of values—most notably the Soviet Union and the Eastern bloc during the Cold War, and China in the most recent period.

As a matter of reality, there was no other choice for Japan but to adopt and to absorb these values after the war, since, after all, the purpose of the U.S. occupation of Japan was to introduce such values into Japan. In this sense, they were given to the nation. However, Japan quickly learned and became aware that these values were indispensably important for the well-being and prosperity of its people. There is no doubt that these values are now deeply imbedded in Japan's economy and society.

Form of the Relationship

Because of their shared values, the economic relationship between Japan and the United States has generally been close and intimate. Needless to say, across the different postwar periods there were some differences in nuance. Between 1945 and 1970, the United States was like a guardian: providing protection to Japan, while teaching Japan the way to reconstruct and develop at the same time. While the United States wanted Japan to take more responsibility in the realm of national security to match the economic power it was achieving, it avoided pressing Japan too hard out of a fear of causing instability in the country. It was a close and strong relationship but was, in a sense, one way.[20] In contrast, after late 1990 the relationship became more balanced. The United States still provides protection, but Japan also shares the burden of the protection. In many areas the two have become more equal partners.

The period between the late 1960s and mid-1990s was different. Starting from textiles and expanding to automobiles and semiconductors, trade frictions brought tension and hostility to the relationship between the two nations.

It is difficult to understand in hindsight why such events took place at a time of the Cold War. Even though the Soviet Union did ultimately collapse, the period saw some serious confrontations with the United States over the deployment of intermediate-range ballistic missiles and the invasion of Afghanistan, among others. Obviously, the United States and Japan should have wanted to avoid confrontation amongst themselves.

The clue may lie in the different trend the two countries were experiencing in terms of macroeconomic performance. On one hand, the United States was gradually losing ground as the largest economy in the world after suffering from chronic low productivity growth and the twin deficit that emerged after its involvement in the Vietnam War. On the other hand, Japan had achieved successive years of high growth and had become the second largest economy in the world with a large current account surplus. The difference heightened frustration in the United States. For a nation that provides protection to Japan, it was intolerable to see the difference in the macroeconomic state.

Such tension gradually receded in the 1990s.[21] A number of factors explain the changes in the political attitude. First, China emerged as a new opposing player in the international power balance game. As already mentioned, China made an important shift in policy stance when it decided to reform and open up its economy in 1979. After a brief interruption starting in late 1989, it resumed its efforts in 1992 and succeeded in expanding trade and achieving remarkable growth. It became a member of the WTO in 2001 and soon overtook Japan to become the second largest economy in the world. China's economic power became prominent in economic development assistance, international policy coordination, and international organizations.

However, despite these achievements, there were concerns over such areas as government intervention (e.g., state owned enterprises), law enforcement (e.g., intellectual property rights), and market norms (e.g., food safety). Trade imbalance is also always a great concern for the United States. The emergence of China became a common challenge for Japan and the United States.

Second, the United States regained its dynamism with the IT revolution. Capital deepening and the increase in total factor productivity in both IT-producing industries as well as IT-using industries raised the labor productivity growth rate above the historical trend. The pickup in growth rate enabled the fiscal balance to record a surplus in the period between FY 1998 and FY 2001. It should not be forgotten, of course, that in the 2000s the subprime mortgage problem and its impact on the financial system led to a global crisis. However, even this event proved that the U.S. economy was flexible and dynamic when it showed a much quicker recovery than Japan.

Third, Japan in contrast began to suffer from long-term stagnation. The average growth rate since the 1990s has been significantly lower than in the past. The output gap has stayed negative, and deflation has become chronic. There are a number of reasons behind this stagnation. Since the 1990s, the current economic system that provides the institutional framework for economic activities (such as the lifetime employment system and the seniority-based wage system) has become inconsistent with recent changes in underlying structural conditions (such as the aging of the population). As a result, limited resources have not been fully mobilized to achieve growth.[22] In addition, in the 1990s and early 2000s severe downward pressures on the economy came from the burst of the bubble. After the mid-2000s, significant downward pressure has been exerted by the aging and declining population.[23]

Fourth, the strength of Japanese exports became a less salient issue in the United States. It is partly due to the loss of its market to Chinese exports, but it is also due to the increase in foreign direct investment by Japanese firms to increase production in the United States so as to replace exports from Japan. Foreign direct investment also created jobs in the United States, which made U.S. society more receptive to Japanese firms and products.[24]

Relationship in the Asia Pacific

These changes worked to reduce tensions between the two countries after the 1990s, and the economic relationship has become more close and intimate in the recent years. One of the main fields in which economic cooperation between the two countries has been successful is the region of the Asia Pacific.

The increase in interdependency across wider Asia has continued to take place. As the region grew (fueled strongly by the establishment of global supply chains), labor costs gradually increased. This provided motivation for investment in a wider range of economies in the region. In order to invite investment and reap its benefits, the free flow of goods, services, and capital was essential. These developments naturally led regional economies to prefer the reduction of barriers to trade, investment, and harmonization of institutional arrangements.

APEC is an organization in which Asian economies, which had become the growth center, are members alongside Japan and the United States. It has committed itself to achieving free and open trade and investment in the region. However, since APEC operates on the basis of nonbinding, voluntary principles, this ambitious program has been difficult to realize.

As a consequence, interest in the Asia-Pacific region gradually shifted to FTAs/EPAs. The APEC economies themselves already had such arrangements—Australia-New Zealand Closer Economic Relations Trade Agreement (ANZCERTA), North American Free Trade Agreement (NAFTA), and ASEAN Free Trade Area (AFTA)—but the number of FTAs/EPAs is increasing at a fast pace. Regional integration continues to expand and deepen.

Japan was slow at first to engage in bilateral free trade agreements because of its focus on a multilateral agreement under GATT/WTO. However, it became evident that the negotiations in WTO faced a stalemate. It led Japan to become more positive toward bilateral negotiations. Japan signed its first EPA with Singapore in January 2002. Japan's share of trade between countries with FTAs/EPAs, even when those that have not yet been ratified such as Trans-Pacific Partnership (TPP) are included, remains low at 39.5 percent in 2015, far behind competitors like South Korea (67.4 percent in 2015). In this respect, the recent successful conclusion of the TPP negotiations in October 2015 should significantly make up for the delay. With the United States and Japan as members, it commands about 40 percent of world GDP and about a quarter of world trade.

In the international finance area, the long-awaited regional monetary organization was finally established when the ASEAN+3 Macroeconomic Research Office (AMRO) started its operation in February 2016. It will conduct regional economic surveillance and supports the implementation of the multilateral version of the CMI, the Chiang Mai Initiative Multilateralization (CMIM). This time, the United States did not oppose its establishment, probably because AMRO has emphasized its closer cooperation with the IMF, and there was growing acknowledgment of a need for regional arrangements after the experience of the Asian financial and European sovereign debt crises.

PROSPECTS FOR JAPAN IN THE WORLD
IN THE TWENTY-FIRST CENTURY

Looking ahead into the middle of the twenty-first century and thereafter, some significant changes are expected to take place both globally and domestically. They should affect Japan's relationship with other countries and its contribution to the world.

Global Changes Expected in the Twenty-First Century

One of the significant changes that is going to take place globally is related to China and India, which continue to grow faster than the developed economies. China, which has already become the second largest economy in the world, is in general expected to continue to grow at a relatively high rate. By extrapolating the past trend of real GDP growth, it is expected that China will eventually overtake the United States and become the largest economy in the world.[25]

However, China will not be able to continue to grow as it has in the past. It is expected to slow down in the long term because of the multiple transitions it will have to make simultaneously. First, a structural transformation from an economy that is dependent on investment to one that is more dependent on consumption has to be made. It is essential in resolving the overcapacity that has become apparent in its heavy industries. Second, the negative impact of the burst of the bubble in the real estate and stock markets has to be overcome. If the nonperforming assets are left unresolved, they will continue to exert negative influence on the economic activities of households, firms, banks, and the government. Third, adaptation to the aging and the declining population that have resulted from the one-child policy has to be made. China's working age population (those aged between 15 and 59) is already declining as of 2012, and the total population is expected to start declining in the 2030s. The decline in population is sure to constrain China's long-term potential growth rate.[26]

Taking into account the difficulties China faces, the average real growth rate could fall to less than 1 percent in the 2040s. However, even if the growth rate is subject to slowing over the long term, China will still be able to maintain its second place ranking, admittedly a great achievement.[27]

What is more spectacular is the fact that India is expected to achieve even higher growth. That is because of its ample room to catch up, its potential to shift to a more market-oriented economic policy, and its young and growing population. After achieving an average real growth rate of 7.5 percent in the 2000s, India is still expected to grow by more than 4 percent in the 2020s and 2030s and above 3 percent in the 2040s. It is expected to overtake Japan to become the third largest economy in the world.[28]

Domestic Changes Expected in the Twenty-First Century

The changes that are going to take place domestically relate to Japan's aging and declining population, which has already become a heavy burden on its economy. Not only will Japan's growth potential continue to be subject to downward pressure, but significant changes are also expected to take place in its external relationships.

According to the official projection shown in Figure 3.2, Japan's total population, estimated at 128.1 million in 2010, is expected to

Figure 3.2   Demographic Projections

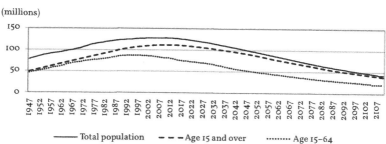

(millions)

———— Total population   − − −Age 15 and over   ·········Age 15–64

Data source: "Population Projections for Japan: 2010–2060" and "Auxiliary Projections: 2061–2110," National Institute of Population and Social Security Research.

Figure 3.3   Old-Age Dependency Ratio

(per 100)

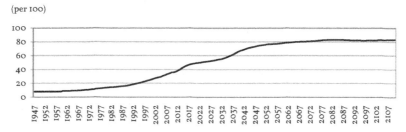

Data source: "Population Projections for Japan: 2010–2060" and "Auxiliary Projections: 2061–2110," National Institute of Population and Social Security Research.

shrink to 86.7 million people by 2060, or to about two-thirds of the 2010 level. In the following 50 years (by 2110), the total population is projected to shrink to 42.9 million people, or to about one-third of the population in 2010.[29]

At the same time, the aging of Japan's population is going to advance further. As Figure 3.3 shows, the old-age dependency ratio—the ratio of the number of people aged over 65 to those between 15 and 64—will rise from 36.1 percent in 2010 to 78.4 percent in 2060, and eventually further to 83.3 percent in 2110.

The rapid decline in population, at an average rate of minus 1.1 percent per annum, will lower the contribution of labor input to the potential growth rate.[30] The current potential growth rate of about 0.5 percent, which already incorporates some of the negative impact of the demographic change, may fall further in the long term. According to one projection, Japan's average real GDP growth rate is expected to fall to –0.1 percent in the 2030s and –0.4 percent in the 2040s.[31]

If the Japanese economy is to grow, it will be necessary to offset the negative effect in some way. To that end, efforts need to be made by the government as well as by the private sector.[32] It is in this sense that Abenomics II, announced in September 2015, is important.

Japan's Contribution to the Twenty-First Century

In view of these changes, there are reasons to expect that the nature of Japan's contribution to the world will also change in the long term.

RECEIVING GOODS, SERVICES, AND CAPITAL

One of the most significant changes to occur in the global context is the fact that Japan will no longer be a net supplier of goods and capital, but will instead become a net receiver of them. Immediately after World War II, Japan was a young country with an ample young labor force and a high household savings rate. This enabled it to achieve high growth with a large current account surplus. Its main contribution to the world during the period was through supplying high value-added goods to other countries. Japan also contributed by providing foreign direct investment and portfolio investment abroad. It contributed in establishing a global supply chain in the Asian region. The external activities of the Japanese economy provided one of the main drivers of growth and development in the region.

Because of the aging and declining population, however, the situation is doomed to change quite rapidly. It means that the household savings rate will eventually turn negative and the current account to a deficit. As Figures 3.4 and 3.5 show, early signs of this are already

Figure 3.4   Household Savings Rate

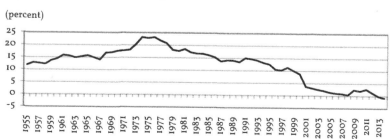

Data source: "Long-Term Data Series," Economic Research Bureau, Cabinet Office.

Figure 3.5   Current Account Balance

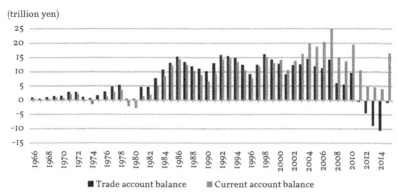

(trillion yen)

■ Trade account balance   ■ Current account balance

Data source: "Long-Term Data Series," Economic Research Bureau, Cabinet Office.

observable in the data. It means that Japan will have to import more goods and services and also to receive more capital inflows in order to finance domestic investment.

Japan has been good at opening up in terms of "going out" but will now have to change to be good at opening up in terms of "receiving in." In this regard, it will be in Japan's interest to remove barriers against transactions of goods and capital if the country is to survive.

ACCEPTING FOREIGN WORKERS

At the same time, Japan will have to change its policy toward foreign workers. Instead of the very restrictive policy that has been in place, it needs to invite more workers from abroad if the negative impact of changing demographics is to be cancelled out in order to secure positive growth.

As already mentioned, the impact of the aging of and decline in Japan's population is expected to exert a negative impact on potential growth in the long term. In order to prevent the potential growth rate from turning negative and to raise it to a comfortable positive rate, which is necessary to sustain fiscal and social security systems, significant efforts are needed. There are a number of options to which Japan could resort.[33] Yet even if all options were implemented, it would still be essential to increase foreign workers in the medium term. This would offset the negative impact on labor input that the aging and declining population may have, and contribute to maintaining growth momentum in the Japanese economy.

Accepting more foreign workers would require a significant change in people's mindsets as well as the social system. It may require some time in order to make it happen. When it does, it should help in maintaining the population in the medium to long term in Japan. At the same time, it should also contribute to equalizing wages across the economies in the region (higher wages for the foreign workers), and also in transferring human capital abroad, probably most significantly to neighboring economies in Asia.[34]

INTEGRATING FTAS/EPAS

Even though many changes are expected to occur, they would not change the fundamental value that Japan places in democracy and a free and open market. As mentioned, Japan has benefited greatly from the international framework for free and open trade and investment as well as the international arrangement for stable foreign exchange. Japan was able to grow at a pace unprecedented in economic history and became one of the largest economies in the world. In return, Japan gradually exerted its influence for the well-being of the international community. In particular, Japan focused on the Asia-Pacific region in establishing a stable environment for development. Japan should continue to promote free and open trade and investment as well as to harmonize institutional arrangements, particularly in the region.

In this respect, close cooperation with the United States, which has the largest influence in international policy setting, will be essential. Japan needs to cooperate in such international institutions as the IMF, World Bank, and WTO. In a more regional sense, APEC is still the main forum for promoting free and open trade and investment and exchanging information and ideas in the region. As two of the main members in the forum, it is important that the United States and Japan continue to cooperate in making it more effective and conducive to growth and prosperity of the region.[35]

As a way of cooperating in the Asia Pacific, Japan and the United States do not need to form a group on all occasions. If the two have deep understanding and trust between them, there could be a division of labor in terms of the area or organization. That attitude did not seem to have been in place when the AMF was proposed in the late 1990s but has since been gradually formed to allow AMRO to be established. In an area as dynamic as the Asia Pacific, it is difficult for either country to be fully visible in all activities in the region. Fostering understanding and trust and engaging in a division of labor deserve serious consideration.[36]

One of the region's more recent features is the proliferation of FTAs/EPAs. The most recent developments include the successful conclusion of the Trans-Pacific Partnership (TPP) negotiations in October 2015, and the creation of the ASEAN Economic Community (AEC) in January 2016. There are negotiations taking place among the ASEAN countries and six countries in the region—Australia, China, India, Korea, and New Zealand as well as Japan—to create a Regional Comprehensive Economic Partnership (RCEP). The realization of a Free Trade Area of the Asia Pacific (FTAAP), which has been proposed by the United States, is also being studied within the framework of APEC. These arrangements could further expand economic interdependency to a wider range of countries.

While pursuing an increase in the number of FTAs/EPAs, the pros and cons of these partial arrangements needs to be acknowledged. Regional agreements inevitably involve a trade diversion effect as well as a trade creation effect. They are clearly less efficient relative to multilateral agreements. If the regional agreements are to be justified, it is only when they are considered to be temporary arrangements that would eventually move toward the final goal of a global arrangement. It is important that countries do not lose track of the importance of reaping the dynamic gains of regional arrangements; the integration of the existing FTAs/EPAs needs to be pursued. Japan and the United States, which are both committed to achieving a global arrangement under the auspices of the WTO, should be ready to play a more significant role in this respect.

EXTENDING HIGH-QUALITY MARKETS AND SOCIETIES

Japan may be at a stage where a new approach toward international society should be taken. This comes from the acknowledgment that Japan should no longer emphasize the size of the economy in contributing to the international community. The size of the economy, being the third largest economy in the world, is not yet that small. However, the decline in the potential growth rate reduces the relative importance of emphasizing its size. Instead, Japan should emphasize the importance of achieving a high-quality economy that would lead to greater well-being for its people. This involves both high-quality markets and high-quality living standards.

The necessary condition for a high-quality market is the freedom to compete and trade with others. However, there are other sufficient conditions for it to be a high-quality market, including such attributes as the transparency and reliability of trade as well as the quality, safety, and punctuality of goods and services. Japan can be considered to be one of the markets that could be seen as successfully achieving such attributes.[37]

The quality of development in Japan can be seen in the longevity of its people. Average life expectancy at birth was 87.05 years for Japanese women and 80.79 for men in 2015. They are both among the best longevity in the world. While aging is often seen as a problem, in particular from the point of view of the social security system, it is still an admirable achievement. Other indications of the high quality of development can be seen in the low infant mortality rate, low homicide rate, low assault rate, and high literacy and numeracy rate, among others.[38] They can be considered to be among the qualitative targets that should be achieved by economic growth and development. Transferring Japan's know-how and institutional arrangements in achieving such a high-quality economy should benefit the development of other economies.

CONCLUSION

Japan is struggling to overcome the problems that it currently faces in realizing a higher growth potential. On the one hand, the current economic system, the origin of which was established in the high-growth period where an ample young labor force was available, has become outdated and inconsistent with demographic changes, and is now preventing the limited resources available to make a maximum contribution to growth. On the other hand, Japan needs to tackle the negative influence coming from the aging and declining population. Its impact on capital input and total factor productivity as well as on labor input will inevitably lower Japan's growth potential further.

The problems in the domestic economy have implications for Japan's position in the global economy. Japan has been overtaken by China in terms of the size of its GDP. Japan has lost confidence in its economic power, which was once the source of its influence in the international community.

From a different angle, however, in terms of the quality of the market and of society, Japan can be regarded as one of the leaders in the world. There are many aspects of the economy of which Japan can be proud. In that respect, by transferring the lessons it has learned during the process of its own development to other countries, Japan should be able to make a significant contribution to other economies that would like to follow its path.

In turn, Japan would benefit from the dynamic expansion of Asian and other economies, which would stimulate Japanese economic activity through global supply chain activities. It would also benefit from the capital and labor that would be supplied to Japan in order to compensate for the negative impact of the demographic changes. In this context, this chapter suggested areas that Japan may be able to contribute to the world and the Asia-Pacific region in particular. They include such areas as integrating the achievements of FTAs/EPAs, facilitating international mobility of labor, and transferring experience and lessons for achieving a high-quality economy.

Most of the areas, however, lack forums for analyzing and discussing the related issues in the Asia-Pacific context. APEC's economic committee has the potential to be one, but it currently focuses on promoting structural policy to remove obstacles to trade and investment and to doing business. PECC used to have a Pacific economic outlook (PEO) project, which discussed economic forecasts and structural issues in an analytical manner, but PEO has ceased its activity as of 2014. At this moment, there is no existing forum that could analyze and discuss these issues.

Creation of such forums in the Asia-Pacific context would be an important first step in securing the prosperity of the region. Japan, in cooperation with the United States, should take the initiative in making such a move. After all, Japan will only be able to develop further by developing along with the Asian and the global economies. Japan's contribution to international society will benefit not only the future of the global economy but also that of its own economy.

NOTES

1. The beginning and the ending years for each of the periods are determined by taking account of the dates of the peaks and troughs of business cycles. The dates are formally identified by an academic committee set up in the Economic and Social Research Institute of the Cabinet Office.

2. Japanese Economic Planning Agency, *Economic White Paper*, 1956.

3. Japanese Economic Planning Agency, *Economic White Paper*, 1960.

4. It is interesting to note that the recession between October 1964 and October 1965, which separates the two phases of the high-growth period, is often called a structural recession. Indeed, it was a structural watershed between domestic demand-driven growth and a period of export-driven growth. In addition, it also opened the floodgates to some structural changes that were unprecedented up until that time. The recession saw the collapse of a number of large firms, accompanied by a financial crisis that led to an emergency liquidity provision by the Bank of Japan. In view of the economic difficulties, government bonds were issued for the first time under the new Fiscal Law of 1947. In fiscal year (FY) 1966, construction bonds, which are for financing asset-creating expenditures, started to be issued (and continue to be issued to date).

5. European countries were not supportive of Japan's membership bid to the OECD, which was, until 1961, called the Organization for European Economic Cooperation (OEEC). Japanese membership was again made possible by the support of the United States.

6. It should be noted that textiles in the early 1970s were not the first VERs to be implemented. In fact, VERs have a long history, going back to a VER on Japanese tuna exports to the United States in 1952.

7. The period is generally called the stable growth period. This terminology is not adopted here because of the fact that the real GDP growth rate, as well as the environment for growth, was far from stable.

8. Trade frictions in the 1970s included those over steel and color TVs, for which VERs were introduced.

9. G5 members are: France, Germany, Japan, the United Kingdom, and the United States.

10. Prior to this period, there were foreign direct investments to purchase rights in the energy sector of energy-producing economies. Foreign direct investment was also made in the United States and Europe to establish production sites within their borders to overcome barriers to trade. The changes in the nature of Japanese foreign direct investment over the years were discussed in Jun Saito, "Deepening of Economic Interdependence in the Asia-Pacific Region: Its Structure and Driving Forces" (paper presented at Economic Planning Agency conference on "Macroeconomic Interdependence in the Asia Pacific Region," Tokyo, Japan, October 1996).

11. The policy rate of the Bank of Japan was changed from an official discount rate to a collateralized overnight call rate in 1995. The "official discount rate" term itself was formally abolished in 2006.

12. For a discussion on the business cycle during the period, see Jun Saito "The Japanese Business Cycle after 1991: How Is It Different, and Why?," *Journal of Asian Economics* 8, no. 2 (Summer 1997): 263–293.

13. The author was responsible for planning and drafting the first *APEC Economic Outlook* in 1995 for the Economic Committee of APEC. The main theme of the *Outlook* was the deepening of economic interdependence within the region.

14. The United States was also very negative about the prospect of Asian countries setting up institutions in the region that did not include itself. The proposal in 1990 by Prime Minister Mahathir Mohamad of Malaysia to create an East Asia Economic Group (EAEG) also faced U.S. opposition.

15. The members of the G20 are: Argentina, Australia, Brazil, Canada, China, France, the European Union, Germany, India, Indonesia, Italy, Japan, the Republic of Korea, Mexico, Russia, Saudi Arabia, South Africa, Turkey, the United Kingdom, and the United States.

16. The timing of Japan receding to third place globally in terms of GDP as mentioned above (and cited often) is based on a comparison of nominal GDPs converted to a common currency by using market exchange rates. If the comparison is made by using purchasing power parity (PPP), the timing would be brought forward to as early as 1999. It reflects the undervaluation of the renminbi in the market relative to its PPP. See the World Bank DataBank.

17. Structural policy has been slow in showing progress. However, more concrete results have started to show up in recent years. One of the most significant is the successful conclusion of the Trans-Pacific Partnership negotiations (October 2015). Other achievements include the designation of nine areas as national strategic zones, where experiments in deregulation will be tested for future extension to other regions (May 2014 and December 2015), and the introduction of a Stewardship Code and Corporate Governance Code (February 2014 and June 2015, respectively). A reduction of the effective corporate tax rate to below 30 percent and the liberalization of the retail electricity industry have also become effective as of April 2016.

18. In June 2016, it was announced that the second consumption tax rate hike to 10 percent would be postponed again to October 2019.

19. The QQE was further strengthened when the Bank of Japan announced that a yield curve control with inflation-overshooting commitment would be introduced in September 2016.

20. This period was concluded by the extension of the Japan-U.S. security treaty in June 1970 and the reversion of Okinawa to Japan in May 1972.

21. The fading of tension did not mean a direct return to intimacy. To use common terminology, after Japan bashing came Japan passing, followed by Japan nothing.

22. Problems with the current Japanese economic system are discussed in Jun Saito, "Economic Growth and Economic System," in *Economics for the Development of a Super Mature Society,* ed. Yoshio Higuchi, Kohei Komamura, and Jun Saito (Tokyo: Keio University Press, 2013), in Japanese.

23. It is often mentioned that Japan has lost two decades, namely the 1990s and 2000s. However, as is indicated, the reasons for the stagnation in each period are quite different. In this sense, the two decades should be decoupled.

24. The establishment of the WTO dispute settlement system in 1995 also contributed to avoiding direct confrontation over specific trade issues.

25. In fact, in PPP terms, China's nominal GDP is estimated to have overtaken the United States' in 2014. See the World Bank DataBank.

26. In a sense, China is about to go through a number of transitions simultaneously that Japan experienced in a sequence. Japan experienced the slowing down from the high-growth period in the 1970s, the resolution of the nonperforming loans in the 1990s and 2000s, and tackling the downward pressure coming from its aging and declining population in and after the 2010s. Even if China is able to draw lessons from Japan's experience, this will still be an overwhelming task.

27. For the details of these projections, see Japan Center for Economic Research (JCER), *Vision 2050: Long-Term Forecast and Policy Proposal* (Tokyo: Japan Center for Economic Research, 2013).

28. For the details of these projections, see JCER, *Vision 2050.* It should be noted that, if nominal GDP is compared in PPP terms, India had already overtaken Japan by 2008. See the World Bank DataBank.

29. For details, see National Institute of Population and Social Security Research, "Population Projections for Japan: 2010–2060," and "Auxiliary Projections: 2061–2110," Tokyo, January 2012. The projections cited assume medium-fertility rate and medium-mortality rate.

30. Applying a simple growth accounting framework, it implies that, even taking into account only its impact on labor input, the potential growth rate would be subject to a downward pressure of 0.7 percent per annum. Similarly, if the calculation is based on the rate of decline in the working age population, which is −1.3 percent, the downward pressure would be 0.9 percent. While acknowledging that the actual magnitude of the downward pressure depends on how the participation and structural unemployment rates behave, it does show that the impact of declining population on the potential growth rate is significant.

31. JCER, *Vision 2050.* It is based on a projection assuming no policy change in Japan.

32. An early discussion of this issue can be found in Yutaka Kosai, Jun Saito, and Naohiro Yashiro, "Declining Population and Sustained Growth: Can They Coexist?," *American Economic Review: Papers and Proceedings* (May 1998).

33. Other important but difficult options include raising the participation rate of women and the aged, raising total factor productivity, and raising the fertility rate. The pros and cons are discussed in Jun Saito, "The Causes of Population Decline and the Measures to Overcome Its Impact," in *Innovation in a Super Aging and Population Declining Society*, ed. Yoshio Higuchi, Kohei Komamura, and Jun Saito (Tokyo: Keio University Press, 2016), in Japanese. A summary of the discussion can be found in Jun Saito, "Agenda for the Second Stage of Abenomics," *Japanese Economy Update*, Japan Center for Economic Research, October 6, 2015.

34. Issues related to accepting more foreign workers to Japan are discussed in Jun Saito, "Immigration: A Solution for Plummeting Population?," *East Asia Forum Quarterly* 6, no. 3 (July–September 2014).

35. While emphasis has been given mainly to the Asia-Pacific region, it should also be given to the relationship between Asia and Europe. Compared to the relationship between Asia and the United States as well as between Europe and the United States, the relationship between Asia and Europe has been limited. The recognition that this missing link needs to be strengthened led to the creation of the Asia-Europe Meeting (ASEM) in 1994 at the governmental level and forums like the Asia Europe Economic Forum (AEEF) in 2006 at a more individual level. Japan can also play a significant role in strengthening this relationship.

36. The suggestion shares the vision similar to the notion of virtual unipolarity. See Michael J. Green and Patrick M. Cronin, eds., *The U.S.-Japan Alliance: Past, Present, and Future* (New York: Council on Foreign Relations, 1999).

37. The author calls this the PQRST (punctuality, quality, reliability, safety, and transparency) of the quality of a market.

38. See, for instance, Organization for Economic Cooperation and Development (OECD), "Better Life Index: Japan," Paris, October 2015; and OECD, "How's Life in Japan," Paris, October 2015. Both documents also suggest areas where Japan should make more improvement.

4. WILL THE SUN ALSO RISE? FIVE GROWTH STRATEGIES FOR JAPAN

Yoko Takeda

INTRODUCTION

As economists Daron Acemoglu, Simon Johnson, and James A. Robinson once wrote, "The most trite yet crucial question in the field of economic growth and development is: why are some countries much poorer than others?"[1]

Japan has undergone two full-fledged political, economic, and institutional reformations since the eighteenth century. The first was prompted by the Meiji restoration in 1867, and the second occurred during Japan's post–World War II reconstruction. As Glenn Hubbard and Tim Kane note, three decades after the Meiji restoration/reformation, Japan's gross domestic product (GDP) per capita had grown by 70 percent, and by 1913 it had doubled outright.[2] By 1938, it had doubled again. Acemoglu, Johnson, and Robinson emphasize the institutional aspects behind the early phase of the Japanese growth story, noting that "by 1890, Japan was the first Asian country to adopt a written constitution, and it created a constitutional monarchy with an elected parliament, the Diet, and an independent judiciary."[3]

In the postwar era, Hiroshi Yoshikawa identifies the 15 years from 1955 to 1970 as the Japanese economy's high-growth period.[4] I largely follow Yoshikawa's definition of the high-growth period in this chapter, but sometimes extend it to cover 1954 to 1973. A few numbers are worth noting: on average, Japan's real GDP per capita

Figure 4.1   Japan's GDP and per Capita GDP

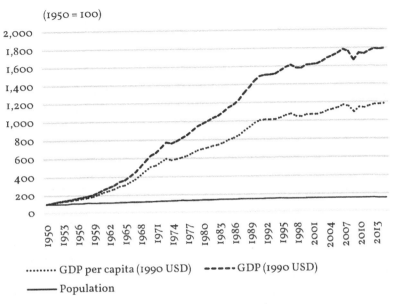

(1950 = 100)

.... GDP per capita (1990 USD)   ----- GDP (1990 USD)

——— Population

Data source: The Conference Board, Total Economy Database.

grew by 8.7 percent annually from 1955 to 1970. Figure 4.1 shows Japan's GDP and per capita GDP. Debate is still under way as to the precise factors that enabled this rapid growth. Most existing studies consider the prime factors to have been demographics (even if per capita GDP is taken into consideration), the so-called catching-up hypothesis, and innovation. The next section of this chapter examines these issues in greater detail.

Since 1990, Japan has been mired in the so-called lost decades—a protracted period of economic stagnation, especially since the late 1990s. It has struggled with problems in the financial sector, illustrated by massive stocks of nonperforming loans (NPLs) and the challenge of long-lasting deflation.

The remainder of this chapter looks briefly at Japan's rise and fall in the postwar period and discusses what has been found and lost since the 1950s. It then focuses more extensively on what Japan lost in the mid-1990s. In some cases, factors that aided Japan's development earlier in the postwar period became entrenched and turned into weaknesses. The "dead hand of vested interests" began to hamper the process of innovation and change.[5] Along with this issue, I consider why Japan lost its strength over the lost two decades. After considering what was found and lost, this chapter then presents a policy package for reinvigorating the Japanese economy composed of five Ds: dynamic labor markets; diversity; destructive innovation; decentralization (or disinvestment from Tokyo); and deleveraging.

WHY JAPAN LOST ITS STRENGTH OVER THE LAST TWO DECADES: SEVEN TURNING POINTS

Japan's Peaking and Soon-to-Be-Declining Labor Force

The National Institute of Population and Social Security Research (NIPSSR) has conducted important estimates of the past and future of Japan's population. Japan's population steadily increased from the Meiji era through 2012, when it peaked at 127 million. According to these forecasts, Japan's population is subsequently beginning the slow process of falling back to the level of that in the Meiji era. By 2060, NIPSSR projects Japan's population will decrease to 87 million, a level comparable to that of the 1950s.[6] Given that Japan's birthrate is expected to remain at the current ultra-low level, the rest of the world could well find Japan a tiny country in 2100, much the way it appeared when the world discovered it at the start of the Meiji era. This is the quiet warning posed by NIPSSR's projection.

Japan's working-age population peaked in 1995 and started declining thereafter. In general, long-term economic growth depends—albeit not necessarily equally—on three factors: labor input, capital input, and technological progress. More workers and capital accumulation contribute to more production. On the flip side, a declining labor force reduces output (see Figure 4.2). Labor input depends on the size of the total working-age population. While the definition of working-age population varies slightly across

Figure 4.2   Japan's Productivity Growth

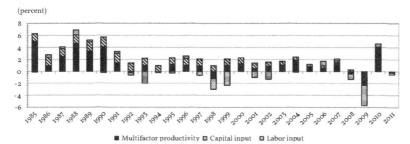

Data source: Organization for Economic Cooperation and Development.

jurisdictions, a popular measure is the number of individuals between the ages of 15 and 64.

Two factors have led to the decline in Japan's working-age population: a declining birthrate and population aging. In 1950, the ratio of over 65-year-olds to the total population was less than 5 percent. By 1970, this ratio had risen to 7 percent, and reached 14 percent in 1994. By this point, the notion of a graying society was well-established. In 2013, 25 percent of Japan's population was over the age of 65.

As noted, policymakers were struggling with NPLs in the mid-1990s. It took time for their efforts to materialize, leading to more than 10 years focused on financial sector reforms. Meanwhile, problems stemming from the ultra-low birthrate went unnoticed. Demographic issues should have been prioritized earlier, but serious discussion did not start until the 2000s. A prime illustration is the shortage of childcare centers. As this shortage has intensified in recent years, it has drawn increasing attention, but policy responses have emerged slowly. This shortage has contributed to a further decline in the birthrate and impeded women's participation in the labor force. Due to the confluence of these trends, the labor force in Japan has been quietly decreasing. In my view, the tapering of the labor force was one of the most important factors during Japan's two lost decades.

End of Two Catch-Up Attempts

The rapid growth of the Japanese economy in the post–World War II period, as well as the modernization of its national economic system and the technological advancement of its private sector, is partly due to Japan's catching up with the U.S. and Western European economies. Japan's per capita GDP, which was 20 percent of the U.S. level in the 1950s, rose to 70 percent by the end of the so-called high-growth era in the 1970s. Hubbard and Kane describe a Japanese supermodel characterized by (1) elite bureaucrats, politicians, and bankers working together in pursuit of a common goal as part of "Japan Inc." and (2) highly educated, diligent workers willing to save for tomorrow rather than consume today.[7] Hubbard and Kane further argue that the supermodel had operated in pursuit of a single national objective since the Meiji restoration: catch up with the United States and Western Europe. This remained unchanged for a long time and was supported by broad popular enthusiasm. In summary, the process of catching up with frontrunners promoted Japan's productivity growth.

In the early 1990s, Japan's per capita GDP reached almost 90 percent of the United States'. That was the end of the catching-up story. Japan not only failed to outgrow the United States, it failed to fully catch up. The explanation Hubbard and Kane provide is that Japan's managed capitalism was a great model for catching up with the frontier, but moving beyond that frontier required replacing Japan Inc. with entrepreneurial capitalism.[8] Japan Inc. had succeeded in providing secure jobs to a massive labor force, but, precisely because it was so successful, there was little incentive for an entrepreneurial spirit to develop. Japan's model did not generate pioneering innovation, which is one of the main characteristics of the American economy. The lack of entrepreneurship may be affecting (and affected by) other issues discussed later in this chapter.

Japan demonstrated a model that a number of countries followed, including South Korea since the 1990s and China since the 2000s. South Korea's GDP per capita increased from 56 percent of Japan's in 1990 to almost 90 percent in 2013. China's GDP per capita is currently around 30 percent of Japan's, but has grown rapidly from 8 percent in the 1990s. Based on Hubbard, Kane, and others, I suggest the following hypothesis on the rise and fall of the Japanese economy: Japan was successful in establishing a supermodel in pursuit of the frontier, but it could not evolve into a new model to push the frontier outward.[9] As a result, while Japan was dawdling a few steps from the frontier, South Korea successfully caught up with Japan.

The International Institute for Management Development (IMD) world competitiveness ranking provides some insights in line with this hypothesis.[10] In the mid-2000s, Japan's IMD rank improved somewhat, and has been climbing since Prime Minister Shinzo Abe's administration took power in late 2012. However, taking a longer perspective, Japan's IMD ranking has been lackluster for years. By comparison, the United States has, by and large, kept the top rank since 1994. Germany, whose rank fell in the mid-2000s, has ranked within the top 10 following a remarkable comeback. In the meantime, Korea and China have been steadily climbing the charts. Back in the early 1990s, Japan ranked above them by a margin of 30 percent. More recently, these three East Asian countries have been engaged in a rivalry with thin margins.

The IMD ranking is computed by integrating multiple submeasures, such as economic performance, government efficiency, business efficiency, infrastructure, and so forth. The 2014 results rate Japan second (after the United States) in terms of scientific infrastructure, which consists of total national expenditure on research and development, scientific articles, Nobel Prizes, patent applications, and other related metrics. A key implication of the 2014 results is that Japan's high competitiveness in scientific infrastructure does not translate into business efficiency, in which Japan ranks 19th. Business efficiency is a combination index, and Japan's evaluations measured by the subcomponents of this index are markedly low. For example, Japan ranks 42nd in adaptability of companies to market change, 54th in flexibility and adaptability, and 55th in entrepreneurship. In sum, Japan has highly valued technologies in basic and theoretical research areas, but such valuable technologies are not well-applied to practical uses. Accordingly, the key challenges for Japan are two-fold: (1) for researchers, possibly with help from business experts, to learn entrepreneurship so that their valuable technologies can be better marketed; and (2) for existing firms to better apply newly invented technologies to their business. For both challenges, better marketing skills are needed to translate in-laboratory technologies into business competitiveness.

Low Turnover, Turnaround, and Small Number of Start-Ups

It has been widely reported that the low productivity of the Japanese corporate sector, and the service sector in particular, stems from low business turnover. As mentioned above, the decline in the working-age population has hampered economic growth since the mid-1990s, but labor input is not the entire reason. Other factors held constant, while the marginal products of both labor and capital have been experiencing decreasing returns, just as articulated in production theory in microeconomics textbooks. Accordingly, as an economy grows with labor and capital, total factor productivity (TFP) increasingly becomes the important factor for sustained growth.

Relatedly, Yoshikawa points out that Japan's high growth rates during the 1960s could be attributed to innovations rather than simply catching up with the frontrunners.[11] Yoshikawa's view, at least in part, contrasts with that of Hubbard and Kane outlined above. Yoshikawa points to two empirical findings. First, Japan has achieved the highest productivity of any advanced industrial nation in machinery and material industries, such as electrical machines, automobiles, iron and steel, nonferrous metals, pulps, and papers. Second, from 1945 to the 1960s, a number of well-known Japanese firms were born that later created new ideas, innovations, and technologies. For example, Tokyo Communication Industry Ltd., which later came to be known as Sony, was founded in 1946. Honda Ltd. and Sanyo were established in 1948 and 1950, respectively.

Bearing this in mind, some may identify low turnover and very few start-ups in the current Japanese economy as the key impediments that hamper economic growth and contribute to the declining trend in TFP. Old firms with low productivity tend to remain in the market, while new entrants with high productivity are rarely observed. As a result, average productivity declines. Takeo Hoshi and Anil Kashyap argue that, although firms with low profitability/ productivity should discontinue their business and leave the market, creditors and governments support these low-performing zombie firms.[12]

If that had been the case, highly skilled labor could have been reallocated more smoothly and quickly from the zombie firms to high-profitability firms. Misallocation of labor due to excessive support for zombie firms undermined labor productivity.[13] At the minimum, I can point to two data points that support Hoshi and Kashyap's view.

First, data on corporate entry and exit rates in Japan show that the entry rate has been on a downward trend, while the exit rate has remained broadly steady at a low level. Until the 1980s, the entry rate was above 5 percent. Since the 1990s, the entry rate has declined to around 3.5 percent. More puzzling is that the exit rate did not rise in the 1990s even as the nonperforming loans issue was drawing significant attention. In the 2000s, when public bailouts were engineered for some firms, the exit rate rose slightly. Most surprisingly, the exit rate remained steady from 2007 to 2009 during the global financial crisis. One reason for this is a public assistance policy known as the Small and Medium Enterprises (SMEs) Finance Facilitation Act, under which cheap money was provided to certain SMEs regardless of their profitability/productivity. In the meantime, as already mentioned, the entry rate remained low. Hence, there is some evidence that potentially promising start-ups were crowded out by the zombie firms.

Second, the level of entrepreneurial activity in Japan is low. The Global Entrepreneurship Monitor (GEM) indicates that Japan ranks 69th in total early-stage entrepreneurial activity among 70 countries.[14] Looking into the key indicators of the GEM reveals that Japan is ranked 70th out of 70 countries in terms of both perceived opportunities and perceived capabilities. Similarly, Japan ranks 64th (among 65 countries) in entrepreneurship as a desirable career choice and 60th (among 66 countries) in high-status successful entrepreneurship. These indicators are not another useless statistic. A cross-country regression confirms a significant positive correlation between this GEM index and per capita real GDP. This evidence suggests that Japan's low productivity, or stagnant productivity growth, can be partly explained by the low activities of entrepreneurs.

In Japan's post-bubble period, researchers observed the absence of the aforementioned replacement mechanism and the low activities of entrepreneurs, which can explain the steady declines in productivity growth rates.[15]

Deteriorating Human Capital

In this section, I discuss issues revolving around human capital, which affects GDP per capita. I examine two aspects of human capital development: issues regarding the tertiary and secondary education system, and intra-firm underinvestment in human capital.

DECAYING EDUCATIONAL INFRASTRUCTURE

Until the late 1990s, there was growing criticism of the then-prevailing cramming education system. Against this backdrop, the curriculum in Japanese public high schools and junior high schools was diluted from the early 2000s. The new system was sarcastically dubbed the pressure-free curriculum education system (or *yutori* education), and later provoked backlash due to significant deterioration of students' abilities in various subjects. In the pressure-free system, the overall curriculum, together with class hours, was downsized by 30 percent. The downsizing of the curriculum may have taken pressure off students, but it simultaneously took away opportunities to gain knowledge and develop human capital during school days. Some negative outcomes of the pressure-free system can be found, for example, in Japan's worsening performance on the Programme for International Student Assessment (PISA) measures published by the Organization for Economic Cooperation and Development (OECD).

Following the introduction of the new system, the PISA results showed noticeable deterioration in the quantitative literacy, reading comprehension, and scientific literacy of Japanese children at the age of 15. The PISA evidence contributed to the backlash against the pressure-free system, which was eventually replaced by a more intense curriculum similar to the old system. Following this shift, the 2012 PISA results showed some signs of Japan recovering its global ranking.[16] Nonetheless, Japan ranked first in mathematics performance in 2000, but seventh in 2012. Some lost capital has yet to be replenished.

For a long time, the Japanese primary and secondary education system has aimed at achieving overall excellence, similar to the United States' no children left behind (NCLB) policy, rather than sorting and screening elites for tertiary education. While an NCLB-style policy facilitated Japan's development of a high-quality mass labor force, its dark side has increasingly been gaining attention. As discussed earlier, during Japan's catching-up process, the NCLB approach was an ideal way to build a high-quality labor force capable of undertaking core roles in mass production industries. On the other hand, in the era of information technology (IT), the knowledge-based economy has increased the need for innovators, highly skilled creators, scientists, well-trained engineers, and highly capable managers. These professionals are competitive individuals in global markets. Investing in human capital leads to successful business, and more profit attracts more human capital: a virtuous cycle now regarded as an essential practice in a number of growing industries.

Japan's tertiary education system is also facing serious challenges from changing global competitors. While Japan's corporate sector is considered top ranked in terms of productivity, the country's universities perform poorly in global rankings. For example, the 2013–2014 *Times* higher education survey ranks Japan's best university, the University of Tokyo, 23rd globally. However, in terms of number of patent applications, reported by the World Intellectual Property Organization (WIPO), Japan ranks second after the United States, which clearly shows its high performance by global standards.[17] Looking at this data in more detail reveals the problem of Japanese educational institutions: among corporations, Panasonic ranks first for patents, and a number of other Japanese manufacturers are also ranked within the top 50. On the other hand, the top five spots for educational institution patent applications are all occupied by U.S. universities, while the University of Tokyo is ranked 15th. The total share of Japanese universities' patent filings has also decreased. Meanwhile, some Asian countries (such as Singapore) are encouraging top U.S./European universities to establish satellite campuses in their countries. This is, again, in sharp contrast to the case of Japan. Japan is losing ground on educational infrastructure.

Because of the declining birthrate since the end of the second baby boom (1971–1974), the number of applicants to universities in Japan has also been decreasing. Given this trend, maintaining a high quality of freshmen would require proportionally downsizing admissions. Japanese universities have not scaled back admissions, which may have resulted in the deterioration of the quality of students' abilities.

INTRA-FIRM UNDERINVESTMENT IN HUMAN CAPITAL

Japan's educational infrastructure has declined not only in relative terms, as its external competition has strengthened, but in absolute terms. Inside Japanese firms, there are also indications of declining investment in human capital. For example, Japanese firms have long traditions of providing financial support for their employees to study abroad, often at top U.S. universities. Many firms would pick a few employees per year and send them to U.S. universities, frequently funding all or part of their expenses, with the expectation that they would return to the firm with new knowledge and upgraded human capital. However, this tradition has been eroded across Japanese firms over the course of the lost two decades. Some survey data indicates that the lack of globally competitive human capital is hampering Japanese firms' efforts to extend their business overseas and, hence, they are missing business opportunities.[18]

A more serious issue in the context of intra-firm underinvestment in human capital is the rapid increase in nonregular workers. This issue is also known as labor market polarization, or the *hiseiki* problem. A number of studies, particularly those by Japanese labor economists, have repeatedly drawn attention to the repercussions of the steady and sizable increase in nonregular workers in Japan's labor market.[19] From the mid-1990s to mid-2000s, labor demand was weak due mainly to the adverse environment surrounding Japanese firms (e.g., intensifying domestic nonperforming loan problems and the Asian currency crisis). During this period, many Japanese firms scaled back their business. By international standards, Japanese firms tend to rely less on layoffs for workforce adjustments, preferring instead to reduce new hiring.[20] The period between 1995 and 2005 is widely known as the ice age for job seekers, meaning that it was very hard for university graduates to find regular positions because Japanese firms had scaled back hiring. The result was that the number of young nonregular workers markedly increased over the period (see Figure 4.3). At that point, each firm likely thought they were adjusting the size of employment in accordance with the macroeconomic conditions. Later, however, the increase in nonregular workers collectively undermined Japanese firms' competitiveness at the aggregate level. As discussed later in detail, Japanese firms have long emphasized intra-firm employee education, including on-the-job training and other study opportunities. However, these intra-firm training opportunities were provided to regular workers only. In the short run, firms were successful in cutting labor costs without shedding employment, but, over the medium to long term, it is likely that hiring more nonregular workers (who subsequently received less training than

Figure 4.3   Ratio of Nonregular to Regular Workers (age 25–34)

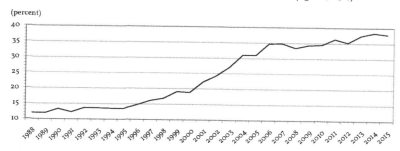

Data source: Japanese Ministry of Internal Affairs and Communications.

their regular counterparts) has led to underinvestment in human capital and, over time, contributed to lower productivity among Japanese firms.

Labor Markets: Illiquidity and Immobility

Since the 1990s, as globalization has progressed, firms have been required to reallocate their resources, both labor and capital, more flexibly. It is critical for multinational firms to shift their resources in a timely manner to places where market demand is high and/or production cost is low. This means that sometimes firms need to retreat from places where they can find no advantages. From a macroeconomic standpoint, high labor market mobility is essential for firms to reallocate their labor forces flexibly across firms and industries.

Japan's labor market is well-known for its low mobility and illiquidity. The Japanese employment system combines synchronized recruitment of new graduates, a seniority-based wage system, and lifetime employment. Freshmen who join large firms as regular workers are generally expected to remain there until retirement. Most undergraduate juniors (third-year students) spend their time job hunting rather than studying. Students do not apply for specific positions, but for membership in a certain firm they wish to join. According to a survey by the Sanno Institute of Management,

7 out of 10 students aspire to join a firm that ensures lifetime employment.

Japan's employment system is rigid by international standards, but this status quo was established not that long ago. Yoshikawa points out that the lifetime employment system was the standard practice in the high-growth period of the 1950–1960s.[21] However, data on separation rates by industry from the 1960s shows that the then-expanding industries, such as the manufacturing sector, wholesalers, and retailers, had high employee turnover rates. Separation rates in those industries were higher than 20 percent. In the 1970–1980s, the separation rate declined, followed by an even clearer drop in the 1990s. In the 2000s, the rate edged up as the first baby boomers began to reach retirement age.

Strict restrictions on the dismissal of workers, a pillar of the lifetime employment system, also remained intact even during the long period of stagnation. In Japan, case law principles work as strict de facto regulations on dismissal. Dismissals for the purpose of restructuring a firm can be legitimate only if four conditions hold: proof of necessity of dismissal; fulfillment of obligation to make efforts to avoid dismissal; rationality of selection of personnel to be dismissed; and validity of the procedures.

From the viewpoint of management, scaling back unprofitable businesses and shifting to promising fronts frequently requires some dismissals. However, with the four conditions, it is extremely difficult to make dismissals in one segment while expanding recruitment in other segments. Effectively, it is almost impossible for many large Japanese firms to flexibly adjust their labor force due to tight dismissal restrictions. Such labor market rigidity, both at the intra-firm and inter-firm levels, also undermines capital mobility, because shifting capital without shifting labor cannot keep businesses alive. Ultimately, labor market rigidity has impeded changes in the industrial structure by making mergers and acquisitions considerably more difficult.

Nonetheless, dismissal restrictions alone cannot explain all aspects of Japan's labor market rigidity. While the lifetime employment system is underpinned by the dismissal restrictions, it is only a piece of the Japanese employment system. The system as a whole imposes labor market rigidity from both the demand and the supply side. These mutually reinforcing points—some institutional and others exogenous—are worth emphasizing for their impact on undermining Japan's labor market liquidity.

THE LIFETIME EMPLOYMENT AND SENIORITY-BASED WAGE SYSTEMS

The combination of long-term employment conventions, the lifetime employment system, and the seniority-based wage system has been applied by many firms *voluntarily*. The voluntary application, rather than forceful regulation by law or through government instructions, implies that both firms and employees have benefited from this combination system. A widely held notion is that the combination of the lifetime employment and seniority-based wage systems was effective in promoting firm-specific professional skills, through which individual firms were actively investing in their own human capital to enhance their unique strengths.

Opponents dispute the benefits of the status quo system.[22] They emphasize that even if such benefits exist, they come with side effects that have increasingly hampered Japan's economic growth. For example, some argue that, under the lifetime employment system and the seniority-based wage system, individual workers have less incentive to invest in their own human capital. This creates a problem of moral hazard, which has increasingly distorted workers' incentives as the restriction on dismissals has been enhanced over time. In an extreme case, the status quo system is protecting those who shamelessly (by the Japanese standard) stick to positions in Gulliver firms, even if they are less motivated and the least productive. In this context, there has been momentum among Japanese Gulliver firms to review the status quo human resources (HR) management system.

This momentum has manifested in some tangible actions. In the mid-2000s, a number of firms replaced existing seniority-based wage systems with merit-based wage systems. However, it should be noted that all new systems, including this new wage system, have been applied to next generations only. In other words, current employees were grandfathered in and remain protected by the old status quo system. Grandfathering can in part explain why most of the new attempts to replace the status quo HR system have failed (at least from the viewpoints of incumbent managers). Other reasons include that existing HR divisions and managers lack capacity, and/ or are not experienced enough to evaluate individual workers' professional skills; and that the coexistence of grandfathering and over-competition within teams undermines teamwork.

More recently, some firms, such as Hitachi and Rakuten, have successfully established a globally uniform HR system, replacing the old status quo. The acute need to attract and manage human resources across countries was the main driver behind such shifts. However, whether those successful cases can prevail has yet to be seen.

DIFFICULTY OF REENTRANCE INTO LABOR MARKETS

Under the status quo system, reentrants into labor markets are subject to sizable handicaps. As mentioned above, Japanese corporate recruiting practices are heavily focused on new undergraduates and mid-career recruiting, and Japan's secondary labor market remains underdeveloped. For a period, intra-firm investment in human capital through on-the-job-training was believed to be a source of the strength of Japanese firms, but this same strength could disadvantage an individual worker leaving their firm to take an outside option. Multiple characteristics of the status quo system strongly incentivize employees to remain in their first jobs, including immobile, firm-specific pensions; separation packages that geometrically increase along with the length of an employee's term; and a lack of regular-worker positions that can be filled by a second job seeker. These create a negative cycle. Because the incentives embedded in the status quo system are well-recognized, the number of second job seekers is small, which results in an illiquid secondary job market where worker-job matching is difficult. Workers recognize the lack of job opportunities in the secondary market, and prefer to stay in their first jobs. To promote inter-firm/industry labor force reallocation, this cycle must be ended.

POLICY MEASURES

Previous policy measures are a third factor in Japan's illiquid and immobile job market. Many administrations have used employment adjustment subsidies to prevent firms from cutting employment. Given the recurring shocks that hit the Japanese economy during the lost two decades, including the global financial crisis in 2008–2009, policy measures aimed at securing jobs deserve some credit. The issue is whether the recipients of subsidies promoted labor market efficiency, especially as firms—not individual workers—were the recipients of these subsidies.

In the aftermath of the global financial crisis, the SME Finance Facilitation Act (FFA) may have kept many zombie firms alive for prolonged periods. The FFA created damaging incentives to hoard labor among firms that would otherwise have closed their businesses. If the FFA was successful in revitalizing the beneficiary firms, it would have promoted labor market efficiency. Conversely, if the zombie firms died after a certain length of time, the FFA was simply delaying labor market adjustment. Evidence suggests this latter scenario is closer to the truth. Subsidies were received by the oldest and least profitable firms rather than workers, and thus impeded workers from moving to more profitable and faster-growing firms or industries. As a result, workers lost opportunities.

Slow Adjustment to Globalization

This section discusses the sluggish adjustment of the Japanese economy to globalization since the 2000s. Two notable aspects of Japan's slow adjustment are the delayed response to the rapid evolution of global value chains (GVCs) and the Japanese economy's persistent low level of openness.

SLOW ADJUSTMENT TO GLOBAL VALUE CHAINS

In keeping with the trends of globalization, Japanese firms, mainly large manufacturers, have been increasing their overseas plants and production sites. Reflecting this offshoring, the overseas-to-domestic ratio of investment capital expenditure (capex) has been steadily increasing (see Figure 4.4). The domestic sales ratio has shown a downward trend, while sales outside of Japan have accelerated.

The offshoring trend started in the 1990s with the relocation of assembly plants overseas. This led to an increase in exports of capital goods and intermediate goods that were used in assembly sites. This pattern of offshoring and exports changed over time, and is noticeable in world export data. World trade collapsed in the wake of the global 2008–2009 financial crisis, but this was followed by a strong rebound to pre-crisis growth trends. Japan was an exception to this rebound, and its exports have been notably weaker than other countries since the crisis (see Figure 4.5). During the same post-crisis period, exports from South Korea and China outperformed Japan in terms of the real growth rate.

Ryo Kato and Saori Naganuma argue that Japanese firms have remained highly competitive in high value-added product mar-

Figure 4.4   Japan's Overseas Production Ratio (manufacturing)

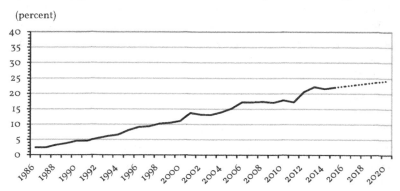

Data source: Japanese Cabinet Office.

Figure 4.5   Export Volume Index

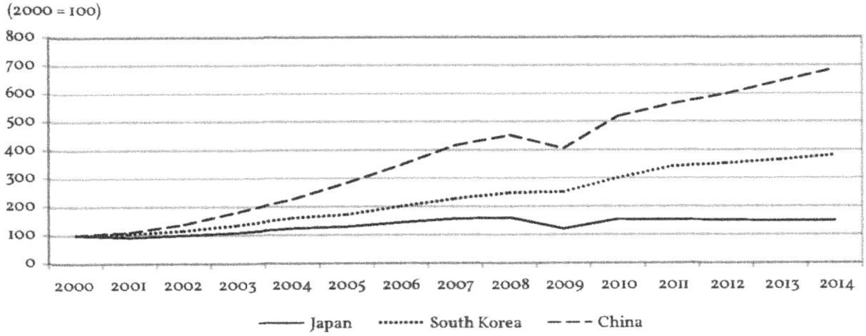

(2000 = 100)

Japan ········ South Korea – – – China

Data source: World Bank.

kets, such as parts, capital goods, and intermediate products.[23] Thus, Japanese firms once held an advantage in the GVC race. However, more recently in several markets where Japanese firms had a stronghold, the shares of new entrants from emerging market economies (EMEs) are growing. In some cases, firms in EMEs are making progress with their high value-added products replacing Japanese products. In other areas, Japanese firms are making slow progress in terms of research and development and are unable to produce new and upgraded products. In both cases, Kato and Naganuma argue that "the competitiveness of Japanese firms has been undermined recently."[24]

The catching-up by EME firms has been facilitated by the quickly evolving management technology of GVCs as a global network develops. In managing GVCs, focusing on the most advantageous and profitable production phase—rather than a single part or product—is essential. A number of firms in advanced economies focus on research and development (R&D), which is the earliest phase of production (sometimes denoted upstream in GVCs), and are making progress in innovating new materials and intermediate goods. On the other extreme, some firms concentrate on maintenance and service businesses—the furthest downstream—and establish large market shares. Many global firms quickly find multiple phases, some upstream and some downstream, and locate business sites in places where they can exert their own strengths most efficiently. In accordance with such strategic positioning in GVCs, both in terms of production phases and geographic locations, globally competitive firms have developed flexible HR management systems. To this end, Japanese firms, as noted, are left behind, with many of them are struggling with the old-fashioned HR system. Looking ahead, Japanese firms will need to upgrade their management systems more quickly so they can evolve with GVCs, while keeping up with their competitors.

LOW DEGREE OF OPENNESS

The low openness of the Japanese economy is another factor that prevents Japan from benefiting from global economic growth as much as other economies. Foreign direct investment (FDI) to Japan has remained low by international standards. Relative to other countries, Japan's ability to attract inward FDI remained stagnant between 1990 and 2013. The World Investment Report published by the United Nations Conference on Trade and Development (UNCTAD) indicates that Japan ranked 28th among the top 30 countries in 2013 for inward FDI.[25] Inward FDI to Japan is 3.5 percent that of the United States and 20.1 percent that of Germany. If judged solely on FDI data, Japan would appear to be continuing its well-known *sakoku* policy of remaining secluded from the outside world.

There are multiple channels through which inward FDI benefits recipient economies. First, it expands both capex and employment, even in the short run. Second, over the medium term, labor force diversity rises, which raises the probability of innovation. New ideas, technologies, and management skills can be incorporated, improving existing practices. In particular, if higher skills are introduced at management levels, inward FDI provides opportunities for domestic firms to evolve into global businesses. Conceptually, all of these positive inward spillover effects can be expected as inward FDI increases.

Looming Uncertainty, Losing Appetite for Risk

This section discusses increasing uncertainty and the resulting weak incentives for consumption and investment. The issue of uncertainty affects both the corporate sector and the household sector.

ABATING RISK TAKING BY THE CORPORATE SECTOR

Until the early 2000s, Japanese firms muddled through balance sheet problems. Some were merged into a larger competitor, others merged with the help of taxpayer money, and some simply closed their businesses. In the aftermath of such painful adjustments, even sound survivors tended to invest less compared to the 1980s. Low investment capex continued as a long-lasting trend while those firms accumulated cash/deposits on the asset side and retained profits on the liability side. Clearly, Japanese firms became more risk-averse in the 2000s. Less risk-taking resulted in lower return on equity (ROE). Hence, the question here is whether businesses' choice of low-risk, low-return strategies are in line with rational behavior.

From a macroeconomic viewpoint, three factors could have provided grounds for firms to move away from risk-taking. First, there was an across-the-board decline in expected returns on investment projects in almost all industries. Firms broadly perceived that the expected growth rate would continue to decline steadily from the mid-1990s to the 2000s, albeit with some fluctuation. The Cabinet Office's survey provides evidence for this hypothesis. However, declines in the expected future growth rate may be a self-fulfilling explanation for low risk-taking. Because firms believe they will earn less, they invest less. The remaining question is why the firms shared this belief. Did they have good reason to believe in lower returns?

The second factor is that risks and uncertainty in Japan have been elevated since the mid-1990s. A sequence of adverse shocks, most of which can be considered exogenous to individual firms, have hit the Japanese economy since the mid-1990s. Instability in the Japanese financial system was sharply elevated in the late 1990s, which was the beginning of the long-lasting headwind spanning from the 1997 Asian currency crisis to the 2008–2009 global financial crisis. The 2011 Great East Japan Earthquake left deep scars, which linger not only in the disaster-stricken areas but in other regions. The disaster destroyed much of Japan's existing supply chain network. These sequential adverse shocks elevated the degree of firms' risk aversion. All of the above-mentioned events could be described as once-in-a-lifetime events, but Japanese firms had to weather such rare storms every few years. Given that, their risk-averse decisions cannot be viewed as irrational. In a nutshell, bad luck reined in capex by Japanese firms with elevated risk aversion.

The third factor is deflation. Deflation means that the prices of goods and services fall as the value of cash rises. Under ongoing deflation and, more importantly, with low (or negative) inflation expectations, it is fully rational to find cash holding more profitable than investing in real activities, including capex.

Can macroeconomic conditions provide a complete and rational explanation for less investment by Japanese firms? That is highly unlikely. There are a number of different views that help explain the low investment and risk-taking by Japanese firms. As noted earlier, the turnover rate in both business entry and exit tends to be low in Japan. In particular, firms' average ages in the material industry and manufacturing are remarkable high, and these older firms tend not to embark on new projects. Because these older survivors were successful in the past, it is even more difficult to restructure the status quo business segments, even if the market for the successful products/business has dissipated.[26] Within older, once-successful firms, any new effort to go into a new market tends to provoke strong objections. Although one may think that this phenomenon is not unique to Japan, it is not that simple. I previously emphasized the importance and overwhelming popularity of the lifetime employment system and seniority-based wage system. In typical older Japanese firms, management board positions are taken by senior executives who were successful in those firms in the past. Under this management structure, new business proposals can be submitted and approved only if the proposals were made as top-down decisions. There are some notable exceptions: Fuji Film, once a world class Gulliver in the film industry, completely changed its core business. They are now primarily running a medical and pharmaceutical business.

In sum, the comprehensive view that I propose here is as follows: until the 1980s, Japanese firms accumulated profits and capital (I will not delve into why they were successful then as there are many early studies on that issue). From the 1990s through the late 2000s, at the individual firm level, marginal profit from rent-seeking was higher than that expected from embarking on new risky businesses. Returns from rent-seeking could have declined more quickly if exogenous bad luck had not occurred so frequently. These events led to a protracted period that incentivized rent-seeking.

Since the mid-2000s, outside conditions surrounding Japanese firms have changed quickly, and the returns from rent-seeking have declined in parallel. Looking ahead, if the expected returns on new business outrun those from rent-seeking, Japanese firms may proceed to uncharted waters, taking more risks. This turnaround could have started earlier if there had been less bad luck, management was more forward-looking, and deflation had ended earlier.

LOOMING UNCERTAINTY OVER FUTURE HOUSEHOLD INCOME

Consumption propensity data by cohorts indicates that people in their 30s and 40s consume less than the baby boomers when the latter were at the same ages. The declines in consumption propensity can be confirmed as a trend, meaning that working generations have cut spending over time (see Figure 4.6). Here, I cite two reasons why that might have happened, both of which are related to elevated uncertainties over future income.

The first is the nonregular worker problem. The nonregular worker ratio started to increase in the mid-1990s. As a result, people who were hired for nonregular jobs (as their first jobs after leaving school) have now reached their 30s or 40s. As mentioned, early empirical studies indicate that those who were hired for nonregular jobs as their first jobs tend to remain in low-income brackets. Under

Figure 4.6   Japan's Propensity to Consume by Age Group

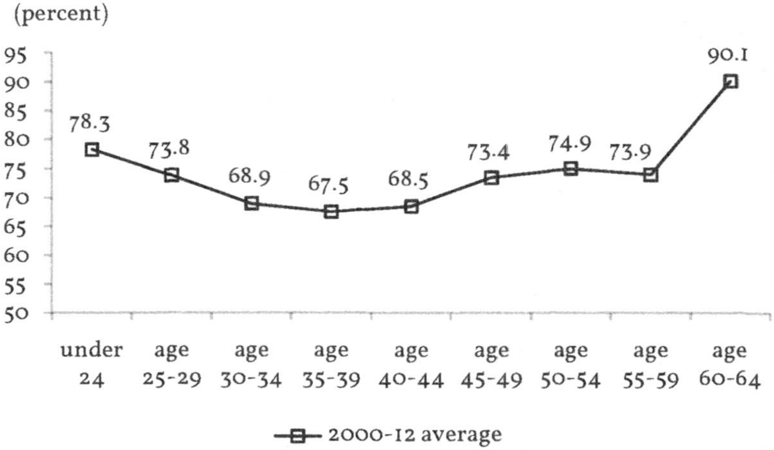

(percent)

——□—— 2000-12 average

Data source: Ministry of Internal Affairs and Communications.

the status quo Japanese labor market, young nonregular workers are given fewer opportunities for on-the-job training by their employers, and are thus disadvantaged in developing their careers later on. As also noted, the immature mid-career job market also places young nonregular workers at a disadvantage. Increases in nonregular workers, as they get older, have resulted in generations who are exposed to more income uncertainty. These groups tend to include low-income households that cannot afford to purchase homes and, given the high uncertainty over their future income, they tend to save rather than spend.

The second factor is the broad concern over Japan's fiscal sustainability. Japan's public debt to GDP ratio was much lower than 100 percent until the mid-1990s. Since then, taxpayers' money was tapped to mop up the nonperforming loans problem and expansionary fiscal policies, characterized by massive public construction projects, were repeatedly deployed in attempts to achieve economic revival. Consequently, Japan's public debt to GDP ratio now stands at 210 percent, higher than that of Greece (170 percent). This is almost the same as the level of public debt in the 1940s.

Concerns over fiscal sustainability include the social security system. Japan's advanced and efficient universal health care system is widely recognized. The system was introduced in 1961, and it has remained intact as national infrastructure. Very few critics raise objections to the roles and contributions the system made in enabling the economy to achieve high growth in from 1960 through the 1980s and improving life expectancies. Japan is also known as a country of longevity. At present, the life expectancy of males and females are 80 and 86 years, respectively, greatly improved from 58 and 61.5 years, respectively, in 1950. The Japanese can be proud of this achievement. At the same time, they have to deal with ballooning pension benefits and payments under the current social security system. Social security–related expenditures dramatically increased from 3.5 trillion yen (about $35 billion) in 1970 to 47.2 trillion yen in 1990. In 2014, it reached 115 trillion yen. Since the early 1990s, Japan's inflation rate has been, by and large, zero or slightly negative. Therefore, those increases should be regarded in real terms.

Japan's pension system is run using a pay-as-you-go (PAYGO) financing method. Like other countries with the same system, benefits are paid directly from current workers' contributions. At present, ballooning benefit payments cannot be fully financed by current workers' contributions and are thus paid for partly through tax revenues. As Japan's population has aged rapidly, the top-heavy demographic structure has increased the burden on younger generations.

In the meantime, rapid aging, together with the rising cost of medical procedures and medication, is increasing total health care–related spending. Under the current social security system, a massive intergenerational transfer is under way. The Cabinet Office has estimated that, as of 2005, those who were born in or before 1943 are net beneficiaries, receiving 49 million yen (roughly $490,000), while people in their 20s (as of 2005) are net contributors, paying 17 million yen. Additional projections indicate that those under the age of 20 (as of 2005) will be subject to even larger (net) income transfers, to the tune of 46 million yen.

The dramatic increase in social security–related expenditures could have been predicted in the 1990s, when the ultra-low birthrate and declining population were already apparent. The super-aging society was quickly approaching. Everyone could have understood well what to do in preparation for such demographic changes.

Politically, the top-heavy demographic structure ensures a situation where the majority of Japanese voters favor the back-loading of burden in pension reform. Older generations make up the majority of voters, making the spend now, pay later option a natural choice. In this context, myopic political strategies taken by the government, albeit often criticized, may simply reflect the average voter's preference in Japan.

NEW AND OLD CHALLENGES AHEAD: FIVE Ds NEEDED

As discussed, Japan experienced many challenges during the lost two decades. Shortly after World War II, Japan grew rapidly, catching up with the United States and European economies. But, later, Japan found itself in a position of being outpaced by emerging Asian economies.

In the meantime, calls for fundamental reforms of industrial structures and other institutional reforms gained strength as globalization, IT innovations, and rapid aging proceeded. However, fundamental reforms did not occur. As a consequence, entrepreneurship failed to grow, labor markets remained rigid and illiquid, and firms lost their appetite for risk. The absence of reforms encouraged rent-seeking under the status quo. Turnover was not stimulated; underinvestment in human capital continued; adjustment to globalization dawdled; and uncertainty regarding future income was elevated for both firms and households. All of these unfavorable developments contributed to undermining Japan's productivity.

Bearing these points in mind, a policy package should be developed to reinvigorate the Japanese economy. I recommend a plan that includes five Ds: dynamic labor markets; diversity; destructive innovation; decentralization (or disinvestment from Tokyo); and deleveraging.

Dynamism of Labor Markets

The first policy priority should be to replenish and enhance Japan's human capital. In World War II, Japan lost 86 percent of its capital stock (business equipment, housing, etc.).[27] Despite this, the country began growing rapidly shortly after the end of the war, eventually becoming the world's second largest economy. The prime factors that enabled prosperity were an ample labor force, previously pooled in rural provinces; the high quality of the labor force, which was broadly well-educated and diligent; and active entrepreneurial activities and innovation.

As discussed previously, after the GDP growth rate peaked in the 1970–1980s, labor market rigidity increased, impeding the smooth transition of the labor force to high-growth firms/industries. Recently, the quality of Japan's human capital has shown signs of deterioration. To reinvigorate the Japanese economy, rebuilding dynamic labor markets and promoting investment in human capital are of paramount importance.

DYNAMIC LABOR MARKET: ACHIEVING SEVEN POSITIVE OUTCOMES

By spurring labor market dynamics, positive outcomes can be achieved for seven problem areas confronting Japan.

1. *Adapting to globalization.* A dynamic labor market would help workers flexibly adjust to global changes in economies and industrial structures. For individual workers, it is frequently a matter of luck when a single firm or industry as a whole falls into a quagmire. A liquid labor market would provide a blanket for each worker to more easily seek a better job. Such a labor market could help reduce poverty.

2. *Encouraging risk-taking by firms.* A dynamic labor market promotes risk-taking by firms. The costs of recruiting human capital that matches the project on which a firm wishes to embark would decrease. Lower recruiting cost is growth enhancing and could indirectly encourage mergers and acquisitions (M&A), as appropriate human resources can be found and allocated more smoothly.

3. *Stimulating FDI to Japan.* A dynamic labor market is compatible with global business, and non-Japanese firms and multinational firms could ramp up FDI to Japan. As discussed previously, the existing Japanese employment system tends to invest in firm-specific skills. If a dynamic labor market can provide more diverse human capital, inward FDI to Japan would be stimulated as the labor force, together with capital, moves back and forth across borders in a less costly manner.

4. *Promoting start-ups.* A dynamic labor market would also promote start-ups and provide fertile ground for entrepreneurs. Over time, an increase in entrepreneurs will generate innovation. As articulated above, second job seekers are subject to significant handicaps in Japan. If a dynamic market removes such frictions, it effectively provides a blanket for failed risk-takers. With such a blanket, reentering the labor market is less costly, so those who have innovative ideas have more incentive to let their ideas materialize. If unsuccessful, they can try another idea in the same or a different career.

5. *Revitalizing regional economies.* In the status quo Japanese employment system, membership in large firms—often lifetime membership—is overemphasized. In contrast, modern IT businesses are more compatible with the skill-based job system. With a dynamic labor market up and running, workers would choose professions rather than membership in a certain firm. With professional skills, workers could move to more profitable firms with less friction. Consequently, there would be less reason to work

in large cities, particularly in Tokyo where the headquarters of Gulliver firms are agglomerated. Conversely, there will be more job opportunities in local provinces as long as each worker keeps his or her own skills and local firms are compatible with such skill-based job matching.

6. *Increasing senior labor participation.* A dynamic labor market naturally increases labor participation by senior workers. With a dynamic labor market, retirement is not the end of a career. Under a skill-based job-matching labor market, senior workers, if they wish, can work in their neighborhood and avoid time-consuming commuting. Although job opportunities may not be well-paid, they are more flexible in terms of working schedules and location choices.

7. *Increasing female labor participation.* A sizeable and essential benefit from a more dynamic labor market is an expected increase in female labor participation, both quantitatively and qualitatively. The quantitative argument needs little explanation. What is more important in this proposal is that a dynamic labor market would help female workers continue developing their careers during and after their childcare period. Reentrants and second job seekers in the Japanese labor market are subject to significant handicaps. As such, female reentrants, after maternity leave and ensuing nursing leave, often choose to work as nonregular workers, typically part-time, and in different jobs/firms from their first employment. A more liquid labor market would reduce such involuntary career choices for nonregular positions.

Labor market reforms may seem like the elder wand of Harry Potter lore. However, this most powerful magic wand cannot be acquired so easily. To obtain and use the wand of labor market reforms, multiple changes must be made through concerted efforts. Those changes would affect complicated labor market institutions, uncodified conventions, and the broadening of the Japanese society's mindset as a whole.

WHAT IS REQUIRED TO CREATE DYNAMIC LABOR MARKETS

Status quo employment practices and conventions need to be rebuilt entirely. The status quo systems to be reformed include the lifetime employment system and its dismissal restrictions; the seniority-based wage/retirement and allowance/pension systems, which incentivize employees to remain in their first jobs; simultaneous recruiting of new graduates; and the resulting polarization of regular and nonregular workers. Ultimately, the basic idea is to change the regime from a membership-based employment system to a skill-based job system. Diverse choices in the labor market must be generated. All choices should be brought to the table for workers: where to work, how to work, how long to work, and whether to join firms or start a business.

During Japan's catching-up era, the membership-based employment system worked in Japan's favor, as previously discussed. To prepare an environment in which innovators and entrepreneurs can flexibly pursue their goals, a regime change is required. With ongoing globalization and a decreasing labor force, Japanese firms must consider applying some sort of skill-based job system.

In addition, the current education system needs a full-fledged review. At tertiary levels, the current system is distorting incentives. Despite the rapidly decreasing number of youths, the number of universities and colleges has increased. As a result, 80 percent of high school graduates move on to tertiary education, even though the returns on Japanese tertiary education generally do not cover the tuition fees. To estimate returns from tertiary education, the OECD has calculated the ratio of the lifetime income earned by an average college graduate to the college tuition fee plus lifetime income earned by an average high school graduate.[28] The OECD's calculations show that the return on educational investment at tertiary levels is lower in Japan than elsewhere. The oversupply of tertiary schools and the resulting deterioration in the quality of the average college graduate must be rectified.

As discussed previously, given the membership-based employment system (combined with mass production manufacturing), the current NCLB-focused system promoted Japan's economic growth during the catching-up period. However, the benefits from complementarities between the status quo employment system and the education system have since been lost. In this regard, Masayuki Morikawa suggests that to raise Japan's TFP, Japan must keep abreast with the world's top-level students.[29] To a certain degree, this calls for more concentration in human capital investment, such as an elite screening system and incentives for highly capable young talents.

One idea worth considering is to separately foster global competitors and contributors to the local economies. Two different pools can be created with different curricula. Equal opportunities in education must be provided to everyone, but equal opportunity does not necessarily mean that every student takes the same classes. More customized curricula, while they may not be exactly equal, could raise the probability that everyone will obtain a better job. Singapore has applied an early-phase sorting system as a national investment strategy. Children are classified into two groups: top elites and the rest at pre-tertiary phases. The former group is given special curricula with the explicit purpose to become national and global leaders. The latter group is expected to acquire professional skills in different programs. The case of Singapore is in sharp contrast with Japan's system in terms of human capital investment.

Matching efficiency needs to be enhanced to achieve labor force reallocation without unemployment. To this end, the policy agenda could include more practical vocational training within industries, upgrading the existing public employment security offices (also known as Hello-work), and revising the tax and subsidy systems to encourage higher rates of labor force participation.

The German experience of broad labor market reform taken up by the Schroeder administration provides useful lessons in this regard. Enhanced matching was perceived as a key to the reduction of the unemployment rate. For example, if people lost their jobs, they received unemployment allowances and the chance to take vocational education. On the other hand, if they rejected a job offer without an appropriate reason, they were penalized through reduction of their unemployment allowances. Furthermore, the German attempts included more concerted efforts for better job matching with the private sector (e.g., recruiting companies). The German practice provides a number of lessons for Japanese labor market reforms.

Diversity

Japan ranks 104th of 142 countries in the World Economic Forum's 2014 Global Gender Gap Report. As noted, Japan's working population ratio peaked in the early 1990s. Around that time, lawmakers enacted bills such as the 1986 Equal Opportunity Act and the 1999 Basic Act for a Gender Equal Society, which aimed to promote female worker participation.[30] However, female worker participation has remained low, particularly among those in their 30s and 40s, compared to other advanced economies (see Figure 4.7).

On the other hand, the gender gap has been diminishing among students enrolling in four-year universities. In 2013, the ratio of males to females was 54 percent to 46 percent, respectively, a significant improvement over the 30-point gap in 1975. In addition, two-year colleges are popular among female high school students and, taking the two-year colleges into calculation, the tertiary education enrollment rate of females exceeds that of males. Those statistics mean that both males and females are paying high tuition fees for tertiary education. By and large, tertiary education does not pay. Human capital investment via the Japanese tertiary education system does not tend to translate into successful career and business achievements.

The bright side is that there is room for improvement in terms of labor participation in Japan. The Abe administration declared its policy target of raising the female labor participation rate among workers age 25–44 from 68 percent in 2012 to 73 percent by 2020. With this target in mind, I estimated the growth-enhancing effects of a rise in female labor participation. My estimations indicate that,

Figure 4.7 Female Labor Force Participation Rate (by age group)

(percent)

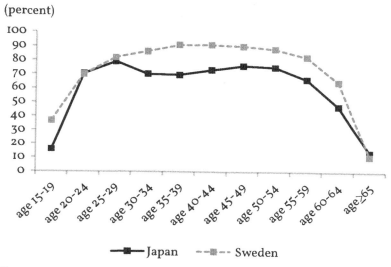

Data source: OECD national accounts data.

if Japan's female labor participation rate were to gradually rise to that of Sweden by 2030, Japan's potential growth rate would increase by 0.2 percent each year.

Aside from female workers' impact on the labor supply, more fundamental benefits could arise from adding diversity to inflexible Japanese organizations. Increased diversity could generate the momentum to change stubbornly outdated Japanese organizations from within. Female managers in Japanese organizations are about 10 percent of the total employees, which is much lower than the United States' and European standards of 30–40 percent. This implies that 90 percent of Japanese firms are run only from the viewpoint of male workers.

A study by Hirokatsu Asano and Daiji Kawaguchi points to a positive correlation between female labor participation and labor productivity in advanced economies.[31] Two hypotheses are suggested: diverse views and ideas reflected in economic activities

Figure 4.8   Female Participation Rate and GDP per Capita Growth (average 2000–2014)

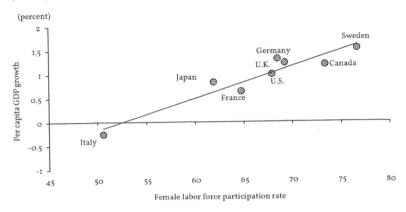

Data source: World Bank.

raise productivity, and countries with a highly liquid labor markets tend to enjoy high labor productivity as a benefit. As noted earlier, a liquid labor market facilitates female labor participation.

Regardless of which hypothesis better explains the facts, any underutilized factor should be reinforced. In this case, encouraging female labor participation would raise potential GDP (see Figure 4.8). What policy measures are needed to facilitate greater female labor participation? The agenda must include measures to increase daycare supply to achieve a zero-waiting list, and pro-work (or at least neutral in terms of labor supply) tax and social security system reforms. Under the current Japanese tax and public pension system, most at-home wives and workers in the lowest income bracket are eligible for tax deductions and pension benefits. The current system effectively incentivizes certain workers and nonworkers, typically at-home wives and female part-time workers, to work less or to not work at all. In terms of tax deductions, if one's spouse earns less than 1.03 million yen (about $10,300) per year, the spouse's income is basically tax free, even if one is in a higher income bracket (thus, one's household may not belong to the low-income class). As a result, the spouse is incentivized not to earn more than 1.03 million yen per year. With regard to the public pension system, if the spouse earns less than 1.3 million yen per year, the spouse is eligible for pension benefits without contributing to the fund. Those who benefit from this system are officially called type-3 beneficiaries of the public pension system. Behind this is an ideology: an ideal family should consist of a single male breadwinner and a stay-at-home mother who concentrates on nursing and housekeeping.

The income distribution of females clearly shows that such incentives are effective. In the distribution, twin peaks can be observed at around 1.03 million yen (about $10,300) and 1.3 million yen. The twin peaks are called the 1.03/1.30 million yen hurdles for female workers. Because of the hurdles, voluntary adjustments in hours worked are frequently made by female workers. Such voluntary adjustments are confirmed by a number of surveys asking women the reasons for not working more and not pursuing other careers. Based on these facts, structural reform of the distortionary tax and social security systems are needed.

Diversity goes beyond female labor supply. The Abe administration is promoting the hiring of highly skilled non-Japanese workers. By 2025, a labor shortage of 300,000 workers is projected in daycare and nursing industries. To fill this shortage, a technical intern training program is being reviewed to increase immigrant workers. As noted previously, if inward FDI were to be stimulated, together with progress in corporate governance reforms, non-Japanese workers and entrepreneurs would increase as a natural consequence.

In a separate vein, it is important for the younger generation to learn diverse views and ways of thinking by studying abroad. Despite the trend toward globalization, the number of Japanese students studying abroad peaked in 2004 and has since declined to early 1990s levels (see Figure 4.9). The rate of decline is disproportionately rapid compared to total population declines. A more detailed inspection of the data reveals that Japanese students studying in the United States decreased the most. What are the possible impediments?

Figure 4.9   Number of Japanese Citizens Studying Abroad

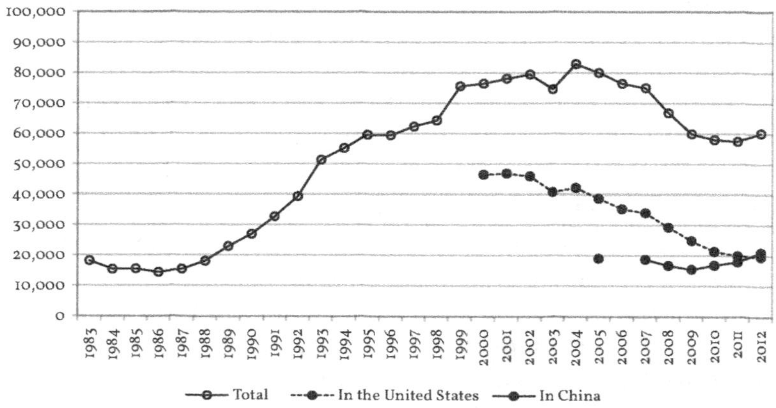

Data sources: Institute of International Education and Japanese Ministry of Education, Culture, Sports, Science and Technology.

According to multiple studies and surveys, respondents suggest three major reasons: studying abroad is disadvantageous for employment prospects because Japanese firms post job openings only for a few months in a concerted manner; there is a shortage of funding for studying abroad; and studying abroad is incompatible with the domestic university system because credits cannot be transferred to Japanese universities. Based on the survey results, a reform agenda could aim to enhance human capital by promoting diversity through enhanced financial assistance for studying abroad; harmonize the Japanese university systems with foreign systems, including changing academic years to start in September; and replace simultaneous recruiting of new graduates in April with a year-round recruiting system in keeping with international practices.

Destructive Innovation

Promoting innovation is likely to be the linchpin of policy measures to spur economic growth. From the mid-1990s up until 2007, Japan's per capita GDP grew by 3 percent annually on average. During this period, Japan's growth was the lowest among the 10 major in-

Figure 4.10 Per Capita GDP Growth in the G7 Nations (average 2001–2015)

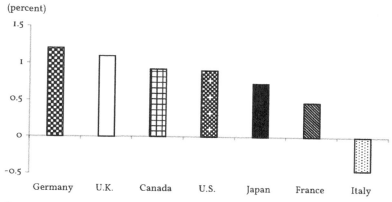

Data source: World Bank.

dustrialized economies. By and large, Scandinavian countries have performed well, but even compared with the major European economies, such as France and Germany, Japan's growth rate was around 1 percentage point lower. Figure 4.10 shows the average 2001–2015 per capita GDP growth in the Group of Seven (G7) nations.

As discussed previously, over the medium to long term, sustainable economic growth requires increases in TFP. Ultimately, only innovation can raise productivity over the long run, as shown by a number of studies. The critical question here is what is preventing, impeding, or discouraging innovation in Japan? In this regard, the *Index of Economic Freedom*, published jointly by the Heritage Foundation and the *Wall Street Journal*, gives some clues to thinking about the crux of the issue (see Figure 4.11).[32]

Even a cursory observation suggests a positive correlation between the levels of per capita GDP, based on purchasing power parity (PPP), and overall scores in the *Index of Economic Freedom*.[33] Additionally, high correlations were detected between the per capita GDP (based on PPP) growth rates and (1) trade freedom (+0.83), (2) freedom from corruption (+0.53), and (3) business freedom (+0.53). As noted, Japan ranks lowest in terms of per capita growth rates

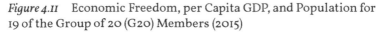

Figure 4.11   Economic Freedom, per Capita GDP, and Population for 19 of the Group of 20 (G20) Members (2015)

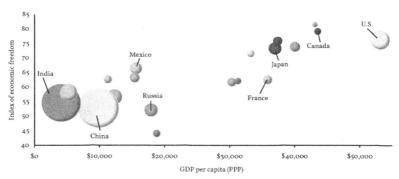

Note: The size of each bubble represents the size of population. Data for the European Union is not shown.

Data source: Heritage Foundation, *2015 Index of Economic Freedom.*

among the 10 major industrialized economies. Therefore, the high correlations of those indicators mean that Japan is given very low scores in each measure.

On trade freedom, the North Atlantic Free Trade Agreement (NAFTA) contributes to the high scores given to the United States and Canada, and the European Union benefits European countries. By contrast, as discussed earlier, Japan's openness has remained low in various measures. Against this backdrop, the low score on trade freedom given to Japan has a clear policy implication: more effort should be made to conclude the Trans-Pacific Partnership (TPP).[34] In a similar vein, Japan has made some progress in negotiating a few bilateral economic partnership agreements (EPAs) and free trade agreements (FTAs), which would also help the economy. More broadly, lifting barriers preventing inward FDI could stimulate not only cross-border trade but also domestic economic activity.

The low score on freedom from corruption should be viewed with serious concern among Japanese policymakers and incumbent businesses. This indicator does not necessarily mean that bribery and extortion are daily practices in Japan. Rather, the problem suggested by this indicator is that there are a number of sheltered sectors to which new entrants are effectively blocked. The Heritage Foundation notes that corruption takes into account the presence of special interest-groups. In Japan, there are a number of industries, such as agriculture, daycare services, and medical services, in which the "dead hand" of vested interests stops innovation, as discussed in Acemoglu and Robinson.[35]

By and large, the low score on business freedom is reflected in the lack of start-up businesses and low turnover in Japan, as discussed previously. It should also be noted that the low scores on business freedom and freedom from corruption share the same root. In Japan, vested interest groups are powerful in more than a few industries, and they are hampering, perhaps unintentionally in some cases, entrepreneurial activities. This is ultimately curbing innovation and productivity growth.

Total early-stage entrepreneurial activity (TEA), as computed by the Global Entrepreneurship Monitor, provides another look at Japan's position in terms of entrepreneurship. Among all countries with higher per capita income than Japan, none have TEA lower than that of Japan. There are some indications that countries with high TEA benefit from innovation, resulting in high per capita income. The plot of TEA against per capita GDP (based on PPP) suggests a U-shape relationship. Richard Dasher highlights this U-shape, noting that countries with per capita GDP higher than $40,000 can rekindle entrepreneurial activities.[36]

Upgrading infrastructure for entrepreneurs and encouraging business partnerships between incumbent large firms and new start-up businesses via open innovations will be critical for destructive innovation.[37] As discussed, an additional D—deregulation—should help promote future destructive innovation in Japan.

Decentralization: Correcting Over-Accumulation in Tokyo

The fourth D is decentralization, or disinvestment from Tokyo. The primary aim would be to rebuild and reassure the sustainability of local economies with declining populations. The new national grand

Figure 4.12   Population Concentration in Major Metropolitan Areas

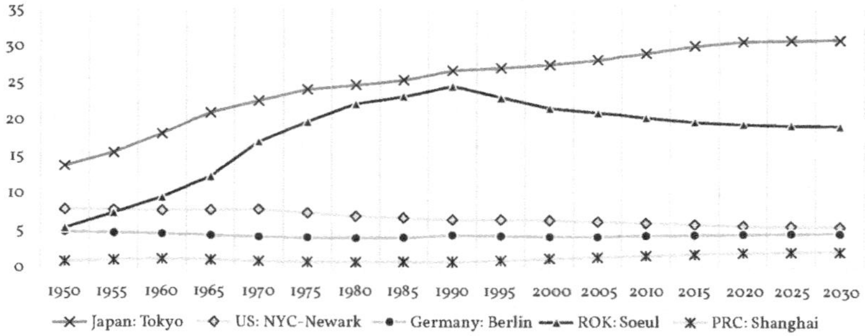

Data source: United Nations, *World Urbanization Prospects* (2014).

design published by the Ministry of Land, Infrastructure, Transport and Tourism projects that between 2010 and 2050, the population will decline by more than 50 percent in two-thirds of local cities and provinces. The biggest challenge posed by this dramatic demographic contraction is how to reinvigorate local economies while keeping administrative services at viable levels and on sound fiscal ground. The cost of civil services is subject to economies of scale. Consequently, to keep municipalities (local administrations) alive, the local economy needs to be maintained at a certain size. To this end, two steps must be taken: encouraging agglomeration in local big cities and, on the flip side, disinvesting from Tokyo and redistributing resources and capital to local cities.

Compared to major cities in advanced economies, Tokyo's rate of population concentration is high (see Figure 4.12). Since 1996, interprefectural migration statistics show that outflows from local cities and inflows to Tokyo have continued in tandem (see Figure 4.13). Hiroya Masuda warns about vanishing municipalities, with projections showing that the population of 20- to 29-year-old females in 896 local cities (out of 1,800) will decrease by almost 50 percent between 2010 and 2040.[38]

To stop population outflows from local cities, job creation and reindustrialization are needed. In this regard, there are some signs of the green shoots of new businesses in local provinces.

Figure 4.13 Japan's Internal Migration Flows in Major Metropolitan and Local Areas

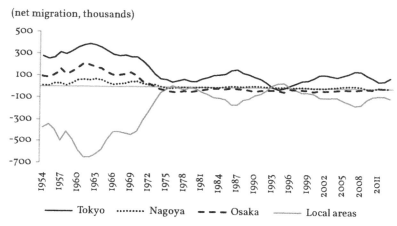

(net migration, thousands)

Tokyo ········· Nagoya – – – Osaka ────── Local areas

Data source: Japanese Ministry of Internal Affairs and Communications.

For example, the rapid diffusion and evolution of the Internet of Things (IOT), which connects multiple plants, factories, offices, and consumers with each other, and digital fabrication, typically represented by three-dimension (3D) printers, provide new business opportunities. With these technologies physical distance matters less. These new technologies can also enhance growth in local cities. In particular, digital fabrication incentivizes venture companies to participate in the manufacturing business in new locations. Manufacturing normally requires experience, but new entrants are now emerging in the manufacturing sector. In Germany, quickly changing the manufacturing business with new technologies has already been deemed Industrie 4.0.

For businesses, location and geography matter a lot, as a poor location could mean less available capital or complicate access to markets. Even if an entrepreneur had a great idea with significant business potential, location disadvantages could hamper success. However, all these headwinds are weakened by the spread of information and communication technologies, and business chances are available in local cities because there will be fewer reasons to work in Tokyo. As business start-ups and entrepreneurs increase in local cities, the Japanese labor market and other old Japanese systems and conventions will lose ground and change accordingly.

Promoting agglomeration in local big cities can save administrative and civil service costs. The idea of a compact city is not new in city planning literature. A number of early studies confirmed statistically significant growth-enhancing effects in highly agglomerated cities. Masayuki Morikawa argues that plants and establishments located in densely populated cities tend to be more productive than those in less densely populated areas.[39] He adds that, in particular, the positive correlation between productivity and population density is more significant for the service sector.

Similarly, the Ministry of Land, Infrastructure, Transport and Tourism indicates that the per capita cost of civil services in local cities falls as the population density of the region increases; there are economies of scale in running local governments. Agglomeration lowers the costs of a variety of civil services, including developing and maintaining transportation networks, daycare services, and police and educational services. The infrastructure necessary for the daily lives of local residents depends on municipal governments confronting the challenges arising from lower population density. At this juncture, the need for compact cities has never been clearer. Taking this opportunity, local communities should gather momentum to move forward toward compact cities. Some local cities will be merged into more efficient bodies. Some others may disappear quietly, but this is an avoidable fate for some local cities that could grow with agglomeration. Early movers will survive. Over time, competition among local cities could stimulate the macroeconomy as a whole.

Deleveraging in the Public Sector

FISCAL CONSOLIDATION

There are growing calls for fiscal consolidation to achieve sustainable growth. As previously noted, Japan's debt-to-GDP ratio is over

200 percent. In the future, if the economy finds a way out of deflation, long-term yields on Japan government bonds (JGBs) are expected to rise. If concerns about fiscal sustainability still loom, the JGB market will face a sizeable risk that the price of bonds could experience a disorderly collapse. Any sharp decline in JGB prices, meaning sharp interest rate hikes, would quickly raise the cost of interest payments and could result in a debt explosion.

The Abe administration decided to postpone the consumption tax rate hike until October 2019, while maintaining its commitment to achieve a zero primary balance deficit by FY 2020. Assuming that the nominal growth rate continues to grow by around 1.9 percent annually (based on the baseline case), the Cabinet Office calculates that a reduction of the deficit by 9.2 trillion yen (about $92 billion) is necessary to achieve this commitment.[40]

Due to the postponement of the consumption tax rate hike, the possibility of achieving a zero primary balance deficit has decreased drastically. Without raising taxes, Japan is left with two measures to cut the deficit: (1) growth-enhancing measures, and (2) the downsizing of social security benefits. However, even if the Japanese economy achieves a high annual average growth rate of 3.1 percent by FY 2020, Japan would need to limit social security benefits to a −0.6 percent growth rate compared to 2.3 percent in the baseline case. Social security benefits and other expenditures would need to be cut considerably even if a high growth rate could be realized.

SOCIAL SECURITY REFORMS

At the root of Japan's fiscal problems are the ongoing demographic changes that are jeopardizing its universal health care system. The key to achieving fiscal consolidation lies in social security reform aimed at making the universal health care system viable given Japan's rapidly aging demographic structure. The population-aging rate (ratio of people 65 years old and over) is projected to reach 40 percent by 2060, up from 25 percent in 2013 (see Figure 4.14). Given this demographic outlook, health care spending is expected

Figure 4.14   Japan's Aging Process

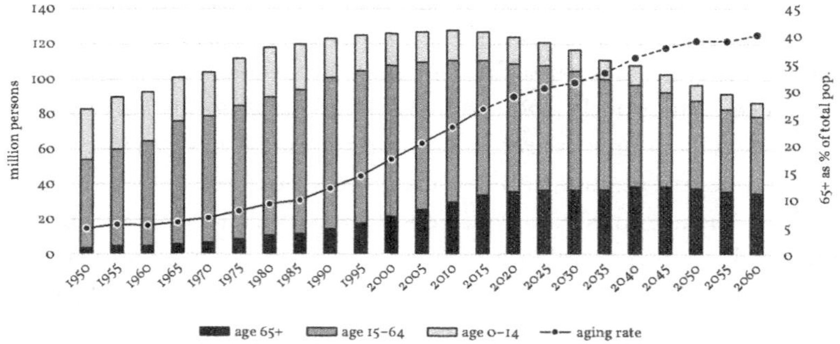

Data source: National Institute of Population and Social Security Research.

to rise by 4 percent per year (see Figure 4.15). Under the current system, these ballooning costs will be financed by public expenditure (ultimately, taxes) and increases in insurance premiums paid by working generations. With the ratio of working population to retired population dwindling, it is evident that this financing system will result in a fiscal crisis or the bankruptcy of working generations.

Avoiding these scenarios will require a two-pronged approach: reforms should be made both to financing structures and to fix the distorted incentives that currently allow for extravagant expenditures. For the financing structures, raising copayments for the retired generations would improve the ever-increasing deficit. At present, the copayment (i.e., the amount paid at hospitals by patients, with the rest covered by the universal health care insurance) is 30 percent for those working, while those age 70–74 pay 20 percent and those age 75 and over pay only 10 percent. The first step would be to raise the copayment of 75-year-olds and older to 20 percent, which would dramatically improve the financing imbalance. The biggest obstacle will be political pressure, given that more and more voters are reaching retirement age.

The second prong is to curb total health care spending. Efforts need to be made to reduce the per capita cost of medications and medical services. Dispersion of per capita health care cost by pre-

Figure 4.15 Estimation of Future Expense of Social Security
Systems in Japan

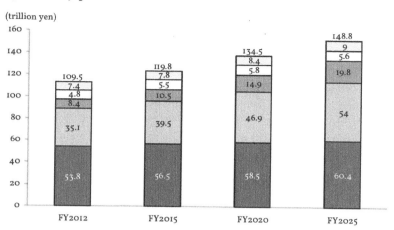

(trillion yen)

■ pensions   ▫ medical care   ▪ long-term care   ▫ child care   ▫ other

Data source: Japanese Ministry of Health, Labor, and Welfare (MHLW), "Overview
of the System and Basic Statistics" (Tokyo: MHLW, January 2012), 24.

fectures cannot be explained by demographic factors only. For example, per capita cost tends to be higher in prefectures in western
Japan where climates are relatively mild than in northeastern
regions. Inspections of cost-increasing factors in an average pre-
fecture's data should be helpful. Other possible sources of
over-expenditure are distorted incentives, which result in over-
prescriptions, over-hospitalization, and other ills. If improvements were made based on empirical analysis, health care–related
expenditures can be curtailed. However, removing pork barrels
from the health care and pharmaceutical industries is a challenge
that remains to be tackled.

Finally, pension reforms would also help improve fiscal imbalances going forward. Correcting excessive intergenerational
transfers is an acute issue. Working generations are already over-
burdened under the current system, and the burden is expected to

increase. Because the current pensions are run under the PAYGO system, the top-heavy demographic structure also increases the burdens of younger generations disproportionately. Quantitatively, retirees reaching the age of 65 by 2014 will be given pension payments worth as much as 62.7 percent of the annual income of the working generation. A realistic projection indicates that those who are 30 years old in 2014 will be given only 50.6 percent when they become 65 years old. Therefore, under the current PAYGO system, burden sharing is not fair and will endanger the entire system over time. One possible reform could be the reduction of pension payments for high-earning beneficiaries. Many of those who are age 65 and over are still earning high incomes.

CONCLUSION

Japan is still combating the deflation of the lost two decades in the midst of strong headwinds: an unprecedented decrease in the working-age population alongside population aging. Whether Japan can raise its per capita growth rate and maintain a high quality of life while overcoming these demographic challenges ultimately depends on the five Ds discussed in this chapter.

Historically, Japan has overcome many difficulties and challenges, as in the aftermath of the Meiji restoration and World War II. Japan tackled these challenges with its resourcefulness.

In the context of the twenty-first century's rapid globalization, however, Japan is losing diversity and flexibility. The weaknesses stemming from this monotonous, nondynamic economy are manifest in working style, career choices, and corporate culture. Promoting diversity in the labor market as well as in corporate culture can change mindsets and heighten the potential of each individual. If Japan can make best use of those with the most talent, it will enable reforms to proceed on various fronts, creating a more liquid labor market, diversifying society, and generating innovation.

Investment in future generations through reform of the education system and social security is also of prime importance. Corpo-

**APPENDIX: PANEL REGRESSION RESULTS FOR ECONOMETRIC ANALYSIS OF
BUSINESS FREEDOM, FREEDOM FROM CORRUPTION, LABOR FREEDOM,
AND TRADE FREEDOM**

Dependent variable: Per capita GDP growth (Fixed effects panel regression)

Variable	Coefficient	Std. Error	t-Statistic	Prob.	Significance
(intercept)	0.0302	0.0018	16.6075	0.0000	***
D(BUSINESS)	0.0007	0.0003	2.1382	0.0339	**
D(CORRUPTION)	0.0032	0.0007	4.4529	0.0000	***
D(FINANCIAL)	−0.0003	0.0003	−1.0684	0.2868	—
D(FISCAL)	0.0008	0.0007	1.0888	0.2777	—
D(GOV)	0.0002	0.0002	0.9620	0.3374	—
D(INVESTMENT)	−0.0004	0.0003	−1.2135	0.2266	—
D(LABOR)	0.0022	0.0006	3.8901	0.0001	***
D(MONETARY)	0.0007	0.0006	1.1742	0.2419	—
D(PROPERTY)	−0.0002	0.0005	−0.3887	0.6980	—
D(TRADE)	0.0041	0.0008	5.2216	0.0000	***

Weighted Statistics	Adjusted R-squared	0.41166
	S.E. of regression	0.02207
	F-statistic	4.77835
	Prob (F-statistic)	0.00000
F-Test Fixed Effects	Statistic	2.4594101
	d.f.	(30,176)
	Prob.	0.00015
Breusch-Pagan Test	Cross-section	150.66973
	Prob.	0.00000
Hausman Test	Chi-Sq. Statistic	27.725673
	Chi-Sq. d.f.	10
	Prob.	0.00200

Note: ** and *** indicate 5 percent and 1 percent significant estimates, respectively. Sample period: 2006 to 2012 (annual frequency). Cross-sections included: 31. Total panel (balanced) observations: 217. Dependent variable: first order difference of 3-year central moving average of per capita GDP.
Source: Author's analysis and calculations.

rations, together with workers, need to move from rent-seeking to risk-taking and explore the possibilities of the future. Only those who do not fear challenges can win gold medals, not only in the upcoming Olympic Games in Tokyo, but also when you stand on frontiers. Tackling those challenges head on will ultimately benefit everyone and lead to prosperity.

NOTES

1. Daron Acemoglu, Simon Johnson, and James A. Robinson, "Institutions as a Fundamental Cause of Long-Run Growth," in *Handbook of Economic Growth, Volume 1A*, ed. Phillippe Aghion and Steven N. Durlauf (Amsterdam: Elsevier, 2005), 388.

2. Glenn Hubbard and Tim Kane, *Balance: The Economics of Great Powers from Ancient Rome to Modern America* (New York: Simon & Schuster, 2013), 165.

3. Daron Acemoglu and James Robinson, *Why Nations Fail: The Origins of Power, Prosperity, and Poverty* (New York: Crown Business, 2013), 297.

4. Hiroshi Yoshikawa, *Koudo Seicho: Nihon wo Kaeta 6000-Nichi* [High Economic Growth: 6,000 Days that Changed Japan] (Tokyo: Chuokoron-Shinsha, Inc., 2012).

5. Michele Boldrin, Salvatore Modica, and David K. Levine, "Why Do Nations Fail?," *Huffington Post*, November 3, 2012.

6. See National Institute of Population and Social Security Research, "Population Projections for Japan," January 2012.

7. Hubbard and Kane, *Balance*, 160–173.

8. Ibid.

9. Ibid.

10. See International Institute for Management Development (IMD), *IMD World Competitiveness Yearbook* (Lausanne: IMD, 2016).

11. Yoshikawa, *Koudo Seicho*.

12. Takeo Hoshi and Anil K. Kashyap, *Naniga Nihon no Keizai Seicho wo Tometanoka: Saisei e no Shohōsen* [What Stopped Japan's Economic Growth: A Prescription for Renewal] (Tokyo: Nikkei Publishing Inc., 2013). In a similar context, see Ricardo J. Caballero, Takeo Hoshi, and Anil K. Kashyap, "Zombie Lending and Depressed Restructuring in Japan," *American Economic Review* 98, no. 5 (2008): 1943–1977.

13. In a similar context, Foster, Grim, and Haltiwanger show that firms with high TFP growth expand employment more quickly than those with low TFP growth rates. More specifically, firms with low TFP growth tend to cut employment, and over time, close their business with high probability. Given their findings, more new entrants, replacing zombies, would raise TFP and increase employment. Lucia Foster, Cheryl Grim, and John Haltiwanger, "Reallocation in the Great Recession: Cleansing or Not?," U.S. Census Bureau Center for Economic Studies Paper, No. CES-WP-13-42, 2013.

14. See José Ernesto Amorós and Niels Bosma, *Global Entrepreneurship Monitor 2013 Global Report* (n.p.: Global Entrepreneurship Monitor, 2013).

15. Fukao and Hyeog Ug point out that manufacturers, raw material firms, and wholesalers and retailers, all of which led Japan's rapid economic growth before the

1980s, were founded before 1974. The ratio of such old survivors amounts to 40–50 percent of all existing firms. Given their findings, they highlighted two characteristics of capital investment by firms. First, relatively younger firms have actively accumulated capital while old-aged firms and their subsidiaries and subcontractors (i.e., *ko-gaisha*) tended to invest less. Second, among old firms, large manufacturers ramped up research and development (R&D) investment and embarked on new projects in pursuit of globalization. A big caveat is that those large manufacturers did not expand domestic production while maintaining high productivity growth. Putting all these findings together, they concluded that the roles undertaken by young firms would be the biggest factor in predicting Japan's future employment, capital accumulation and, ultimately, productivity growth down the road. Kyoji Fukao and Hyeog Ug Kwon, "Nihon Keizai Seicho no Gensen wa Dokoni Arunoka: Micro Data niyoru Jisso Bunseki," RIETI Discussion Paper Series, 11-J-045, 2011.

16. See Programme for International Student Assessment (PISA), *PISA 2012 Results in Focus: What 15-Year-Olds Know and What They Can Do with What They Know* (Paris: OECD, 2012).

17. See World Intellectual Property Organization (WIPO), *Patent Cooperation Treaty Yearly Review: The International Patent System* (Geneva: WIPO, 2015).

18. See PricewaterhouseCoopers Co., Ltd., "Global Human Resources Management Survey 2010," press release, February, 3, 2011.

19. See Yuji Genda, "Jobless Youths and the NEET Problem in Japan," *Social Science Japan Journal* 10, no. 1 (2007): 23–40.

20. I will discuss Japan's labor market rigidity and why dismissals and layoffs are rare in Japan in greater detail later.

21. Yoshikawa, *Koudo Seicho*.

22. Takao Komine, *Nihon Keizai Ron no Tsumi to Batsu* [The Crime and Punishment of the Japanese Economic Theory] (Tokyo: Nikkei Publishing Inc., 2013).

23. Ryo Kato and Saori Naganuma, "Guroubaru ka to Nihon Keizai no Taiou Ryoku" [Globalization and the Resilience of Japan's Economy], Bank of Japan Working Paper Series, No. 13-J-13, 2013.

24. Ibid.

25. See UN Conference on Trade and Development (UNCTAD), *World Investment Report 2014: Investing in the SDGs: An Action Plan* (Geneva: UNCTAD, 2014).

26. The other possibility is that it is necessary for the older firms, which are facing an aging population, to hold cash for pension payments.

27. Masaaki Shirakawa, "The Transition from High Growth to Stable Growth: Japan's Experience and Implications for Emerging Economies" (remarks at the Bank of Finland 200th Anniversary Conference, Helsinki, May 5, 2011).

28. See OECD, *Education at a Glance 2014: OECD Indicators* (Paris: OECD, 2014).

29. Masayuki Morikawa, "RIETI no Seisansei Kenkyu ni tsuite: Update" [About RIETI's Research on Productivity: Update], RIETI Policy Discussion Paper Series, 13-P-010, 2013.

30. The official title of the law is Act on Securing, etc. of Equal Opportunity and Treatment between Men and Women in Employment.

31. Hirokatsu Asano and Daiji Kawaguchi, "Male-Female Wage and Productivity Differentials: A Structural Approach Using Japanese Firm-level Panel Data," RIETI Discussion Paper Series, 07-E-020, 2007.

32. See Terry Miller and Anthony B. Kim, *2015 Index of Economic Freedom: Promoting Economic Opportunity and Prosperity* (Washington, D.C.: Heritage Foundation and Wall Street Journal, 2015).

33. A formal econometric analysis confirms that business freedom, freedom from corruption, labor freedom, and trade freedom have statistically significant positive effects on per capita GDP growth. See Appendix for details of the panel regression.

34. Petri, Plummer, and Zhai point out that adding Japan to the TPP increases global benefits from the agreement from $75 to $223 billion per year and Japanese benefits (income gains) increase from –$1 billion to $104 billion (these values are for 2025, relative to the authors' baseline projections, and are expressed in 2007 dollars). Peter A. Petri, Michael G. Plummer, and Fan Zhai, "Adding Japan and Korea to the TPP," Asia-Pacific Trade, March 7, 2013.

35. Boldrin, Modica, and Levine, "Why Do Nations Fail?"

36. Richard B. Dasher, "Open Innovation, As Seen from Silicon Valley" (presentation for Japan Users Association of Information Systems Stanford University, November 3, 2014).

37. Dasher makes a similar argument in ibid.

38. Hiroya Masuda, "Jinkou Genshou Mondai to Chihou no Kadai [The Problems of Population Decline and the Challenges for the Rural Area]" (presentation for Sentaku Suru Mirai Iinkai, January 30, 2014).

39. Masayuki Morikawa, "Economies of Density and Productivity in Service Industries: An Analysis of Personal-Service Industries Based on Establishment-Level Data," *Review of Economics and Statistics* 93, no. 1 (2011): 179–192.

40. Japanese Cabinet Office, "Economic and Fiscal Projections for Medium to Long Term Analysis," July 2016.

Part III. JAPAN'S POSTWAR INSTITUTIONAL AND DEVELOPMENT POLICIES

5. MULTILATERALISM RECALIBRATED: JAPAN'S ENGAGEMENT IN INSTITUTION BUILDING IN THE PAST 70 YEARS AND BEYOND

Akiko Fukushima

INTRODUCTION

In the 1980s, the international community criticized Japan for free riding on the international order without paying its dues. But did Japan actually undermine institution building in the 70 years after the end of World War II? No—on the contrary, Japan never opposed multilateral institutions either at the global level, such as the United Nations (UN), or at the regional level in the Asia Pacific. Emerging from the ashes of the war, Japan did not engage in visible leadership in building multilateral institutions, nor was it expected to take such leadership by the international community. Instead, Japan was expected to be on the receiving side of the international order created by the victors of the war.

Japan, however, has consistently been an active supporter of institutions throughout the past 70 years. On the global front, although Japan was not a party in establishing institutions, particularly in the earlier decades after the war, Japan sought ways to contribute as a loyal member. On the regional front, after the end of World War II the Asia-Pacific region was infertile ground for institution building, in sharp contrast to Europe, as demonstrated by the failure of the Southeast Asia Treaty Organization (SEATO). The only exception was the subregional Association of Southeast Asian Nations (ASEAN) and track two institutions such as the Pacific Basin Economic Conference (PBEC) and the Pacific Economic Cooperation Council (PECC).

Since the 1990s, however, the Asia-Pacific region has witnessed budding regional institutions with varying geographical footprints in East Asia and the Asia Pacific more broadly. Some of these institutions have competed against each other. In some areas there are too many overlapping institutions, what is described as an "alphabet soup" or the "noodle bowl." During this evolution of regional institutions spanning the past three decades, Japan has sought to pursue its own initiatives but was perceived to lack leadership in proportion to its economic strength. As a result, some have claimed that Japan "led [regionalism] from behind."[1]

This chapter reviews how Japan has engaged in global and regional institutions since the end of World War II, particularly in response to the international community's increasing demands for Japan to pay its dues as its economy grew. The chapter then considers how Japan's multilateralism has been recalibrated to fulfill its responsibilities as a legitimate global citizen for international peace, security, and prosperity against the backdrop of geopolitical changes including the end of the Cold War, deepening global interdependence, increase of transnational issues, and rise of emerging countries on both global and regional fronts.

SEEKING TO BE A LEGITIMATE CITIZEN OF THE INTERNATIONAL COMMUNITY

Japan's debut to multilateralism goes back to its accession to the Geneva Convention in 1886 and the Hague Convention of 1899. As a civilized country, Japan tried to demonstrate that Japan honored internationally recognized laws of war during the 1894–1895 Sino-Japanese War and 1904–1905 Russo-Japanese War. The emperor specifically instructed the Japanese military to abide by these international laws even in the event the enemy did not reciprocate. The International Red Cross recorded that the Japanese military treated hostages and the wounded according to the Geneva Convention during these two wars.[2]

These steps were taken because Japan wished to be recognized as a civilized member of international institutions on par with other European and American powers after the Meiji restoration. The motive behind its zeal to engage in institutions was to rectify inequality in bilateral treaties signed at the time of the opening of the country after its long period of seclusion. By engaging in international institutions, Japan strongly hoped to get out of a second-tier citizen status and to climb up to a first tier. This was the origin of Japan's penchant for universalism.

After the end of World War I, Japan was invited to participate in the Paris Peace Conference and joined the League of Nations in 1919 as one of the victorious powers. This was a milestone in Japanese multilateral diplomacy while it pursued a bilateral alliance with the United Kingdom. The League created a supreme executive Council of Ten, to which Japan was invited to join. Japan felt that it was finally recognized as a power not only in Asia but also in the international community. Reporting on the Paris Peace Conference, the Japanese media proudly trumpeted that Japan had finally become a "First-Class Country."[3]

The Japanese delegation to the Paris Peace Conference proposed that a racial equality clause be included in the Covenant of the League of Nations, asking for equal treatment of Japan and its nationals. This was the extension of its demand for equal status with the Western powers. Being a victorious power of World War I, Japan wanted to make sure that it was treated as a peer in the League. Despite the majority vote to approve the Japanese proposal, it was not approved due to the strong opposition from the United Kingdom and United States. Instead of a majority vote, they demanded a unanimous vote for the clause. As a result, the racial equality clause was defeated. This case left bitterness, dissatisfaction, and a sense of alienation on the part of Japan. Inazo Nitobe, the Japanese diplomat who served in the League of Nations as under-secretary general from 1920 to 1927, felt strongly dissatisfied with the decision. Meanwhile, in 1924, the U.S. Congress unilaterally repudiated the agreement to receive 146 Japanese individuals a year to immigrate to the United States and passed the Oriental Exclusion Act, forbidding any Japanese to immigrate to the United States. Nitobe was outraged by the act. Moreover, the Oriental Exclusion Act by the United States made Japan feel evermore alienated in the international community.

Another multilateral forum that Japan was invited to attend was the Washington Naval Conference, which was held from November 1921 to February 1922. By that time the naval armaments race among the United States, the United Kingdom, and Japan had become so fierce that the financial burden was too heavy to bear during the recession. The United States took the initiative to host a conference on naval arms control and invited Japan, the United Kingdom, France, and Italy to Washington, D.C. The conference produced the Washington Treaty, which reduced the number of warships and carriers to a ratio of 10:10:6 among the United States, the United Kingdom, and Japan. The Japanese delegation had insisted upon a naval power reduction to a ratio of 10:10:7 and remained dissatisfied with this much deeper cut. Despite Japanese dissatisfaction over the outcome of the Washington conference, Foreign Minister Kijyuro Shidehara did try to honor the agreement to maintain multilateral cooperation with the United States and the United Kingdom. Nevertheless, the sense of alienation on the part of Japan deepened.

Ultimately, the League of Nations became concerned with Japanese expansionism in China. It sent an investigatory mission headed by Victor Litton in response to the case, brought to the League's attention by China. Upon the adoption of a Litton report blaming Japan for events in Manchuria, on February 24, 1933, the Japanese delegation voted "no" to a resolution recommending that Japan withdraw its occupation troops and restore Manchuria to Chinese sovereignty. The resolution was adopted 42 to 1. Yosuke Matsuoka, the head of the Japanese delegation, left the hall of the General Assembly and remarked, "We are not coming back." This marked Japan's withdrawal from the League.[4] From that point on, Japan was isolated from the international community and sought other means of increasing its influence in Asia, as exemplified in its vision of the Greater East Asia Co-Prosperity Sphere. Isolation led Japan to turn its back on universalism and to shift to pan-Asianism. Pan-Asianism is another ideology that Japan embraces, which surfaced most strongly during this era.

After World War II ended, Japan wanted to avoid isolation and aspired to return to the international community as a legitimate citizen. Japan shifted back to universalism and regarded international institutions, such as the United Nations and Bretton Woods institutions, as a critical platform for Japan.

The Japanese people have embraced both universalism and pan-Asianism since the Meiji restoration. Japan is geographically an Asian nation but has aspired to be accepted as one of the Western countries as a citizen. Forced to sign unequal treaties with Western countries when it opened the country after 300 years of Tokugawa seclusion, Japan has sought to be accepted as an equal partner by Western societies. While it pursued universalism until the early twentieth century, Japan turned to pan-Asianism when it was isolated by the Western powers. Japan's quest for universalism was expressed again when Japan sought to return to the international community after the end of World War II. In its diplomacy, Japan has tried to reconcile the two different perspectives of universalism and Pan-Asianism. This double perspective also helps explain Japanese engagement in multilateralism over the last 70 years.[5]

Applying for Membership in the United Nations

Thus, on June 16, 1952, not long after the signing of the San Francisco Peace Treaty in 1951, Foreign Minister Katsuo Okazaki sent a letter of application for membership to UN Secretary General Trygve Lie and stated, "The Government of Japan hereby accepts the obligations contained in the Charter of the United Nations, and undertakes to honor them, *by all means at its disposal* from the day when Japan becomes a member of the United Nations."[6] The application to the United Nations, however, was rejected by one of the five permanent members (P5), namely the Soviet Union. Japan's application was denied three times due to the fact that diplomatic relations between the Soviet Union and Japan had not resumed because the Soviet Union did not sign the San Francisco Peace Treaty. Another reason for the Soviet denial of Japanese membership was the Cold War divide between the Soviet Union and the United States, during which both wanted to prevent the other's sphere of influence from expanding by adding new members. Finally, after the arrival of the Khrushchev administration and the proposals to admit new members from both sides of the Cold War divide, Japan was accepted as the 80th member of the United Nations on December 18, 1956.

Japan's UN-Centered Diplomacy

Following Japan's accession, Prime Minister Nobusuke Kishi stated in a February 4, 1957, speech to the Japanese Diet that the basis of Japan's postwar diplomacy would be an attempt to further world peace and prosperity. Kishi outlined the three pillars of the country's postwar foreign policy: (1) centering its foreign policy around the United Nations, (2) cooperating with the free, democratic nations of the Western alliance, and (3) identifying closely with Asian nations. The second pillar has subsequently been realized and maintained particularly through cooperation with the United States based on the Japan-U.S. security treaty, as well as reflected in Japan's *National Security Strategy* (NSS) released in December 2013. The strategy describes the relationship as follows in the Strengthening the Japan-U.S. Alliance section:

> For more than 60 years, the Japan-U.S. Alliance, with the Japan-U.S. Security Arrangements at its core, has played an indispensable role for peace and security in Japan as well as peace and stability in the Asia-Pacific region. In recent years, the Alliance has also played a more critical role for peace, stability, and prosperity in the international community. The Japan-U.S. Alliance is the cornerstone of Japan's security.[7]

Also revealed in the strategy is the emphasis in recent decades on cooperation with other like-minded countries and regional organizations, including the United Kingdom, France, and Germany, and their regional organizations, namely the European Union (EU), the North Atlantic Treaty Organization (NATO), and the Organization for Security and Cooperation in Europe (OSCE).[8]

Similarly, the third pillar—cooperation with Asia—has been maintained and implemented up until now in terms of Japan's relations with Asian countries and ASEAN. The *National Security Strategy* names the Republic of Korea (ROK), Australia, India, and China as other partners with which Japan can collaborate.[9]

The first pillar—UN-centered diplomacy—however, was withdrawn one year after its enunciation due to the ineffective functioning of the United Nations. While UN-centered diplomacy appeared in the beginning section of the 1958 *Diplomatic Bluebook*, the phrase was pushed to the latter section and subsequently disappeared from the annual *Bluebook*. This was in response to criticism that the United Nations, and particularly the UN Security Council (UNSC), was paralyzed by the Cold War and could not hammer out policies for peace and security. There was no UN policy on which to center Japanese diplomacy. The phrase "UN-centered diplomacy," however, was occasionally used by prime ministers and foreign ministers in speeches to the Diet and the UN General Assembly.

Another element that bothers Japan in the United Nations is the former enemy clause that still remains in the UN Charter pertaining to Articles 53, 77, and 107. The Charter reads, "Nothing in the present Charter shall invalidate or preclude action, in relation to any state which during the Second World War has been an enemy of any signatory to the present Charter." This means member states can take any action without abiding by the Charter to former enemies including Japan. Japan has long asked for the deletion of these former enemy clauses from the Charter. In 1995, the Special Committee on the Charter of the United Nations and the Strength of the Role of Organization recommended deleting the former enemy clause, and the General Assembly adopted a resolution to delete the clauses when the Charter is next amended. Despite the resolution, the former enemy clause has yet to be deleted because the Charter has not been amended since the 1995 resolution.

Despite these misgivings, Japan has remained a loyal supporter of the United Nations and a contributor in key areas, such as economic issues. Japan did not make contributions on security due to its constitutional constraint against sending troops overseas, even though Foreign Minister Okazaki said that Japan would undertake its responsibility as a member by using "all means at its disposal." Since the day the letter was prepared, there has been an active debate within Japan on what "all means at its disposal" includes.[10] The debate still continues in the context of the new Japanese peace and security law in terms of how far Japan can contribute to UN collective security measures.

Japan's Contribution to United Nations

Japan has certainly contributed financially to the United Nations. Its assessed contribution exceeded 10 percent in 1983, and peaked at 20.6 percent in 2000 (see Figure 5.1). From 2013 through 2015, the Japanese contribution was 10.8 percent, making it the second largest contributor after the United States, ahead of the other P5 members. In the assessments for 2016 through 2018, Japan's contribution declines to 9.7 percent while China's contribution is 7.9 percent, rising from 5.2 percent in the preceding period. Japan remains the second largest contributor; meanwhile China has surpassed Germany and France.

However, in terms of its peacekeeping operations (PKO) assessed contribution, after long being the second largest contributor after the United States, Japan declined to third in 2016 while China has surged from sixth in preceding years to the second largest contributor after the United States, surpassing France, Germany, and the United Kingdom.[11] What kind of impact this change will bear on Japan's position in the United Nations or for that matter on China's position remains to be seen.

Japan was also instrumental in establishing and developing the UN Peace Building Commission (PBC). The PBC was established to promote a more coordinated, coherent, and integrated approach to post-conflict peace building and recovery, and was the result of UN

Figure 5.1   Japan's Assessed Contributions to the UN Regular Budget

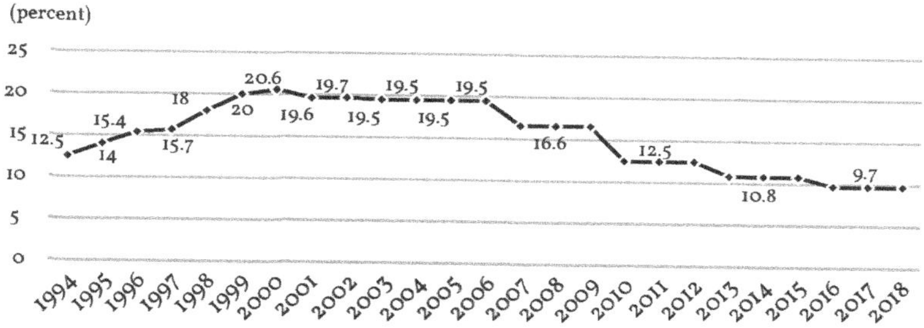

(percent)

Data source: United Nations, Committee on Contributions.

reform around the United Nations' 60th anniversary. Japan was a founding member of the PBC in 2005 and served as a chair June 2007–January 2009. Japan also assumed the chairmanship of the PBC Working Group on Lessons Learned in 2011. Despite the shortcomings of the PBC, Japan has strived to make it more effective in supporting peace building operations.

Thus, although Japan failed to realize the original meaning of UN-centered diplomacy enunciated by Prime Minister Kishi, Japan has been supporting the functions of the United Nations. This includes the core function of international peace and security in collaboration with like-minded countries, and not limited only to the United States. This case demonstrates how Japan positively contributed to global multilateralism.

Fitting the United Nations into the Current International Order

Japan wishes to engage more proactively in global institutions, including the United Nations. This is reflected in Japan's *National Security Strategy* document. The strategy declares that Japan will play an active role in the peace and stability of the international community as a "Proactive Contributor to Peace" based on the principle of international cooperation and stresses "strengthening diplomacy at the United Nations." The strategy specifically expressed Japan's intention to further engage in active efforts by the [United Nations] for the maintenance and restoration of international peace and security. Moreover Japan will actively contribute to diverse UN-led efforts including UN peacekeeping operation (PKO) and collective security measures; diplomatic efforts such as preventive diplomacy and mediation; seamless assistance efforts from the phase of post-conflict emergency humanitarian relief to recovery and reconstruction, as well as assistance through the UN Peacebuilding Commission.[12]

In this context, Japan regards the UN Security Council as the core UN organ of a collective security system for maintaining international peace and security. The strategy also called for its reform.[13] The Security Council was reformed once in 1965, when nonpermanent seats were increased from 6 to 10. This was in response to the increase in the number of member states due to decolonization. Although the number of member states grew due to the continuation of decolonization and the end of the Cold War, the core composition of the Security Council has been maintained since then, making the Security Council less representative than it was when the organization was founded (see Table 5.1).

While Japan has expressed its interest in obtaining a permanent seat on the Security Council, it will not become a reality unless the UN General Assembly approves changes in the composition of the Security Council and the revision of the Charter,

Table 5.1   Ratio between Members of the United Nations and the Security Council

	UN Members	Security Council Members	Permanent Security Council Members	Nonpermanent Security Council Members	Ratio (approximate)	% of UN Members on Security Council
1945	51	11	5	6	1:5	21.5
1965	115	15	5	10	1:8	13.0
2016	193	15	5	10	1:13	7.8

Data Source: Information compiled from United Nations website.

because Article 23 stipulates the specific names of the permanent members.

Since the developing member states have complained that the UN Security Council does not represent the interests of the UN general membership equitably, they have tabled many ideas for Security Council reform over the years. They argued that the United Nations, in its current structure, is a relic of World War II, which needs to be remodeled to suit the post–Cold War world.

In 1992, during the 47th session of the General Assembly, India and other nonaligned countries took the initiative to submit a resolution on Security Council reform. This resolution was unanimously adopted by the General Assembly and led to a questionnaire survey by the secretary general that resulted in the establishment of an open-ended Working Group on the Questions of Equitable Representation and Increase in the Membership of the Security Council in 1993. The working group was established by the General Assembly to debate reform but found it very difficult to create consensus.

In the first half of 1997, Security Council reform began to gain momentum. On March 20, 1997, Malaysian ambassador Razali Ismail, president of the General Assembly and a chairman of the working group, presented a paper synthesizing the majority view regarding expansion of the Security Council and proposed to increase Security Council membership from 15 to 24 by adding five permanent members (one each from the developing states of Africa, Asia, and Latin America and the Caribbean, and two from the industrialized states, generally recognized as Germany and Japan) and four nonpermanent members (one each from Africa, Asia, Eastern Europe, and Latin America and the Caribbean). Razali's proposal, however, failed to secure enough support.

While the momentum for Security Council reform seemed stalled, four member states (Japan, Germany, India, and Brazil, the so-called G4), in 2005 started their campaign to be permanent members. Their draft resolution failed at the last minute when the African nations could not come to a consensus on supporting the draft resolution. Meanwhile the United States expressed its support for a permanent seat for its ally Japan, but was passive in supporting the G4 campaign. U.S. ambassador to the United Nations John Bolton often said, "Don't try to fix it when it isn't broken."[14]

For the period from 2016 through 2018, Japan sits as a nonpermanent member of the Security Council for the 11th time. Japan is exploring ways to contribute to international peace through the United Nations such as peace keeping and peace building. It is also running a new G4 campaign to adjust the makeup of the UNSC to make it fit better with the current size of the organization. This time around, the G4 concept is seeking to create a new category of semi-permanent seats, which would allow Japan to stay on the UNSC for longer than the current two years allowed for nonpermanent members and allow it to be elected when the term expires without waiting for another two years, though these seats would not enjoy a veto. This would make the Security Council more representative and viable. One experienced Japanese ambassador posted to the United Nations, Kenzo Oshima, uses the analogy of adding business class to an airplane that has only first class and economy class today. He asks whether Japan can fly business class.[15]

The G7 Summit as an Important Venue for Japan

Another illustration of Japan's participation in a global institution has been in the global economy, namely the summit meetings of the Group of Seven (G7) nations (Canada, France, Germany, Italy, Japan, United Kingdom, and United States). Since its first meeting in 1975 at Chateau Rambouillet in France, Japan has been a founding and loyal participant in G7 summits and has explored ways to contribute to the G7 agenda. The G7 was very significant to Japan because it was the only summit-level meeting that Japan participated in, unlike other members who had the NATO summit, European Council summit, and other occasions for leaders to meet. Since the G7 was originally a meeting on economic issues, Japan did not have any constitutional constraints in contributing. Thus, the value of the G7 was extremely high for Japan.

Then, in 1997, the G7 summit expanded to include Russia (G8) due to the initiative of President Bill Clinton and Chancellor Helmut

Kohl, which was realized in the Birmingham summit of 1998. President Clinton's motive was to encourage Boris Yeltsin to promote economic reform and to maintain a neutral position on the expansion of NATO. With this expansion, the G7 summit lost some of its significance and momentum in Japanese eyes. Certainly there were voices in favor of enlarging the membership of the summit; France even invited African countries to the Evian summit. However, African countries were dissatisfied because their summit was a side event, which subsequently led to the creation of the G20. Enlargement diluted the ability of the G7 to show solidarity and to act on a common agenda. Gradually the G8 summit was positioned as just another summit meeting. Some criticized the G8 summit for becoming a mere talk shop. On the other hand, others criticized its lack of representativeness as the combined gross domestic product of the G7 declined to one-third of global GDP. The G20, which includes emerging countries like China, India, and Brazil, has 85 percent of global GDP.

The G7 seems to have regained its momentum when it was transformed back into the original G7 due to Russia's seizure of Crimea and invasion of Ukraine. In 2015, Chancellor Angela Merkel noted,

> The G7 cannot meet these challenges alone; we will need many other partners. Nevertheless, I am convinced that the G7 can be, indeed must be, the driving force for a world worth living in, in the long term. . . . That is the value-added that can be expected from G7 summits. And that is the standard against which we should measure our actions.[16]

Despite all the criticisms about the relevance and power of the G7 Summit, it is an important institution for Japan to be part of "a like-minded coalition of market democracies dedicated to the international rule of law."[17]

On global trade, Japan has supported the Uruguay Round of General Agreement on Tariffs and Trade (GATT) negotiations, serving in the quadrilateral trade ministers meeting along with the United States, European Union, and Canada. The quad was instrumental in leading the negotiations. However, in the Doha Round agriculture was the main challenge, meaning that Japan, which has a strong agricultural lobby, could not lead, and the quad was disbanded. The Japanese agricultural lobby compromised in the Uruguay Round and was not ready for another major compromise for opening of the Japanese agricultural market.

These are a few examples that demonstrate Japan's record of participation in global institutions. Though it faces legal constraints, which led to criticisms of Japan's contributions to multilateralism, Japan has made efforts in building and developing global institutions. With the changes mentioned above and in geopolitics, Japan has an opportunity to engage more proactively in these international institutions, if it so wishes. Japan is now turning into a proactive contributor to international order, which reflects Japan's leaning toward universalism.

LEADING REGIONAL COOPERATION "FROM BEHIND"

Now turning to the regional level, how has Japan promoted its association with the Asia-Pacific region (the third pillar of Japanese diplomacy mentioned previously) in the past 70 years? While the Asia Pacific could not launch regionalism until the 1980s—except in track two processes—it embraced mega-regionalism with an Asia-Pacific framework in the 1990s, including through Asia-Pacific Economic Cooperation (APEC) and the ASEAN Regional Forum (ARF). Then, from the end of the 1990s to the 2000s, East Asian institutions such as ASEAN+3 and the East Asia Summit (EAS) emerged. This created competition between the geographic footprint of the Asia Pacific and East Asia. However, from the late 2000s onward, the tide has flowed back toward the Asia Pacific. The EAS now includes the United States, as does the recently concluded Trans-Pacific Partnership (TPP), but East Asia groupings have not faded away (see Figure 5.2). Rather, these institutions coexist, offering a multilayered architecture for regional cooperation.

This flourishing of the alphabet soup of institutions represents a sea change in the region, which had been characterized by a web of bilateral ties in the post–World War II period. All military alli-

Figure 5.2   Regional Architectures in the Asia Pacific

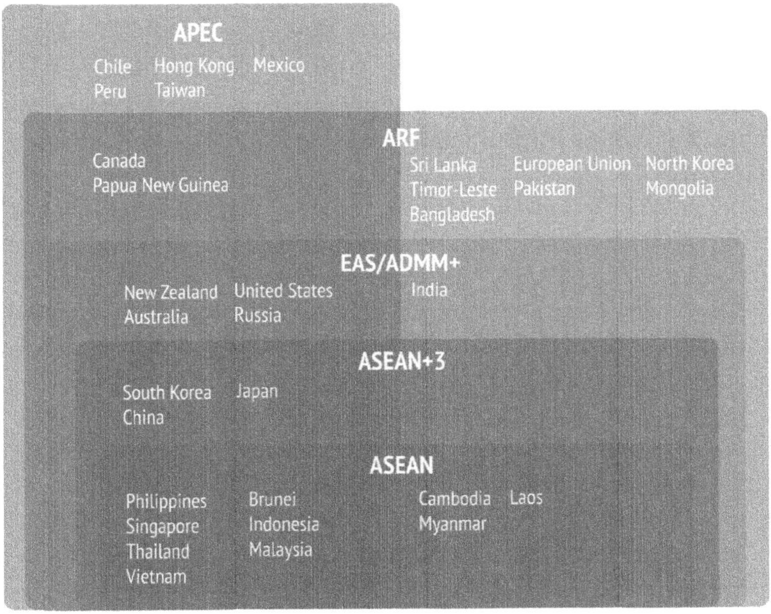

APEC
Chile   Hong Kong   Mexico
Peru   Taiwan

ARF
Canada
Papua New Guinea
Sri Lanka   European Union   North Korea
Timor-Leste   Pakistan   Mongolia
Bangladesh

EAS/ADMM+
New Zealand   United States   India
Australia   Russia

ASEAN+3
South Korea   Japan
China

ASEAN
Philippines   Brunei   Cambodia   Laos
Singapore   Indonesia   Myanmar
Thailand   Malaysia
Vietnam

Source: Michael Green et al., *Asia-Pacific Rebalance 2025: Capabilities, Presence, and Partnerships* (Washington, DC: Center for Strategic and International Studies, 2016), 109.

ances in the region are bilateral, as are free trade agreements (FTAs) and economic partnership agreements (EPAs), and regional economic mechanisms did not emerge in the first three decades except the subregional Association of Southeast Asian Nations.

Taking Initiative in Launching PBEC and PECC

Soon after World War II, Japan engaged the region, most notably Southeast Asia, through the provision of official development assistance (ODA) to assist economic development. This was reflected in Japan's relations with ASEAN. Successive prime ministers paid official visits to the region and made speeches to enhance relations, most notable among which were the heart-to-heart relations of

Prime Minister Takeo Fukuda, the human security assistance provided by Prime Minister Keizo Obuchi after the region was hit hard by the 1997 currency crisis, and the five new principles for Japanese diplomacy toward Asia by Prime Minister Shinzo Abe in 2013.[18] Prime Minister Abe mentioned that Japan's relations with ASEAN form "a supreme vital linchpin" for Japan's diplomatic strategy during his visit to Jakarta in January 2013.[19]

Even in the earlier days after the end of World War II, Japanese business leaders took the initiative in launching a regional grouping of Pacific Rim countries. Japan was instrumental in launching the Pacific Basin Economic Conference (PBEC) in 1968. PBEC has hosted annual plenary meetings ever since. It has been a venue for business professionals in the region to exchange views. The president of the Japanese Chamber of Commerce and Industry, Noboru Goto, nicknamed "Mr. Pacific," was known for his strong leadership in PBEC when he served as chairman of the chamber. Successive presidents of the chamber have inherited his spirit and developed the institution. This institution has served as a platform for Asia-Pacific Economic Cooperation (APEC) at the governmental level, and business leaders advise APEC before the leaders meeting every year.

Japan took yet another initiative by launching a track two dialogue with Australia called the tripartite process, including government experts in their private capacity, business leaders, and academics. In 1978, Prime Minister Masayoshi Ohira created a committee to study cooperation among Pacific Rim countries, which was chaired by Dr. Saburo Okita. This group proposed the creation of a pan-Pacific Association in its May 1980 final report, hoping to promote free trade, transfer of capital, market openness, economic and technological cooperation by developed countries, and self-help efforts by developing countries, to mitigate North-South issues. In January 1980, Prime Minister Ohira met with Prime Minister Malcolm Fraser of Australia and agreed to host an international seminar on the pan-Pacific in Australia, which was subsequently held in Canberra later that year. Scholars, business people, and government officials from Australia, the United States, New Zealand, Japan, ASEAN, South Korea, Papua New Guinea, Fiji, and Tonga participated and agreed to launch the Pacific Economic Cooperation Conference (PECC) to promote regional cooperation. This tripartite process was produced in response to strong reservations by ASEAN countries to establish an intergovernmental organization that could be swallowed up by the big powers in the region.[20] PECC offered another intellectual infrastructure to create a habit of dialogue in the region, which served as another platform for APEC.

In founding PECC, Japan thus took initiative not alone but with Australia to make the proposal more acceptable to regional members. This method of working with like-minded countries rather than taking initiative alone has been the modus operandi of Japanese leadership in promoting regional institutions. Some observe that this is due to its historical legacies and to a possible association with the pre-war Japanese Greater East Asia Co-Prosperity Sphere. Others argue that it comes from the fact that Japan did not want to impose its leadership in light of its dominant regional economic power. This has, however, frustrated some Asian countries, which complain that Japan does not exercise its full leadership potential in the region.

The Case of Asia-Pacific Economic Cooperation

Since there was no regional institution until the end of the Cold War, it was significant that the Asia-Pacific Economic Cooperation (APEC) conference at the intergovernmental level was born in November 1989, the same month that the Berlin Wall came down in Europe.

In creating APEC, Japan again worked closely with Australia. The idea originally came from the Japanese Ministry of International Trade and Industry (MITI), which thought it would be beneficial for the region to have an institution to promote regional trade and investment. This view arose against the background of deepening economic interdependence and the emergence of regional institutions elsewhere, such as the single market in Europe and the North American Free Trade Agreement (NAFTA).

In January 1987, MITI minister Hajime Tamura proposed to organize a pan-Pacific industry ministers meeting when he visited

Australia. This proposal aimed to gather ministers in charge of industry in Japan, the United States, Canada, Australia, and New Zealand to discuss their economic situations, industrial restructuring, technologic development, and small and medium industries. MITI followed up on Minister Tamura's proposal by creating the Asia-Pacific Trade Development Study Group within the ministry in 1988. The study group recommended that Asia-Pacific countries should promote cooperation by consensus, should pursue a gradual approach, and should maintain outward looking cooperation rather than building a fortress. This idea was conveyed to the Australian Minister of Commerce and Industry during his visit to Tokyo in September 1988. The Asia-Pacific trade ministers meeting proposal promoted the negotiation of the Uruguay Round of negotiations and helped reduce trade barriers in the region and promote common economic interests in the region.[21]

MITI, instead of launching the idea itself, left the task to the initiative of Australia, which was also interested in the idea and was looking to participate in a multilateral venue, since it was excluded from the G7. Thus, during a visit to South Korea in January 1989, Australian prime minister Bob Hawke officially proposed the idea to create a consultative body working toward open regional cooperation. After the speech, both the Japanese government and the Australian government visited capitals in the region to explain and to ask them to participate. Some potential members were interested in launching an institution without the United States but Japan persuaded them to include the United States. In June 1989, U.S. secretary of state James Baker mentioned in a speech in New York on Asian policy that he would also like to promote a mechanism for pan-Pacific economic cooperation in collaboration with Prime Minister Hawke and MITI minister Hiroshi Mitsuzuka. This led to the launch of the foreign and trade ministers conference in November 1989 under the APEC name.

APEC was further fortified by President Bill Clinton's initiative, with Australian support, to organize a leaders meeting of APEC participants in Seattle in 1993. In July 1993, President Clinton also proposed the creation of a new Pacific Community during a speech in San Francisco. APEC was another case of institution building in which Japan spawned an idea and asked Australia to lead while Japan remained behind the scenes but made strenuous efforts to get everyone on board.

The Case of the ASEAN Regional Forum (ARF)

For regional security, the creation of the ARF was a watershed. In this case, Japan proposed the creation of an institution, but it was eventually left to the management of ASEAN. Witnessing the successful evolution of APEC in the economic sphere, the impetus for a regional security framework grew gradually.

In fact, there were proposals on regional security cooperation that preceded the ARF. It was General Secretary Mikhail Gorbachev of the Soviet Union who proposed a Pacific Ocean Conference (which was not accepted) along the lines of the Helsinki Conference in his Vladivostok speech of July 1980.

In July 1990, Gareth Evans, Australian minister for foreign affairs, proposed a Conference on Security Cooperation in Asia (CSCA)—an Asian version of the Conference on Security and Cooperation in Europe (CSCE)—for addressing the apparently intractable security issues that exist in Asia.[22] Also in July 1990, Joe Clark, Canadian minister of foreign affairs, gave a speech at the Foreign Press Club in Tokyo and suggested that it was time to create an Asia-Pacific security organization.[23] These proposals, however, were received coolly by ASEAN member states, if not rejected outright. ASEAN was concerned that such an organization might force them to adopt European-style human rights, which were perceived as a central theme of the Helsinki Final Act. On the other hand, the United States was concerned that if the CSCA emulated the CSCE, it would possibly focus on arms control, which might in turn be dominated by the Russian proposal to reduce naval arms in the Pacific.[24]

In the early 1990s, Japan was also reluctant to participate in the multilateral regional security framework, because it was originally proposed by the Soviet Union. It was perceived as propaganda masking a hidden agenda that aimed to drive a wedge in the

Japan-U.S. security relationship. Thus, Japan also rejected the idea on the grounds that security in Europe and Asia were different and therefore required different mechanisms to maintain security. Prime Minister Toshiki Kaifu said in July 1990 that it was too early for an Asian CSCE.[25]

Although the major powers in the region rejected the creation of a regional security institution in the early 1990s, these proposals slowly influenced their mindset. Asia-Pacific governments that were initially negative on institution building gradually became more receptive to the idea of less institutionalized and less formal security cooperation in the form of a dialogue process, following in the footsteps of APEC.

The first clear change of attitudes came from the ASEAN Institutes of Strategic and International Studies (ASEAN-ISIS). ASEAN countries held a conference in Jakarta in June 1991 to discuss recommendations for the fourth ASEAN summit to be held in Singapore the following year. Directors of ISIS proposed to consider creating a multilateral security framework using the existing ASEAN Post Ministerial Conference (PMC). Mindful of these changes, Japan reversed its position after Gorbachev's visit to Tokyo in April 1991. Foreign Minister Taro Nakayama gave a speech at the ASEAN PMC in July 1991 proposing the creation of a security and political framework for dialogue within the annual ASEAN PMC in order to enhance peace and security in the region. Nakayama's proposal was in line with the recommendations of the ASEAN-ISIS. However, the ASEAN countries did not receive this proposal warmly. The Nakayama proposal was too early as ASEAN-ISIS recommendations were intended for the January 1992 ASEAN Singapore summit. Also, Foreign Minister Nakayama's proposal was tabled too abruptly without building sufficient support in advance from the United States and ASEAN member states. Another explanation for its rejection was that the initiative should not have come from a large power in the Asia Pacific. It would have been more palatable if it had come from one of the smaller regional powers.[26]

Two years later, in July 1993, the ASEAN PMC in Singapore did agree to create the ARF along the lines that Nakayama proposed. By this time the United States had shifted its position in regard to a multilateral security dialogue. This shift was reflected in James Baker's comment, "Asian security increasingly is derived from a flexible, *ad hoc* set of political and defense interactions. Multilateral approaches to security are emerging."[27] Since then, the ARF has embraced members from the Asia Pacific and has functioned as a framework for confidence building measures.

Shifting to East Asian Cooperation

While the institutional framework of the Asia Pacific—so called mega-regionalism—flourished in the 1990s, it started to stall after a decade. Both APEC and the ARF were perceived as not achieving tangible results. Japan, which had been promoting Asia-Pacific institutions since the 1960s, reduced its efforts due to the domestic economic recession of the 1990s. Other members also lost their high hopes. Some labeled APEC and ARF as mere talk shops.

The region shifted its focus from the Asia Pacific to East Asia. This change was triggered by Malaysia's Prime Minister Mahathir Mohamad's proposal to create the East Asia Economic Group (EAEG) in December 1990. His idea was not accepted by ASEAN member states, except for Singapore. Watching the negative reactions in the region, the ASEAN economic ministers meeting in October 1991 renamed the proposal the East Asia Economic Caucus (EAEC), which was an ASEAN way to say no politely to Malaysia. The idea was shelved.

However, the idea started to simmer in the minds of East Asia countries and was realized in a different format through initiatives by ASEAN, first by Singapore and then by Malaysia. In October 1994, Prime Minister Goh Chok Tong of Singapore visited France and proposed the Asia-Europe Meeting (ASEM). This led to a first meeting of ASEM in March 1996. In preparing for this meeting, while Europe decided to make EU member states participants, it was decided that Asia, lacking a comparable regional institution, would include Japan, China, and the Republic of Korea, in addition to ASEAN. This happened to include exactly the same members as the earlier EAEG proposal.

Meanwhile, Prime Minister Mahathir proposed to invite Japan, China, and the Republic of Korea to an informal ASEAN summit in 1997, which was intended to be a one-time event. However, due to the unexpected Asian currency crisis in the summer of 1997, this group decided to meet annually, and would be called ASEAN+3.

At the time of the currency crisis, Thailand, which was hard-hit, asked for International Monetary Fund (IMF) assistance. However, the IMF did not offer major assistance, nor did the United States, to Thailand's disappointment. Instead, Japan and other Asian countries and the Asian Development Bank (ADB) came to Thailand's aid.

Witnessing the turn of events after the crisis, the Japanese Ministry of Finance proposed the creation of an Asian Monetary Fund (AMF) to assist countries hit by the crisis and to prepare for future crises. However, the United States opposed the AMF because the draft proposal was not clear in terms of AMF's relations with IMF, and because the United States was not included as a member. The United States was also concerned about possible moral hazard problems if Asia created its own financial institution, undermining the Washington consensus. On the other hand, ASEAN wholeheartedly endorsed the AMF. When the IMF/World Bank annual meeting was held in Hong Kong, the United States expressed its opposition very strongly. Australia joined the United States in opposing the AMF. China was also not forthcoming.[28] As a result, the AMF failed.

Japanese finance minister Kiichi Miyazawa then offered a new initiative of $30 billion to assist regional states hard hit by the Asian currency crisis that started in Thailand and Malaysia. Furthermore, Prime Minister Keizo Obuchi introduced the concept of human security to assist countries hit by the Asian currency crisis and announced a new special yen loan of $60 billion in 1998 at the time of the second ASEAN+3 summit in Vietnam.

The Asian currency crisis reminded members at the ASEAN+3 summit meeting of the need to have their own grouping to respond to crises as well as to prevent crises from recurring. They agreed to have a regular annual summit meeting as ASEAN+3. Meanwhile, the United States, which strongly opposed the EAEG, did not oppose

ASEAN+3. The United States did not see ASEAN+3 as undermining U.S. interests.[29]

After the ASEAN+3 summit had been regularized and fortified by ministerial meetings (and after the Chiang Mai Initiative was established to prepare for crises), an effort to expand and to strengthen the institution started. The initiative this time around was taken by the Republic of Korea. Korean president Kim Dae-Jung proposed to establish an East Asia Vision Group (EAVG) of eminent persons to consider the future of ASEAN+3, including the possible creation of an East Asia Community. ASEAN+3 leaders accepted the proposal, and the group announced its recommendations in 2001. The EAVG report proposed a community for prosperity and sustainable development as well as stability and peace in East Asia. The group recommended including not only the economy but also politics, security, and social issues. It also called for embracing a common identity.[30]

Although the intergovernmental group discussed the report, community building in East Asia was perceived as something in the distant future. Thus, when Malaysia proposed to host the first East Asia Summit, opinions were divided about whether such a summit should be organized. Some were in favor while others were either reluctant or opposed. Witnessing the confusion over EAS and the concept of an East Asia community, the Japanese government took its own initiative to sort out the issues by preparing an issue paper on the East Asia community. The paper was submitted to ASEAN+3 senior officials meeting (SOM) and the ASEAN+3 foreign ministers' meeting in the summer of 2004. Although this was titled an issue paper, it included the Japanese vision of an East Asia community, regional cooperation, and an East Asia summit. The paper noted the momentum for East Asian cooperation since the 1997 Asian currency crisis, and the growing needs for regional cooperation that included both economic and security issues. The issue paper also recognized the key role played by ASEAN in East Asian cooperation. As an approach for East Asian regional cooperation, the paper recommended functional cooperation, future architecture building, and development of a community identity. As for the membership of EAS, it suggested inclusion of Australia, New Zealand, and India.[31] Prime Minister Junichiro Koizumi had already proposed this expansion of the framework of East Asia in his speeches in Singapore on January 14, 2002, which proposed an Initiative for Development in East Asia (IDEA)[32] and for Australia on May 1 2002,[33] which expanded the community to include Australia and New Zealand. In these speeches, the Japanese prime minister made an unequivocal call for democratic norms, departing from the emphasis on Asian values struck in the region. Prime Minister Koizumi emphasized regional cooperation so much that some were concerned whether he intended to substitute international cooperation with regionalism. Singapore also suggested including India, Australia, and New Zealand to balance the influence of China and Japan. Indonesia agreed. However, Malaysia and China insisted on keeping participants to ASEAN+3 members only.

Furthermore, Japan proposed to include the United States as an observer. Some ASEAN members and China did not agree to this proposal. ASEAN, instead of negating the proposal, gave a condition that participants to EAS must sign the Treaty of Amity and Cooperation in Southeast Asia (TAC), which the United States was reluctant to sign. ASEAN thus strove to take a leading role in regionalism. Meanwhile, the United States expressed that it would not participate in EAS as an observer.

The first EAS meeting was held in December 2005 in Kuala Lumpur with ASEAN, Japan, China, the Republic of Korea, India, Australia, and New Zealand. The distinction between ASEAN+3 and EAS was an issue. While the EAVG recommended developing ASEAN+3 into the EAS in order to create an East Asian community, Malaysia proposed to host EAS alongside ASEAN+3. This confused the situation. China wanted to promote ASEAN+3 so that it could keep its strong influence in a smaller group, while Japan was promoting EAS as a wider group including other like-minded countries and to discuss a whole array of issues. In the respective declarations of the summit meetings, the functions of the two were described as follows. The "Kuala Lumpur Declaration on the East Asia Summit" stated that EAS should play *a significant role* in building a community in the region," and also positioned EAS as "a forum for dialogue on broad strategic, political, and economic issues of common interest and concern with the aim of promoting peace, stability, and economic prosperity in East Asia."[34] On the other hand, the "Kuala Lumpur Declaration on the ASEAN Plus Three Summit" stated that the "process will continue to be *the main vehicle* in achieving the maintenance of regional and global peace and security, prosperity, and progress."[35] It also acknowledged that the ASEAN+3 process contributed to community building in East Asia. The difference between "significant role" and "the main vehicle" was left open to interpretation.

These Japanese institution building efforts in East Asia stemmed from the observation of Chinese aggressive diplomacy in liaising with ASEAN. This was demonstrated by their swift conclusion of an FTA in November 2001 and China's efforts to be a leader in East Asia and beyond, as demonstrated by the launch of the Shanghai Five in 1997 and by its extension into the Shanghai Cooperation Organization (SCO) in 2001. Japan, mindful of China's emergence on multilateralism, sought to take its own initiative, as exemplified in its issue paper for EAS. Due to its two-decade-long recession, Japan was gradually losing economic weight in the region and was making efforts to remain on the radar screen of other countries. Japan was concerned that it might be marginalized in the geopolitical game. These efforts, however, led to a perceived competition between Japan and China in regionalism, as illustrated by the aforementioned tug-of-war between ASEAN+3 and EAS. Perceiving a competition between China and Japan in regional institution building, ASEAN complained that it did not want to be placed in a position to choose one of the two proposals.

ASEAN also did not want to lose its leadership in Asian regionalism and started to appeal to centrality in regionalism. ASEAN used the phrase "ASEAN in a driver's seat of regionalism" to describe its leadership role, but switched it to "ASEAN centrality" or an "ASEAN-centered approach." This was demonstrated in their decision to host the East Asia Summit only in ASEAN countries and to not allow other members to host the summit. This was also included in the declaration of EAS, denying the wishes of China to host the second EAS. ASEAN created the ASEAN Defense Ministers Meeting (ADMM) in 2006, and later the ADMM Plus, which includes defense ministers of ASEAN as well as Japan, China, New Zealand, the United States, Australia, the Republic of Korea, and India. This includes Asia-Pacific members in addition to East Asian ones. This is the only defense ministers meeting in the region at the intergovernmental level to exchange views on security issues and to explore security cooperation. Its joint exercises on humanitarian assistance and disaster relief (HADR) have given more substance to the institution, beyond the ARF. While the ARF gathers foreign ministers, ADMM Plus gathers defense ministers and is the only venue for defense ministers in the region to participate, except the track two Shangri-La Dialogue.

Japan cherishes its relations with ASEAN. This was clearly demonstrated in the importance the joint statement commemorating the 40th anniversary of Japan-ASEAN relations placed on ASEAN's centrality in regional architecture on December 14, 2013, expressing the commitment to work "hand in hand."[36] Japan opted to allow ASEAN to take the lead in institution building in the region. It was more acceptable for smaller countries. Japan felt comfortable in generating ideas and leading from behind rather than running upfront. Otherwise it worked with like-minded countries in the region to lead institution building.

Back to the Regional Framework of the Asia Pacific?

One should also note that the United States is back in Asia with its own rebalancing or pivot to Asia policy. The Asian side decided to enlarge the scope of East Asia and to include the United States in the EAS in 2011. The United States also participates in ADMM Plus. These changes gave a facelift to the institutional footprint of the Asia Pacific. This was further fortified by the United States participating in and leading the Trans-Pacific Partnership (TPP) negotiations. Japan did not join in its initial phase but has participated since 2013 and played an important leading role, both working with and balancing the United States. With the signing of TPP in February 2016, a new regional architecture may unfold. TPP does not include all regional states at this point, but members are required to be from Asia-Pacific countries. Some ASEAN members are not participants. Yet, there is another framework under negotiation, namely the Regional Comprehensive Economic Partnership (RCEP), between ASEAN members plus China, ROK, Japan, Australia, New Zealand and India. It seems the framework of regional cooperation evolved from pan-Pacific, Asia Pacific, East Asia, and now back to Asia Pacific or Indo Pacific. However, this time around, various institutions with differing frameworks coexist without losing relevance and also are further fortified with smaller footprints of trilaterals or quadrilaterals. Japan is a member of almost all of these regional institutions and is trying to let each organization have its respective role while Japan also seeks to be a leading power in maintaining peace, security, and prosperity in the region. Japan certainly engages in Asia and explores its future course by navigating these multilayered architectures in addition to its traditional bilateral diplomacy. However, at the regional level the scene seems to be complicated with leaders and a whole spectrum of issues. Being complicated with competing leaders and agendas, some regional practitioners and scholars question whether the current regionalism can sustain its utility.

MULTILATERALISM RECALIBRATED

Liberal Institutionalism to Recede?

As the international order undergoes changes, it is asked whether liberal institutionalism can sustain itself or is at the verge of extinction. G. John Ikenberry, however, observes that the system of liberal institutionalism still holds sway and argues that "states continue to have deep—and indeed growing—interests in an international order that is open and at least loosely rule-based, i.e., a system of multilateral governance." He analyzes that the future of multilateralism hinges on "the ability of states rising and falling, advanced and developing, Northern and Southern in redistributing authority, negotiate new bargains and generate collective leadership." He concludes by asserting that the "alternative is disorder."[37]

In the twenty-first century, institutions certainly seem to matter more than ever. Simply put, due to the advent of globalization, national agendas today demand transnational cooperation more than before. There is no denying that global interdependence across the economic and security domains is deeper than ever. In addition we are witnessing an increase of trans-boundary issues such as international terrorism, pandemics, large-scale natural disasters, and climate change. These challenges cannot be effectively managed by a single country but only by transnational cooperation under an institutional framework of some sort. Overcoming obstacles to instituting cooperation is always difficult and it is wiser to have a framework for cooperation in place. Furthermore, these threats may develop into combined hazards rather than an eruption of isolated single crises. This was amply illustrated by Great East Japan Earthquake in 2011, which combined a tsunami with a nuclear meltdown. Accordingly, measures to meet these hazards must not be fragmented; they must be comprehensive. These challenges demand that countries do more to cooperate. This reality has given birth to the term "global governance," which did not exist 70 years ago. The term was coined when globalization surged as a phenomenon and suggests the need to use the whole spectrum of institutional tools.

In the past 70 years, the United States has been the major driving force of global governance and liberal internationalism. Will it remain a leader? The United States promoted a liberal internationalist vision of world order, democracy, capitalism, openness, the rule of law, and human rights.[38] Has it given up? It seems not. President Obama in his 2016 interview with Jeffrey Goldberg in the *Atlantic* identified himself as an internationalist, among four paradigms of foreign policy including isolationism, realism, and liberal interventionism. Goldberg observes that President Obama is devoted to strengthening multilateral organizations and international norms.[39] Judging from his remarks, it seems that the United States is prepared to lead in the years to come.

Bearing in mind the geopolitical changes under way, liberal institutionalism should not recede but remain relevant. Therefore, institutions that were created at the end of World War II may need to be recalibrated. As described in the introduction, the history of liberal institutionalism dates back to the nineteenth century when the Geneva and Hague conventions were agreed upon. Liberal institutionalism was led initially by the European powers, and then subsequently by the United States in collaboration with the other advanced industrialized countries in the twentieth century. Over the past two centuries, the order created by liberal institutionalism has been challenged by wars and economic upheavals but has persevered. Now standing in the twenty-first century, it seems it is again challenged not by wars, but by changes in the distribution of power with the rise of new powers such as China, India, and Brazil. At the time of the creation of existing institutions, these countries were at the margins of the international society. Today they are renegotiating their positions for more authority, weight, and voice.

The most prominent emerging country is China, which has risen to become the second largest economic power after the United States. China also has been building its military strength at a rapid pace. As China has gained power, it has sought greater weight internationally, commensurate with its comprehensive national power. At the global level, China, for example, has sought reforms from the International Monetary Fund (IMF) and the World Bank, which have been led by Americans and Europeans since their creation. Upon strong urging by China in the aftermath of the world financial crisis, the IMF approved reforms to the increase of voting rights of emerging countries. However, the U.S. Congress was concerned with diluting the influence of the United States at the Bretton Woods institutions and rejected the IMF reforms. Emerging countries were disappointed. After the Chinese announcement of the creation of the Asian Infrastructure Investment Bank (AIIB), however, the U.S. Congress approved the reforms in December 2015. This has revised the United States' share of voting rights down from 16.7 percent to 16.5 percent and Chinese voting rights up to 6 percent from 3.6 percent, making it the third largest in the IMF. India's share of voting rights also increased. The United States still retains its veto. IMF also approved the inclusion of the Chinese renminbi in the Special Drawing Right (SDR) basket in November 2015.[40] Although the reforms have taken longer than China hoped, the IMF reforms were realized with enhanced positions for emerging countries.

Also at the United Nations, China's assessed contribution has risen. Its voice and weight may increase accordingly, although UN votes are not weighted because of its one country, one vote principle. Meanwhile China has responded to UN requests for the dispatch of peacekeepers and has played its role as the permanent member of the Security Council, such as hammering out the resolution on North Korea's test launch of missiles in March 2016. Thus, at the global level, emerging powers have renegotiated their standing and influence in existing institutions but have not taken initiatives to launch new institutions that replace existing ones.

In contrast, at the regional level China has taken more assertive actions. China has taken initiatives to create new institutions and is keen to lead and expand its sphere of influence. In the early 1990s, China was not involved in launching APEC or ARF. Other countries in the region were anxious to engage China in these multilateral institutions. As described previously, China has since turned out to be more aggressive in engaging East Asian institutions. This was first manifested in its swift conclusion of the ASEAN+1 FTA ahead of others. As noted, China favors ASEAN+3 over EAS and opposes the inclusion of the security agenda in EAS because it believes it can exercise more influence with a smaller group than a wider one. China is willing to discuss economic issues in a wider group but security only among Asian members, excluding the United States.

Recently China has also taken leadership in launching new institutions where it was not content with existing institutions. As a first-tier citizen of the international community, China is no longer an object to engage but is instead leading the engagement of others through the institutions it creates. One such illustration is the creation of the Asian Infrastructure Investment Bank (AIIB). China has long been dissatisfied with the Asian Development Bank (ADB), which was founded in 1966 by the initiative of Japan to reduce poverty in Asia through economic cooperation including loans, grants, and technical cooperation. Witnessing the creation of development banks in other regions such as the Americas, Takeshi Watanabe, of Japan's Ministry of Finance, organized his private study group and conceived a plan to create a development bank in Asia in 1963. It was a time when Japan hosted Olympic Games in Tokyo for the first time in Asia and its economy became the second largest in the world four years later. Although Watanabe hesitated to make the proposal himself, as he wrote in his memoirs, the Japanese government eventually proposed the idea and gathered 67 member states including those advanced industrialized countries outside of the region to make the funding base more stable. Although it expected to place the headquarters in Tokyo, Manila won the seat in the election by the 18-member committee. Moreover, Japan did not lead ADB alone but with the United States. The equity contribution of Japan was 15.7 percent versus 12.7 percent from the United States; respective voting rights were 12.8 percent for Japan and 12.7 percent for the United States. Since its founding, the presidents of the ADB have all been Japanese. China was not satisfied and tried to put in place a Chinese president after Haruhiko Kuroda left office to become president of the Bank of Japan but failed. Other members are not necessarily satisfied with consecutive Japanese presidents either but did not object, as the Japanese contribution to the Asia Development Fund has been significant. China has attempted to have more influence including voting rights at the ADB but has not seen much success.

Thus came Xi Jinping's proposal to create the AIIB, which was inaugurated in January 2016 with its headquarters in Beijing. The AIIB is headed by a Chinese official with 56 other members, including European states. Since there are several trillion dollars of demand for infrastructure development fund in Asia, a China-led AIIB is very enticing for countries in Asia. China emphasizes connectivity in its lending policy, reflecting its recent foreign policy to engage surrounding countries. Meanwhile, the United States and

Japan decided to not join the AIIB on the ground that it lacks transparency in its management. Nevertheless, the United States has decided to send an American to AIIB management. Takehikoko Nakao, president of the ADB, expressed his intention to cofinance with AIIB and promote cooperation with ADB field offices. Prime Minister Abe expressed that Japan would invest $110 billion over the following five years to finance infrastructure projects in Asia to respond to such needs. Because the ADB and AIIB are redundant in their missions, there are concerns that competition between the two may loosen lending conditions on human rights, the environment, and labor protections.[41]

China has taken other initiatives, such at the One Belt, One Road (OBOR) Initiative and the Silk Road Fund to enhance connectivity in Greater Asia. As a matter of fact, Japan has taken a similar path to engage with countries in the region. With Central Asia, Prime Minister Ryutaro Hashimoto announced his Silk Road Diplomacy in 1997, through which Japan would strengthen its ties with these countries through ODA and other means.[42] In 2005, Foreign Minister Yoriko Kawaguchi followed up this initiative by launching the Central Asia plus Japan Dialogue, which was further supported by the track two Tokyo Dialogue used since 2007 to strengthen cooperative relations with Central Asian countries. These dialogues have promoted cooperation in agriculture, border control, water resource management, distribution system, and drag control, among others.

With Central Asia, Xi Jinping in his keynote speech at the Fourth Summit of the Conference on Interaction and Confidence Building Measures in Asia (CICA) in May 2014 in Shanghai proposed to create a "new regional security cooperation architecture" and develop CICA into "a security dialogue and cooperation platform" for all of Asia. He proposed China's new regional security concept, accusing U.S. military alliances of being outdated. His proposal was to create a regional security architecture of Asia by Asians, excluding external actors such as United States so that security in Asia should be maintained "by Asians themselves."[43]

Because of these Chinese initiatives, the United States has been seen as more keen to engage in Asian multilateralism, as exemplified by its signing of TAC, participation in EAS, and summit meetings with ASEAN. This is reflected in the U.S. pivot, or rebalancing, to Asia and its efforts to garner support of like-minded countries in the region.[44] At the regional level, one observes multilayered architectures. There are inclusive large institutions such as APEC and ARF, more exclusive plurilateral institutions such as the Six-Party Talks; trilateral institutions such as Japan-China-ROK and Japan-Australia-U.S.; bilateral institutions such as alliances; topic focused institutions either for economic, financial, environmental or security such as ADMM+, TPP, and RCEP; and comprehensive multilateralism, where for example EAS is moving forward to include both economic and security issues. In recalibrating multilateralism in the region, members ought to ask how they want to develop the architecture and toward what purposes.

Meanwhile, there is an observation that powers are competing over institution building, rather than cooperating. On the other hand, institutions once built are difficult if not impossible to dismantle. Having ample layers of institutions, the region may wish to devise ways to refit, reconcile, and utilize existing institutions not for immediate reciprocity but for diffused reciprocity. As an illustration, how TPP will develop hinges on the ratification process and on the willingness of nonparticipants to join the process. The region must also consider how it wishes to develop the Regional Comprehensive Economic Partnership (RCEP), which includes ASEAN+3 members as well as Australia, New Zealand, and India. Rather than excluding certain countries, the prize would be for TPP to include countries in the wider region in order for all the economies to share a common set of rules. Another challenge is how to reconcile with other institutions proposed such as RCEP, the Free Trade Area of the Asia Pacific (FTAAP), and others.

Another leader or convener of regional institutions has been ASEAN. While ASEAN has sat in the driver's seat to promote regionalism and now sits in the center of regional architectures, its future role lacks clarity. Despite their move toward community building, ASEAN member states suffer from rifts. Positions differ over relations with China. Moreover, with active Chinese leadership in regionalism, ASEAN may need to devise a new way to keep its centrality focus. As illustrated in the making of ASEAN+3 and EAS, China and Japan have been portrayed as competing over leadership and initiatives. A region that once lamented a lack of leadership may now suffer from a competition for leadership, in terms of the inclusion or exclusion of the United States and topics to be covered (in particular security) with which framework. For the multilateralism to be recalibrated, the global theater need not be profoundly affected by emerging powers but can adapt. However, the regional theater is crowded with leaders and requires an enlightened approach with a thorough understanding of mutual interests, motives, and diffused benefits.

CONCLUSION

In conclusion, given that such a recalibration is already under way, how ought Japan engage in institution building in the twenty-first century in cooperation with the United States and other like-minded countries? Japan's traditional reactive approach has allowed it to wait and see how the international order is shaped. However, in order to make proactive contribution in shaping the international order, Japan has to design its approach to pay its dues.

Japanese Universalism vis-à-vis Pan-Asianism

In considering a way forward, one needs to go back to the question posed in the introduction of the paper, namely how Japan reconciles its twin foreign policy ideologies Japan has oscillated between universalism and pan-Asianism since the Meiji restoration. Yet as Inazo Nitobe, who served as an under-secretary general of the League of Nations, once put it, this may be partly because Japan has long aspired to be a bridge over the Pacific—a bridge between East and West. This spirit lives on in Japanese multilateral diplomacy. After World War II, Japan's universalism came to the forefront in its pursuit of regaining a legitimate seat in the international community through its engagement in the United Nations and Bretton Woods institutions. Japanese pan-Asianism was not visible in the postwar decades because the region did not witness the construction of a host of regional institutions comparable to Europe. Nevertheless, Japanese Asianism did work in building track two processes such as PBEC and PECC. As Dr. Michael J. Green in his book *Japan's Reluctant Realism* observed, in the early 1990s the growing security threat from North Korea and economic recession at home led to a greater expression of the Japan's Pan-Asianism. With the rise of China, "Japan needs ties in the region to constrain China from moving in [an] unfavorable direction and to sustain Japanese economic growth."[45] This prompted Japan to put more emphasis on Asia in making strategy and policy as illustrated in its efforts to create APEC, ARF, and AMF. However, as APEC has become driven more by the United States and Australia as it failed to lead ARF, Japan turned to universal institutions such as the World Trade Organization (WTO) and IMF in defining Japan's trade and financial agenda. This has placed Japan's focus on universalism over the last decade.[46]

Also in the 1990s, Japan's quest for universalism can be found in its pursuit of common/universal values in its diplomacy, as depicted in the 1996 U.S.-Japan joint security declaration. The preamble of the declaration emphasizes the common values that bond the United States and Japan as allies.[47] Liberal democracy became a key term in Japan's foreign policy beginning in 2006. This led to the Arc of Freedom and Prosperity speech by Foreign Minister Taro Aso in 2006.[48] Aso stated that Japan must go beyond its U.S. ally and neighbors and add a new pillar to its foreign policy, one that engages "the successfully budding democracies that line the outer rim of the Eurasian Continent from an arc." Aso also called for Japan to work with the United States, Australia, India, the European Union (EU), and members of the North Atlantic Treaty Organization (NATO) to expand this zone of rule of law and good governance. This was Japan's new orientation in its foreign policy to advance liberal democracy, human rights, and the rule of law from the Baltics to Southeast Asia. Although the arc concept was not promoted by successor governments of the Democratic Party of Japan (DPJ), the concept to promote liberal democracy and emphasize values in diplomacy still survives in the second Abe administration, even if the phrase "liberal democracy" is no longer used. The *National Security Strategy*, previously cited, specifically mentions that "Japan will strengthen cooperative relations with countries with which it shares universal values and strategic interests."

On the other hand, the WTO, which was expected to govern international rules on trade and investment, has long failed to garner consensus in the negotiations after the Uruguay Round. Countries have set their sights on bilateral and regional FTAs or EPAs. Japan, too, has concluded EPAs with countries in Asia and beyond and has participated in TPP and RCEP for the regional FTA.

It has also been observed that the unresolved legacy of history has held back Japan from its engagement in Asia, despite the official apologies it has offered. While this historical legacy question remains, Japan has made efforts to solve history-related issues. As an illustration, on August 14, 2015, Prime Minister Shinzo Abe apologized by stating, "On the 70th anniversary of the end of the war, I bow my head deeply before the souls of all those who perished both at home and abroad. I express my feelings of profound grief and my eternal sincere condolences." He expressed "deep repentance for the war" and "deep remorse and heartfelt apology" for Japan's actions during the war and pledged to work for peace.[49] Regarding the perennial problem of comfort women that has plagued relations, Japan and the Republic of Korea agreed to resolve the issue in December 2015. Japan issued a sincere apology and agreed to pay $1 billion to a fund to be created in Korea for the surviving victims. The Republic of Korea has reciprocally promised to "finally and irreversibly" end the dispute. The agreement might not have satisfied all the parties concerned, but it has allowed the two governments to move toward future-oriented ties. These events will not resolve the historical legacies from which the region suffers but will at least allow Japan to work for the future with countries in Asia.

Thus, this time around, Japanese pan-Asianism is not receding. Rather, Japan is seeking ways to contribute more in terms of regional cooperation. As mentioned previously, Japan has led and taken initiatives in promoting institutions in the Asia Pacific with varying footprints. It is observed that "Japanese diplomacy since 2010 has sought to strengthen ASEAN's integrity as a bulwark of regional stability, to promote political reform . . . [and] advance ASEAN's own ambition to strengthen its regional role."[50] Prime Minister Abe in his second administration visited all 10 ASEAN members within his first year in office and pledged some $19 billion in aid and loans. He announced his Asia policy and hosted the 10 leaders of ASEAN at a December 2013 summit in Tokyo. Standing within the twenty-first century, as reflected in its *National Security Strategy* document, Japan seeks both universalism and pan-Asianism for its own national interests as well as for regional and international peace, stability, and prosperity. Japan tries to balance both concepts in its diplomacy.

Japan and Multilateralism in the Twenty-First Century

How will Japan reconcile the two identities and embrace its multilateralism in the years to come? The *National Security Strategy* describes its policy in terms of how "Japan will continue to . . . contribute to ensuring [the] peace, stability, and prosperity of the international community more proactively than before, as a major player in world politics and the global economy, while achieving its own security as well as peace and stability in the Asia-Pacific region."[51] The NSS describes its policy as cooperating with the United Nations and other institutions at the global level and to cooperate with individual countries as well as multilateral institutions in the Asia Pacific. The strategy document, acknowledging that multilateral and multilayered structures contribute to the development of mutual understanding and enhancement of joint response capabilities, specifically mentions that it is important to further promote and develop these multilateral initiatives for regional stability.[52] In promoting global and regional cooperation through institutions, Japan needs to join hands with its ally the United States and also with like-minded countries. The venue for the cooperation will not be limited to Asia or the Asia Pacific but may span to Africa where common interest exists for peace, stability, and prosperity.

Collaborating on UN Peacekeeping Operations

Beyond UN Security Council reform, there is room for Japan-U.S. cooperation at the United Nations. One such example is peace-keeping/peacebuilding operations. While the United States has not been active in sending UN peacekeepers, this position seems to have changed. This was demonstrated at the first leaders summit on peacekeeping at the United Nations hosted by Vice President Joe Biden in 2014. Michael O'Hanlon observed that President Barack Obama chose to highlight the future of UN peacekeeping. President Obama, at the second summit in 2015 when he himself chaired the meeting, mentioned that he had issued

> new presidential guidance—the first in more than 20 years—to expand our support for the UN peace operations. We'll work to double the number of U.S. military officers serving in peacekeeping operations. We will offer logistical support; including our unrivaled network of air- and sealift. . . . [W]e'll undertake engineering projects like building air-fields and base camps for new missions. And we'll step up our efforts to help build the U.N.'s capacity, from identifying state-of-the-art technology to offering training to protection against IEDs [improvised explosive devices].[53]

Prime Minister Abe has cohosted the summit with the United States since 2014 and in the second summit mentioned that "Japan has enacted a series of Peace and Security legislations where International Peace Cooperation Act was revised to allow Japanese Peace Cooperation personnel to adapt to diversifying UN PKOs [peace-eeping operations]." Second, he referred to support for the UN Project for African Rapid Deployment of Engineering Capabilities, a pioneering effort along the lines of the triangular partnership model. Japan has contributed approximately $40 million to the UN Secretariat. Engineering personnel from East African Troop Contributing Countries and the Japan Ground Self-Defense Force (JGSDF) are working in Nairobi, Kenya, conducting a training trial on the operation and maintenance of heavy engineering equipment. Japan plans to develop this project into a full-scale training mission. He mentioned that Japan supports the African Peacekeeping Rapid Response Partnership and seeks to develop coordination further.[54] Japan is also supporting training programs to build the capacity of peacekeepers. Japan therefore showed its commitment to the U.S. initiative of reforming and enhancing UN PKOs. The engineering aspect of PKOs is what Japan has been best at and has a good track record in its contribution.

Moreover, the United States did not mention sending combat troops to UN PKOs. If these developments imply a fundamental shift of U.S. policy on UN PKOs, combined with Japan's perennial interest in its cooperation on UN PKOs, this may open another area of cooperation between the two. Furthermore, Japan, as well as the United States, provides capacity building to future peacekeepers in Asia separately. These trained Asian peacekeepers can assist in capacity building efforts elsewhere, including Africa. This combination can generate an amplifying effect.

Promoting Human Security Together

While Japan has been promoting the concept and practice of human security since 1998, the United States has been negative on the concept, calling it a "muddled notion."[55] However, such ambiguity has been resolved by the adoption of UN Resolution A.Res/66/290 on common understanding of the notion. The resolution states that "human security is an approach to assist member states in identifying and addressing widespread and cross-cutting challenges to the survival, livelihood, and dignity of their people." More specifically, the resolution explains that human security includes the right of people to live in freedom and dignity, free from poverty and despair. All individuals, in particular vulnerable people, are entitled to freedom from fear and freedom from want, with an equal opportunity to enjoy all their rights and fully develop their human potential."[56] Japan's *National Security Strategy* document also describes human security in its global issues. In the 2015 Development Cooperation Charter, human security "is the guiding principle that lies at the foundation of Japan's development cooperation." As Akihiko Tanaka observes,

> Threats to human security, if broadly defined, appear so numerous that a simple theory of deterrence and mutual deterrence, which dominated security studies during the Cold War, would not be sufficient. Not only are threats diverse and numerous: possible measures to cope with them seemingly encompass almost all social measures. If threats to human security include sudden financial market fluctuation, earthquakes, epidemics, civil wars, and so on, measures of human security may include all of the policy tools that the entire government bureaucracy disposes of.[57]

Noting the views by many security studies specialists who are critical of such a broad definition and argue for a narrower definition on freedom from fear, Tanaka argues that "human security cannot be reduced to a subset of traditional security studies" and suggests putting the concept in a truly interdisciplinary perspective by creating a new theoretical framework.

The UN resolution gave the international community a common understanding of the concept, which has come to be used by development aid practitioners in the U.S.-Japan Development Dialogue. In fact, the term human security was included in the U.S.-Japan joint statement announced on April 25, 2014, during President Obama's visit to Japan.

> The United States and Japan are committed to promoting peace, stability, and economic growth throughout the world, including in Africa. Through our recently launched senior-level U.S.-Japan Development Dialogue, we are expanding our development cooperation in these areas. Furthermore, the United States and Japan are continuing bilateral policy coordination to address other global challenges and promote

> our common agenda, such as women's empowerment [and] human security.[58]

If this joint statement suggests a policy change on human security by the United States, this opens another avenue for Japan and the United States to cooperate for international peace, security, and prosperity. Such cooperation can take place at the United Nations as well as in the region. Asia-Pacific countries have embraced the notion to varying degrees. The concept would allow regional states to cooperate on humanitarian assistance and disaster relief, peace building, and development assistance. Japan's experience in assisting the Philippines after Typhoon Hainan, along with the United States and other countries, provides lessons for the future. There are also other cases in Asia and Africa that Japan and like-minded countries can integrate efforts into the human security framework.

Engaging Regional Institutions in the Asia-Pacific Region

Turning to the Asia Pacific, how can Japan navigate regional institutions? The region abounds with shared concerns ranging from cybersecurity to refugees to terrorism (especially with the possible return of radicals from training with the Islamic State in Iran and Syria terrorist group), which threaten to undermine political and physical security in the region. Combined efforts are essential. The question is how. Given emerging countries in the region, Japan's strategy should be tailored to fit the changing geopolitical situation and multilateralism under recalibration. Emerging powers are neither comfortable nor satisfied with institutions built when they were smaller powers. In the 1990s, a cliché in the region was that emerging countries could be encouraged to integrate into the existing order through a multilateral process of engagement. This is no longer realistic. These states ask for reform or change of the existing institutions, which were built some time ago. When their requests are not heard, they do not hesitate to create gridlock in the process, such as happened at the Doha Round, and to create new institutions that may overlap with existing ones. It is still not clear whether the states are ultimately aiming to duplicate the existing system or replace the system with new institutions of their own making.

Such a move may destabilize the Asia-Pacific region, forcing countries to choose. This would place smaller powers in a difficult spot in having to choose among options with uncertain consequences. The cases of the Asian Infrastructure Investment Bank (AIIB); the New Development Bank, or so-called BRICS Bank, led by Brazil, Russia, India, China, and South Africa;[59] and the Silk Road Fund come to mind. Behind these moves are appetites to take a leading position and for expanding influence in the region.

At the same time, one should note that some of the initiatives taken by emerging countries meet Asian needs for infrastructure capital. The need is said to be 90 trillion yen (approximately $900 billion), which cannot be met by bilateral ODA, the World Bank, or the ADB alone. When many countries join such an initiative, the new institution gains legitimacy and adds authority to the country that sponsored it. This in turn may reduce the authority of the existing institutions, such as the ADB, which Japan and the United States have led.

Previously, in the case of the EAEG or the AMF, countries in Asia followed the policy of the United States and did not endorse the initiatives. This time around, in the case of AIIB, for example, the United States made overtures to countries to not join. Although Japan opted not to join, many others did join. Japan should consider how it wants to act under these circumstances; its policy needs to be consistent.

Meanwhile, the region has multilayered regional institutions with varying footprints. The task of managing these institutions is daunting. Prime Minister Kevin Rudd of Australia attempted to integrate all these architectures into a single body—the Asia-Pacific Community (APC)—in 2008, but failed due to lack of support from countries in the region, except the Republic of Korea.[60] This episode demonstrates how difficult it is to synthesize regional architectures. Rather than scrapping existing bodies and building new institutions, Japan has to promote institutions that can function as platforms for cooperation. This demands informed idea leadership. In other words, if Japan wants to stay relevant, it has to seek more enlightened approaches to multilateralism.

Second, in contributing to regional institutions, Japan has to join not only with like-minded countries, but to devise a way to get disagreeing countries, including emerging states, on board as well. In promoting regional cooperation for regional public goods, Japan needs to find a key common denominator with the United States and like-minded countries and yet that is still palatable to disagreeing countries. Such a common phrase might be liberal democracy or human security. Such an idea may be difficult to translate into reality, but it ought to be embraced sooner rather than later so that it is hijacked and used for other well-intentioned motives.

Third, the United States has been implementing its rebalance to Asia. This offers further opportunity for Japan to collaborate in the region. For example, in February 2016, the United States hosted the U.S.-ASEAN summit meeting for the first time, which ASEAN member states requested. President Obama stressed, "the United States has increased our maritime security assistance to our allies and partners in the region, improving our mutual capabilities to protect lawful commerce and to respond to humanitarian crisis."[61] All states face imminent maritime threats in the region. This issue has to be solved for regional peace and security. Again, this requires diplomatic skill, knowledge, and innovative ideas. A more enlightened approach to multilateralism is in order.

Challenges for Japan in engaging in recalibrated multilateralism are daunting. Seeking to be a navigator and responsible rider of multilateralism, Japan ought to weave ways to collaborate with its peers both in the West and the East to provide international and regional public goods. This will certainly benefit Japan at a time of ever deepening global interdependence. The path ahead for Japan is the pursuit of enlightened approaches to multilateralism.

NOTES

1. Michael J. Green, *Japan's Reluctant Realism: Foreign Policy Challenges in an Era of Uncertain Power* (New York: Palgrave Macmillan, 2001).

2. Hisaichi Fujita, "Sensohou kara Jindohou he" [From War Law to Humanitarian Law?], in *Nihon to Kokusaihou no 100 nen: Anzen Nosho* [100 Years of Japanese

International Law Research: Focusing on Security], ed. K. Abe (Tokyo: Sanseidou, 2001), 145–146.

3. Akiko Fukushima, *Japanese Foreign Policy: Emerging Logic of Multilateralism* (London: Macmillan Press, 1999), 161.

4. Steward Brown, "Japan Leaves the League of Nations," United Press, February 24, 1933, http://www.johndclare.net/league_of_nations6_news.htm.

5. I thank Dr. Michael Green for this insightful framing.

6. Fukushima, *Japanese Foreign Policy*, 56–57. Emphasis added.

7. Government of Japan, *National Security Strategy of Japan* (Tokyo: Cabinet, December 2013), 58.

8. Ibid., 61–62.

9. Ibid., 60–61.

10. Regarding the details of the domestic debate on "all means at its disposal," see Fukushima, *Japanese Foreign Policy*, 55–59.

11. Assessed contribution is based on Japanese Ministry of Foreign Affairs data available at http://mofa.go.jp/mofaj/gaiko/jp_/pko_yosan.html, accessed March 11, 2016.

12. Government of Japan, *National Security Strategy*, 62–63.

13. Ibid.

14. Kenzo Oshima, "Sengo 70 nen: Kokuren Anpori Kaikaku no Yukute" [UN Security Council Reform after 70 Years], *Kasumigaseki Kai*, July 3, 2015.

15. Ibid., 4–5.

16. Stewart M. Patrick, "The G7 Summit: An Exclusive Club—But a Global Role," *The Internationalist* (blog), Council on Foreign Relations, June 3, 2015.

17. Ibid.

18. Shinzo Abe, "The Bounty of the Open Seas: Five New Principles for Japanese Diplomacy" (press release, Ministry of Foreign Affairs of Japan, January 18, 2013). The speech was scheduled to be delivered in Jakarta. Prime Minister Abe did not actually deliver his speech because he had to cut his schedule short and return to Japan to deal with the Algerian hostage crisis. The full text was subsequently posted. The prime minister has referred to his principles later on at numerous occasions. In the speech, the prime minister "wholeheartedly welcomed the American rebalancing to the Asia-Pacific region."

19. Takaishi Shiraishi, "Abe's Visit to Southeast Asia and Japan's Five New Diplomatic Principles," Nippon.com, January 30, 2015.

20. Fukushima, *Japanese Foreign Policy*, 168.

21. See Ministry of Economy, Trade and Industry, "APEC: The History of APEC," last accessed on March 10, 2016, http://www.meti.go.jp/policy/trade_policy/apec/history/organize.html.

22. Gareth Evans, "Australia Is Catching up with Its Geography" (speech, Institute for Contemporary Asian Studies launch, Monash University, July 19, 1990).

23. See *Canada News*, no. 18, September 18, 1990.

24. Fukushima, *Japanese Foreign Policy*, 139–141.

25. Eiichi Katahara, "Japan's Concept of Comprehensive Security in the Post–Cold War World," in *Power and Prosperity: Economics and Security Linkages in Asia-Pacific*, ed. Susan L. Shirk and Christopher P. Twomey (Piscataway, NJ: Transaction Publishers, 1996), 214.

26. Fukushima, *Japanese Foreign Policy*, 143–144.

27. James A. Baker III, "America in Asia: Emerging Architecture for a Pacific Community," *Foreign Affairs* 70, no. 5 (Winter 1991): 1–18.

28. Mie Oba, *Jusoteki Chiiki toshiteno Asia* [Asia in a Multi-layered Architecture] (Tokyo: Yuhikaku, 2014), 119–121.

29. Ibid., 130.

30. East Asia Vision Group, *Towards an East Asia Community: Region of Peace, Prosperity and Progress* (Jakarta: ASEAN, October 2001).

31. Issue papers prepared by the government of Japan, June 25, 2004.

32. Junichiro Koizumi, "Japan and ASEAN in East Asia: A Sincere and Open Partnership" (speech, Singapore, January 14, 2002).

33. Junichiro Koizumi, "Japan and Australia toward a Creative Partnership" (speech, Asia Society, May 1, 2002).

34. "Kuala Lumpur Declaration on the East Asia Summit," December 14, 2005. Emphasis added.

35. "Kuala Lumpur Declaration on the ASEAN Plus Three Summit, Kuala Lumpur," December 12, 2005. Emphasis added.

36. Ministry of Foreign Affairs of Japan, "Joint Statement of the 40th Commemorative Japan-ASEAN Summit," press release, December 14, 2013.

37. G. John Ikenberry, "The Future of Multilateralism: Governing the World in a Post-Hegemonic Era," *Japanese Journal of Political Science* 16, no. 3 (2015): 400.

38. Ibid., 408.

39. Jeffrey Goldberg, "The Obama Doctrine," *Atlantic*, March 11, 2016.

40. International Monetary Fund, "IMF's Executive Board Completes Review of SDF Basket, Included Chinese Renminbi," press release, November 20, 2015.

41. "Chugoku shudo no AIIB to Nihon shudou no ADB wo kurabete wakarukoto" [Comparison of China-Led AIIB and Japan-Led ADB], *Newsweek Nihon ban*, October 23, 2015.

42. See Christopher Len, "Understanding Japan's Central Asian Engagement," in *Japan's Silk Road Diplomacy: Paving the Road Ahead*, ed. Christopher Len, Uyama Tomohiko, and Hirose Tetsuya, (Washington, DC and Stockholm: Central Asia-Caucasus Institute and Silk Road Studies Program, 2008), 31–46.

43. Xi Jinping (remarks at the Fourth Summit of the Conference on Interaction and Confidence Building Measures in Asia, Shanghai, May 21, 2014).

44. Author's interview with U.S. state department official, March 2016.

45. Green, *Japan's Reluctant Realism*, 26, as well as based on Dr. Green's comments to an earlier draft of this chapter in March 2016.

46. Green, *Japan's Reluctant Realism*, 27.

47. Ministry of Foreign Affairs of Japan, "Japan-U.S. Joint Declaration on Security–Alliance for the 21st Century," press release, April 17, 1996.

48. Taro Aso, "Arc of Freedom and Prosperity: Japan's Expanding Diplomatic Horizons" (speech, Japan Institute of International Affairs, Tokyo, November 30, 2006).

49. Cabinet of Japan, "Statement by Prime Minister Shinzo Abe," press release, August 14, 2015.

50. Daniel M. Kliman and Daniel Twining, *Japan's Democracy Diplomacy* (Washington, D.C.: German Marshall Fund of the United States, July 2014), 25.

51. Government of Japan, *National Security Strategy*, 38.

52. Ibid.

53. Michael O'Hanlon, "Time for American GIs to Become UN Peacekeepers," *National Interest*, October 5, 2015.

54. Shinzo Abe, "Statement by His Excellency, Mr. Shinzo Abe, Prime Minister of Japan At the 2nd Leader's Summit on Peacekeeping" (speech, UN Trusteeship Council Chamber, New York, September 28, 2015).

55. James Jay Carafano and Jane Smith, "The Muddled Notion of Human Security," Backgrounder #1966, Heritage Foundation, September 1, 2006.

56. UN General Assembly Resolution, A.Res/66/290, September 10, 2012.

57. Akihiko Tanaka, *Toward a Theory of Human Security*, JICA-RI Working Paper (Tokyo: JICA Research Institute, 2015), 4–5.

58. Ministry of Foreign Affairs of Japan, "The United States and Japan: Shaping the Future of the Asia-Pacific and Beyond," press release, April 25, 2014.

59. See "BRICS Bank announces first set of loans," *Bricks Post*, April 16, 2016, http://thebricspost.com/brics-bank-announces-first-set-of-loans/#.WBqP43fCPow.

60. Frank Frost, *Australia's Proposal for an "Asia-Pacific Community": Issues and Prospects* (Canberra: Parliament of Australia, December 1, 2009).

61. Barack Obama, "Remarks by President Obama at Opening Session of the United States-ASEAN Summit" (speech, Sunnylands Center, Annenberg Retreat, February 15, 2016).

6. DEVELOPMENT ASSISTANCE FOR INCLUSIVE GROWTH: A FIELD FOR JAPAN-U.S. COOPERATION?

Akiko Imai

INTRODUCTION

This chapter considers the feasibility of active cooperation between Japan and the United States in the provision of development assistance in Asia, with a focus on economic inclusiveness. It argues that addressing social issues (such as women's empowerment) based on a horizontal division of labor between the two countries—and with the involvement of the business community and civil sector in both countries—could advance regional human dignity and quality growth. At the same time, such a broad-based, cross-sector approach would strengthen the Japan-U.S. alliance and enhance their soft power projection in Asia.

THE IMPORTANCE OF INCLUSIVENESS

Rapid economic growth in the emerging economies of the Asia Pacific has boosted both production power and purchasing power, leading to the emergence of a huge middle class in the region. However, improvements in countries' public administrations and markets have tended to neglect the needs of their sizable low-income populations. Low-income populations are additionally burdened by the poverty penalty, a term which refers to the paradoxical finding that the poor tend to pay more than their richer compatriots for the basics of everyday life. As a result, an increasing number of people are being left behind, unable to enjoy the benefits of growth.

A similar phenomenon has been seen in the United States, Japan, and other advanced economies as they have grown over the course of the past century. In India, China, and elsewhere in Asia, a region which accounts for half of the world's population, the number of disadvantaged people is substantial. In today's rapidly globalizing economy, the engines of growth are shifting at a dizzying pace and there is little hope that conditions will improve through the trickle-down effect that may have operated in the past. Achieving inclusive growth is an issue that needs to be addressed with deliberate action.

According to the Asian Development Bank (ADB), after years of rapid growth, many Asian countries have advanced to middle-income status, but the transition to higher income brackets can be a slow process. As the ADB notes, "More than 15 countries globally have been 'middle income' for at least the past 50 years, including three in Asia—Malaysia, the Philippines, and Thailand. . . . China became an upper-middle-income country in 2010." Based on its research, the ADB recommends that middle-income economies focus on "upgrading and diversifying their industrial bases" to avoid the middle-income trap.[1]

Inclusiveness is not just a concern for individual countries: its scope transcends national borders and its root causes must be addressed by the international community as a whole. A chronic situation in which human dignity is slighted and basic human needs are not met contributes to the growth of crime and terrorism, and exacerbates the effects of pollution and natural disasters. The resulting weakening of domestic structures can pose a threat to neighboring nations' security.

Recognizing this, countries extending development assistance have been making inclusiveness part of their strategic agendas, seeking to enhance the social capital of recipient countries by creating the foundations for sustainable livelihoods and freeing the disadvantaged from dependency on aid.

ADDRESSING SOCIAL ISSUES THAT GOVERNMENT
ALONE CANNOT RESOLVE

The Japanese public has tended to think of environmental protection, human rights, women's advancement, and addressing poverty mainly as the job of the government, but the situation has become more complex. There are limits on the capability of government to deal with public issues. In order to cope with these complex and interconnected issues, we must call on the resources of society as a whole. For example, when we consider the factors contributing to poverty in Japan—including unemployment, dysfunctional families, and lack of education—it is apparent that the Ministry of Health, Labor, and Welfare, which is notionally responsible for government policy in this area, cannot resolve the issues on its own. Cooperation with businesses and communities is essential. In the case of large-scale disasters like the Great East Japan Earthquake of March 2011, the impact is felt in every aspect of people's lives and cannot be addressed solely within the framework of public administration.

Figure 6.1   Development Assistance Flows from OECD Development Assistance Committee (DAC) Countries

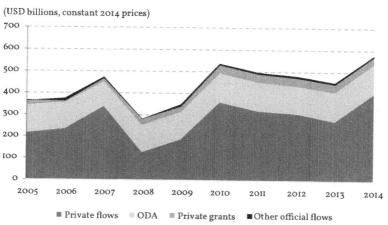

(USD billions, constant 2014 prices)

■ Private flows   ▨ ODA   ▨ Private grants   ■ Other official flows

Data source: Organization for Economic Cooperation and Development.

Every social problem is an amalgam of diverse individual woes and its solution must involve efforts not just by the government, but by all sectors and strata of society based on a sense of their respective responsibilities. In particular, heightened expectations are being directed at the corporate sector, a result of its organizational and technological strengths and funding clout. It is hoped that corporations can bring these strengths to bear in initiatives to fight infectious diseases, such as HIV/AIDS, malaria, and Ebola, as well as to tackle issues like women's empowerment, access to education, and climate change.

Data from the Organization for Economic Cooperation and Development (OECD) on financial flows to developing countries show a marked increase in funds from the private sector around the year 2000. These private flows have exceeded official flows—consisting mainly of official development assistance (ODA)—since 2005 (see Figure 6.1). As of 2012 they were roughly 2.5 times the latter in volume.[2] As noted in Japan's 2014 ODA White Paper, developing countries (particularly in Africa), which formerly depended almost entirely on ODA for external funding, are now drawing attention from the private sector as investment targets and consumer markets.[3] This is a welcome result of globalization.

Another factor behind the increased emphasis on the role of the private sector in development assistance is the deterioration of public finances in donor countries. This is a salient concern in Japan, with its sizable and growing national debt. Restoring fiscal discipline is a key priority for the current administration. When Prime Minister Shinzo Abe decided in November 2014 to postpone a scheduled tax hike in the face of a sagging economy, he made a point of excluding the possibility of further postponement beyond April 2017, even if the economy remains weak. To underline his administration's commitment to cutting the deficit, he called a snap general election in December 2014 to secure a renewed popular mandate for his economic policy agenda.

Restoring fiscal discipline will be a difficult task in view of the many demands for public funds. The aging of Japan's population is causing an inexorable rise in social welfare costs. Efforts to revitalize local economies rely heavily on revenue sharing from the national government. Meanwhile, the success of Abenomics (the government's signature economic policy initiative) may depend on generous outlays for public works. In contrast to these types of government spending, whose effects are readily visible to the public, the budget for ODA is a hard sell.

This is not just a Japanese concern. The difficulty of securing funding for public services in the face of severe budgetary constraints is evident throughout the developed world. In Britain, public services have been overhauled and are being provided not just by the national treasury, but by tapping financial resources from society as a whole, including the private sector, local communities, and the voluntary sector.

Japan is no longer in a position to hand out the fruits of rapid economic growth to other countries in hopes of promoting its own national security. Instead it needs to fulfill its responsibilities as a member of the international community through initiatives that will promote peace and stability around the world without draining its own coffers.

However, this does not mean that Japan can stop increasing its ODA outlays. National security and supporting global peace are primarily the responsibilities of government. Private funds should be seen as a powerful complementary tool for maximizing the impact of ODA, but not as a substitute.

JAPAN'S NEW DEVELOPMENT COOPERATION CHARTER

Many in Japan's development community hope for the promotion of economic inclusiveness and the cooperative combination of public and private funding. In February 2015, the government set forth its current stance with a Cabinet decision approving a new development cooperation charter (replacing the ODA charter first adopted in 1992 and last revised in 2003).[4]

The Cabinet decision referred to development as "encompass[ing] such activities as peacebuilding and governance, promotion of basic human rights and humanitarian assistance," and noted the importance of "securing the stable foundations of development such as peace, stability, rule of law, governance and democratization." It referred to "inclusive development that leaves no one behind," declaring, "It is important to ensure that a wide range of stakeholders in society, including women, participate in every phase of development." It further noted, "The world is facing more diverse and complex challenges. These challenges are increasingly widespread, transcending national borders as the world is increasingly globalized. In a world faced with such difficult challenges, individual countries are required more than ever to exercise ingenuity and take action."

The decision also considered the role of nongovernmental actors:

> In the present international community, various actors, including private companies, local governments and nongovernmental organizations (NGOs), play an increasingly important role in addressing development challenges and supporting sustained growth of developing countries. It is therefore important to mobilize a wider range of resources that are not limited to ODA. In this context, ODA, as the core of various activities that contribute to development, will serve as a catalyst for mobilizing a wide range of resources.

Other noteworthy features of the new charter are its explicit references to "inclusive, sustainable and resilient growth" as "essential for the stable growth of the global economy as a whole," and its explicit references to Japan's national interests. The charter concludes, "To secure its national interests, it is essential for Japan, as a 'Proactive Contributor to Peace' [and] based on the principle of international cooperation, to work together with the international community, including developing countries, to address global challenges."

Up to now, Japan's ODA policies have addressed specific countries or issues. The new charter introduces policies that target entire regions. As Tokyo Foundation research fellow Ippeita Nishida observed in a November 2014 review of a preliminary draft of the charter, the existing set of policies "did not match the actual situation in regions like Southeast Asia and Africa, where the emergence of regional and quasi-regional institutions is coming to have an increasing political impact."[5] Nishida also referred to "the need for measures to address cross-border developments such as large-scale natural disasters, infectious diseases, terrorism, and piracy," a need that forms the basis for the adoption of policies for wide-area assistance.

The new charter notes, "Asia is a region that has a close relationship with Japan and high relevance to its security and prosperity," and it declares that Japan will extend development cooperation to the region on the basis of this recognition. The charter continues: "Japan will support the establishment of the [Association of Southeast Asian Nations (ASEAN)] Community as well as the comprehensive and sustained development of ASEAN as a whole." It refers specifically to seven focus areas:

1. development of both physical and nonphysical infrastructure;
2. reduction of disparities within both the region and individual countries;
3. strengthening assistance to the Mekong region;
4. assistance in human resource development and other areas for countries that have already achieved a certain level of economic growth to keep them from being caught in the middle-income trap
5. strengthening of disaster risk reduction and disaster relief capabilities
6. promotion of the rule of law, which constitutes the basis for stable economic and social activities
7. cooperation with ASEAN as a regional organization to support united efforts to tackle its challenges

Promoting inclusiveness with a view to global security and to humanitarian concerns involves efforts to address structural social issues that cross national borders. It is an undertaking that cannot be accomplished through assistance from a single nation, even if private-sector funding sources and civil-sector organizations work in cooperation with the government. While each donor nation has its own philosophy of development assistance set forth in a charter or similar mission statement, the most effective and resource-efficient approach is to cooperate by participating in multilateral undertakings like the United Nations Global Compact and cross-sector initiatives led by organizations like the World Economic Forum.

With respect to the ASEAN region, where we hear much talk of the importance of policy cooperation in areas like maritime security and the rule of law, the long-established alliance between Japan and the United States can make a major contribution in the field of development assistance.

THE POTENTIAL OF JAPAN'S CORPORATE SECTOR
AS A PARTNER IN ADDRESSING SOCIAL ISSUES

Overview of Japan's Corporate Social Responsibility
and Social Issues

In the pursuit of Japan-U.S. cooperation in development assistance, how can we draw the two countries' private funds and civil sectors into the process using a horizontal division of labor? Here I will consider the role of Japanese firms' corporate social responsibility (CSR) programs in addressing social issues. In 2014, the Tokyo Foundation conducted a survey of CSR programs of 218 companies (213 of which responded), consisting largely of corporations listed on the First Section of the Tokyo Stock Exchange.

The most commonly cited areas in which companies view their domestic CSR activities as having produced good results are: (1) environmental protection; (2) cultural preservation, including efforts to keep local festivals going and to pass on traditional culture to the next generation; and (3) maternal health, including improved maternity leave programs (see Table 6.1). Outside of Japan, while environment-related efforts are by far the most commonly cited as successful, Japanese companies are undertaking initiatives in areas conducive to economic and social inclusiveness, addressing issues like poverty, human rights, and public health.[6]

Table 6.1 Cases Deliberated vs. Actions Taken by Issue

	Deliberation > Action			Deliberation ~ Action			Deliberation < Action		
	Issue	Cases	Actions	Issue	Cases	Actions	Issue	Cases	Actions
In Japan	None			Women	149	144	Poverty	20	31
				Maternal health	154	150	Child poverty	36	50
				Other	133	132	Culture	129	154
				Environment	193	200	Human rights	132	146
				Public health	57	62			
Overseas	None			Women	63	62	Poverty	59	74
				Other	79	78	Maternal health	38	48
				Human rights	81	84	Culture	58	70
				Environment	134	140	Child poverty	64	75
							Public health	52	61

Data source: Tokyo Foundation CSR Survey 2014.

The survey also looked at companies' level of interest in resolving particular issues and the areas in which they have taken concrete action. It does an issue-by-issue breakdown of the answers to two questions: "How much interest do you have in resolving the following social issues?" and "Which of the following issues are you taking concrete initiatives to resolve?" The results of this breakdown are interesting. For many issues, the number of companies that have taken concrete action is higher than the number that have held repeated meetings to discuss the matter. When it comes to business management, a company would never skip the deliberation process, including advance studies, but in the case of CSR they often move straight to implementation.

Of course there are some areas, such as the environment, in which Japanese companies are proficient and have been active for many years. On issues like these, it is quite conceivable that companies completed their deliberations at an earlier stage and were already at the implementation stage at the time of our survey. However, the results overall seem to indicate a strong bias toward action. This is also seen in the areas of poverty and human rights, which are fields in which companies will be expected to do more in the future.

Asked whether their company engages in dialogue with various stakeholders as part of its CSR activities, many of the respondents said they did (see Figure 6.2). However, when it comes to the nature of the dialogue partners, the survey found that the number of companies conducting dialogue with socially vulnerable persons—the actual or prospective beneficiaries of their activities—was quite small, much smaller than the numbers for other types of stakeholders. Companies are used to conducting business-related dialogue with their customers but have relatively little experience in non–business-related dialogue with counterparts in the government and social sectors. They may also hold back from dialogue with groups that advocate particular ideologies or causes because they want to avoid the reputational risk of getting drawn into the fray over controversial issues.

Respondents were also asked whether their company is working together with others in conducting CSR activities. As with dialogue,

Figure 6.2　Dialogue with Stakeholders

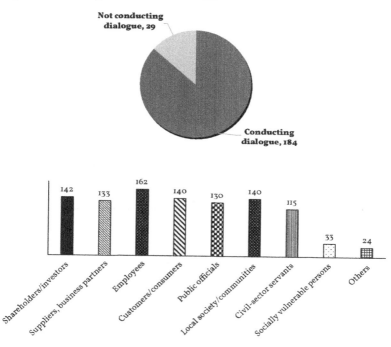

Data source: Tokyo Foundation, "Overview of CSR in Japan: Ideals, Intentions, and Realities at Advanced Companies," September 2014.

a major portion of the surveyed companies reported that they are (see Figure 6.3). Asked what they expected from their partners, the respondents cited help in such areas as finding or proposing social issues to address, acquiring deeper knowledge of these issues and know-how for their resolution, and increasing their capacity to implement programs.

Meanwhile, the scale of philanthropic outlays by Japanese corporations is substantial, partly as a result of long encouragement from business organizations, such as the Keidanren (Japan Business Federation). According to Keidanren surveys, total expenditures for corporate philanthropic activities came to 173.5 billion yen in fiscal

Figure 6.3　Areas of Cooperation

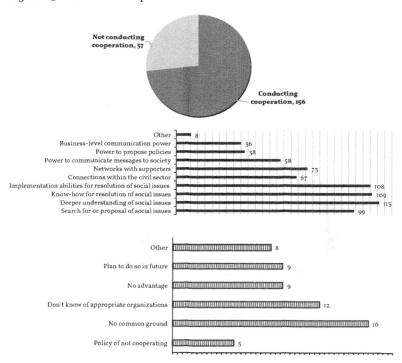

Data source: Tokyo Foundation, "Overview of CSR in Japan: Ideals, Intentions, and Realities at Advanced Companies," September 2014.

year (FY) 2013. Of the average 482 million yen outlay per company (up 8.1 percent year-on-year), 72 percent was donated.[7]

In sum, Japanese companies are providing large amounts of money for philanthropic purposes, but they have relatively little know-how or experience in identifying issues to address as a corporate citizen or in directly implementing projects to address such issues. As a result, they tend to rely on others—such as civil-sector organizations and social enterprises—to do this for them. If Japanese firms want to truly fulfill their social responsibilities, it is not enough to simply outsource their CSR activities to external partners and publish the results in their sustainability reports. They need to work together with their partners to determine which social issues that they will address, carefully consider how best to tap their in-house resources, craft plans accordingly, and then implement them with their partners' cooperation, thereby building up their own store of know-how and experience. This sort of cross-sector approach could enhance the learning curves of Japanese businesses.

Meanwhile, some Japanese companies that are operating internationally have already started initiatives to address social issues through their own business operations based on the concept of creating shared value. We also find companies that are looking at various possibilities in the area of bottom of the pyramid (BOP) business not as CSR activities, but as a field for business investment. In a recent survey of 943 major listed and unlisted corporations conducted by business publisher Toyo Keizai, 95 companies, or about one-tenth of those surveyed, reported that they were already involved in BOP business. Another 79 said they were considering entering this field. Furthermore, out of 768 companies that responded to a question about how they viewed BOP business activities, 364 replied that it was primarily philanthropic, 276 identified it as offering future business opportunities, and 55 said it was already a commercial business for them.[8]

The Need for Japanese Companies to Implement CSR in Asia

According to a survey of overseas business activities by Japan's Ministry of Economy, Trade, and Industry (METI), as of the end of FY 2012 (March 31, 2013), Japanese corporations had a total of 23,351 overseas affiliates—44.6 percent in manufacturing industries and 55.4 percent in nonmanufacturing industries. By region, the number of overseas affiliates in Asia had risen to 15,234, accounting for 65.2 percent of the total (up 2.4 percentage points from a year earlier) (see Table 6.2 and Figure 6.4).[9]

Given the large and growing scale of Japanese presence in the economies of the region, Japanese companies are facing expectations that they will behave responsibly as good corporate citizens.

Table 6.2   Distribution of Overseas Affiliates by Region

	FY 2011	FY 2012
All regions	19,250	23,351
	100.0%	100.0%
North America	2,860	3,216
	14.9%	13.8%
Asia	12,089	15,234
	62.8%	65.2%
China	5,878	7,700
	30.5%	33.0%
ASEAN4	3,111	3,776
	16.2%	16.2%
NIEs3	2,238	2,605
	11.6%	11.2%
Other Asian countries	862	1,153
	4.5%	4.9%
Europe	2,614	2,834
	13.6%	12.1%
Others	1,687	2,067
	8.8%	8.9%

Note: ASEAN4 is a grouping of four members of the Association of Southeast Asian Nations: Thailand, Malaysia, Indonesia, and the Philippines. NIEs3 refers to three of the region's four so-called newly emerging economies: Singapore, Taiwan, and South Korea.
Data Source: Ministry of Economy, Trade, and Industry, "Summary of the 43rd Basic Survey on Overseas Business Activities," July 2013.

In addition, as Japanese firms serving domestic markets have globalized their operations, they have had to substantially adjust their mindsets with respect to CSR. In the case of the pharmaceuticals industry, for example, the global-scale regrouping and consolidation process has brought mergers with foreign companies, with the result that people at corporate headquarters in Tokyo must deal directly with issues that previously never crossed their minds. These include issues associated with conflict minerals, military

Figure 6.4   Trends in Distribution Ratio of Overseas Affiliates by Region

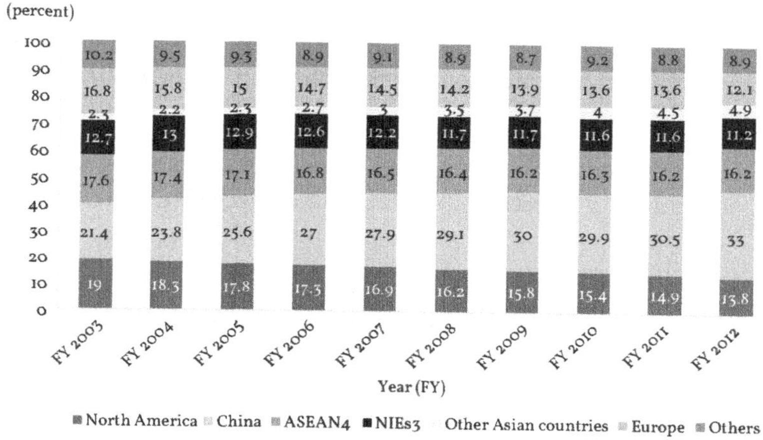

(percent)

■ North America China ■ ASEAN4 ■ NIEs3   Other Asian countries Europe ■ Others

Data source: Japanese Ministry of Economy, Trade, and Industry, "Summary of the 43rd Basic Survey on Overseas Business Activities," July 2013.

clashes, terrorism, absolute poverty, and infectious diseases. As Japanese corporations have encountered these challenges, they have rapidly developed a more sophisticated awareness of CSR.[10]

With the rise in the global share of foreign direct investment going to emerging and developing countries, the impact of regulations in the target countries on the business activities of international corporations has increased, and free trade agreements between states have come to include provisions concerning conditions for business. The Trans-Pacific Partnership (TPP) agreement now being negotiated is expected to contain sections on the environment and labor. For Japanese and U.S. companies the conditions imposed under such agreements should not be particularly difficult to meet, but it is clear that firms extending their operations internationally will need to heighten their sensitivity to the social issues in the countries where they set up shop.

Meanwhile, governments of many Asian countries are expecting the CSR activities of companies in the region to play an important role in contributing to the establishment of a fair and just business environment and to sustainable growth, as stated in 2008 Asia-Pacific Economic Cooperation leaders declaration.[11]

What kind of concrete CSR initiatives are companies expected? A recent article from CSR Asia, a Hong Kong–based advisory and research organization, identified the following as key issues:

- climate change and water
- supply chains, human rights, and slavery
- community investment and the emerging development agenda
- corporate governance, disclosure and anticorruption
- wealth gaps, poverty and social imbalances[12]

Looking at this agenda, we can see that the issues relate directly to the building of a base for sustainability in market economies.

To sum up, Japanese corporations are expected to behave responsibly in the Asian countries in which they operate and must conduct risk management accordingly. They are aware that they do not have sufficient know-how in identifying areas to address and implementing corresponding initiatives. In areas such as human dignity and inclusiveness, the agenda they are expected to address coincides with key elements of Japan's development cooperation charter and major themes of Japan-U.S. development cooperation, meaning that there is a strong possibility of meaningful collaboration between the business community and government organs.

ASIAN VIEWS OF JAPAN AND THE UNITED STATES

We have seen that Japanese corporations have a strong interest in Asia, but how are the people of other Asian countries likely to respond to Japan-U.S. development cooperation?

A survey of seven ASEAN member countries (Indonesia, Malaysia, Myanmar, Philippines, Singapore, Thailand, and Vietnam) commissioned in 2014 by Japan's Ministry of Foreign Affairs (MOFA) found that views of Japan were generally positive. Asked to choose which of 11 countries (Australia, Britain, China, France, Germany, India, Japan, New Zealand, Russia, South Korea, or the United States) they considered most reliable, 33 percent picked Japan, more than twice the figure for the United States, which came in second at 16 percent. Japan placed top by this measure in every one of the surveyed countries except the Philippines and Singapore, where the United States was first and Japan second. This suggests that the environment is good for Japan-U.S. cooperation with ASEAN.

In addition, 92 percent of the respondents from all seven countries affirmed that Japan was playing an active role in the development of Asia, 89 percent believed that Japan's economic and technological cooperation was helpful for their country's development, and 95 percent indicated that they welcomed the expansion of Japanese companies into ASEAN. When respondents were asked to name the areas in which they wished for Japan to contribute to the ASEAN region, "economic and technological cooperation" came first (cited by 77 percent), followed by "trade promotion and private investment" (67 percent). This indicates that respondents had expectations for the economic aspects of Japan's international contribution.[13]

Regarding Asian views of the United States, the Pew Research Center's 2014 global attitudes and trends survey found that views of both the United States and Japan tended to be highly favorable in ASEAN countries. In countries where ratings of the United States were not so high, such as Indonesia and Malaysia (59 percent and 51 percent, respectively), Japan's figures were higher (77 percent and 75 percent), illustrating the potential for cooperation that takes advantage of each country's respective strengths.

According to the same survey, within ASEAN, Indonesians and Malaysians cite the United States as the greatest threat (though Indonesians also say that the United States is their greatest ally, revealing the ambivalence of their feelings).[14] However, in the MOFA survey cited above, Indonesians and Malaysians most often cited Japan as the most important partner for ASEAN, with citizens of both countries ranking it ahead of China and the United States by large margins.

In light of these findings, it seems likely that Japan-U.S. development cooperation can help improve views of the United States in countries with highly favorable views of Japan—and that in places where both are viewed favorably, such cooperation should further enhance views of the United States and Japan as open economies and democratic countries.

Japan-U.S. complementarity should not be limited to public diplomacy; it should also be tapped to address concrete social issues. Support packages should take into account each country's respective strengths and weaknesses, along with the similarities and differences between them and the Asian countries they seek to assist.

In terms of government organization, Asian countries generally have centralized systems more similar to that of Japan than the federal system of the United States. They are also subject to similar types of natural disasters, notably earthquakes, typhoons, and tsunamis. As a result, they are likely to find it easier to use Japan as a model for assigning disaster-related responsibilities to government organs. In the United States, by contrast, it is the corporate sector whose power and flexibility have stood out in cases like the response to Hurricane Katrina. The resources that the corporate sector has deployed have, in some cases, been on the scale of a small country's annual gross domestic product (GDP).

When it comes to helping Asian countries develop their national and local government disaster-response systems, the Japanese government could take the lead, while the U.S. business community could serve as the model for emergency humanitarian aid and supply of resources. With respect to community rebuilding and inclusive growth for post-disaster recovery, it would be ideal to draw on collaborative efforts by social innovators from both countries. This sort of cooperation was seen in many cases and worked to good effect in the response to Japan's March 2011 earthquake and tsunami.

THE CURRENT STATUS OF JAPAN-U.S. COOPERATION IN DEVELOPMENT ASSISTANCE

On February 10, 2015, the second Japan-U.S. development dialogue was held in Tokyo (the first was held in Washington in 2014). This senior-level dialogue was launched on the basis of an agreement reached during Vice President Joseph Biden's visit to Japan in December 2013. The "Fact Sheet on United States-Japan Global Cooperation"[15] issued on that occasion referred to humanitarian assistance/disaster relief and development assistance (particularly focused on Southeast Asia, the Pacific region, Africa, global health, the Millennium Development Goals, and empowering women) as critical areas of cooperation. The dialogue is being conducted based on the view that "enhanced cooperation on development between the two countries will widen the scope of the bilateral relations and contribute to constructing more multi-faceted and strengthened bilateral relations."[16]

The agenda shows a deliberate effort to incorporate the combined soft power of the two countries into their development assistance policies. According to the joint press release issued after the session, the two sides discussed "a broad range of development priorities and challenges on issues such as global health including the Ebola outbreak, women's and girls' empowerment, the Post-2015 Development Agenda, disaster risk reduction, as well as opportunities for development assistance cooperation in Asia Pacific, Africa, and other regions."[17]

By way of historical context, although Japan was a modern state even in the period before World War II, its postwar economic growth was accompanied by its development as a democracy and, over the seven decades since the end of the war, it has become one of the world's biggest economic powers without once engaging in military conflict. For the United States, which supported Japan's development through the postwar occupation, Japan is a natural partner in supporting and advancing the development of Asia based on freedom and democracy.

Japan can serve as one model for developing countries seeking to free their people from poverty. Japan's development assistance was originally implemented as a form of war reparations, but it is now in a position to draw on its experience in using the fruits of economic growth to strengthen its own social capital as a tool for assisting other countries' development.

THREE REQUIREMENTS FOR DEVELOPMENT COOPERATION

As a practical matter, it will not be easy for Japan and the United States to collaborate on development assistance. Given the large number of actors involved, making plans, deciding on roles, and moving ahead in tandem toward shared goals may prove quite difficult.

The idea that I would like to advance, however, is not the creation of an aid-giving club where everybody plays together, but an increase in the options that actors have to tap their particular strengths, enhance networks linking specialized participants on both sides through collaboration in development, and better meet the needs of developing countries.

Social problems that hinder quality growth in developing countries are persistent because in most cases they are rooted in the norms, values, and culture of a society. They are adaptive challenges for the society.[18] To mobilize people to change in the desired direction, broader social awareness is required, and the best way to promote the inclusion of many strata of society is through a cross-sector approach. Promoting social reforms, in other words, is better pursued through open and multifaceted efforts at various levels by various actors using various approaches, while a siloed approach is liable to be wasteful. To enable cross-sector development cooperation, a minimum of three requirements need to be met.

1. Actors must share a common theory of change for creating collective impact.
2. They must agree on a modality of public-interest funding versus for-profit funding.
3. There must be leaders capable of setting clear roles and responsibilities for the various actors and projects.

I will discuss these requirements in the following sections.

The Importance of Collective Impact

In seeking to marshal the power of multiple actors to achieve a common goal, it may be helpful to refer to the concept of collective impact presented by John Kania and Mark Kramer in an article under that title in the *Stanford Social Innovation Review*. As the authors note, "Social problems arise from the interplay of governmental and commercial activities, not only from the behavior of social sector organizations. As a result, complex problems can be solved only by cross-sector coalitions that engage those outside the nonprofit sector."[19]

Kania and Kramer identify five conditions for the achievement of collective impact:

1. *Common agenda*: "Collective impact requires all participants to have a shared vision, one that includes a common understanding of the problems and a joint approach to solving it through agreed upon actions."[20]

2. *Shared measurement system*: "Collecting data and measuring results consistently . . . across all participating organizations not only ensures that all efforts remain aligned, it also enables the participants to hold each other accountable."[21]

3. *Mutually reinforcing activities*: Participants' activities must be differentiated while still being coordinated "through a mutually reinforcing plan of action."[22]

4. *Continuous communication*: Consistent and open communication is needed across the many players to build trust, ensure mutual objectives, and create "common motivation."[23]

5. *Backbone support*: "Creating and managing collective impact requires a separate organization and staff with a very specific set of skills to serve as the backbone for the entire initiative" and coordinate participating organizations and agencies.[24]

Among these, the key determinant of success lies in whether prospective partners can establish a solid support backbone. To create collective impact, the backbone organization has to provide leadership in areas like good governance, strategic planning, community involvement, and evaluation and improvement. A variety of organizations, including funders, nongovernmental organization (NGOs), government bodies, and steering committees, are able to accomplish these tasks. Each has its pros and cons; the important issue is whether the backbone institution can exercise "adaptive leadership; the ability to mobilize people without imposing a pre-determined agenda or taking credit for success," and secure long-term funding that will support resilient results through gradual improvements over time.[25]

Among prospective Japanese aid providers, the Japan International Cooperation Agency (JICA), Japanese grant foundations, and corporate CSR activity organizers are well-qualified to serve as backbone organizations. However, because of the long practice of isolated-impact approaches, where funders seek the most promising solution individually and evaluation and reporting systems are often designed to isolate a particular organization's impact, it will be very hard for any of them to catalyze connections for collective impact initiatives.

In the Japanese aid community, there have already been numerous initiatives between JICA and international institutions, international NGOs, civil society groups, small- and medium-sized enterprises, BOP initiatives, and foreign private-sector bodies. Many experts involved with these initiatives have expressed concerns about the increased transaction costs of such initiatives.

Two major bottlenecks can be seen here. First, each player has its own mandate and accountability to pursue with its limited human and capital resources. Hence, it is often much more cost- and time-effective for an organization to work separately according to its own theory of change.

A theory of change provides a divided, layered set of goals toward the ultimate solution of social issues. For example, in the case of hunger, three stages are set: shifts in community capacity and conditions; community impact; and formation of country-led strategies. In each stage, there are subsets of goals relating to the causes of poverty, income generation, gender and human rights, health and nutrition, education and literacy, and so on.[26]

One would hope to see a common theory of change for the united impact of partners. In a collective impact approach, however, backbone organizations must understand that each partner—whether government agencies, grant foundations, or other possible partners—has its own theory of change, but these do not preclude cooperation. While these partners all "have unique priorities . . . [they] increasingly work together to align their investments."[27]

In "The Role of Grantmakers in Collective Impact," Lori Bartczak points out the need for network officers, who spend time in-country learning about places, ongoing good work, and potential partners.[28] In a collective impact approach, grantmakers or funders must function alongside other actors, rather than solely acting according to their own theory of change.

There are some examples of best practices that can be found in past cases of cross-sector collaboration. The KokoPlus project in Ghana was led by the Japanese food company Ajinomoto Group. In 2009, the CSR division of the company started to play a role as a backbone organization of an effort to improve the infant mortality rate through their food business. Ajinomoto had a strong incentive to commit to this project because it was started in order to commemorate the company's centenary anniversary and nutritious food promotion matched the corporate mission of improving people's dietary lives.

Koko, a traditional Ghanaian porridge for infants made from fermented corn, lacks some important nutritional elements when measured against World Health Organization (WHO) standards. Ajinomoto decided to develop a supplement for the porridge, called KokoPlus, developed jointly with the University of Ghana and an NGO, the International Nutrition Foundation. This eventually led to the formation of a league of 11 organizations including JICA, the U.S. Agency for International Development (USAID), Care International, Ghana Health Service, and a local social marketer.[29]

In another good example of the collective impact approach, the Nippon Foundation, one of Japan's largest grantmaking organizations, has been acting as a backbone organization to eliminate leprosy worldwide for about 35 years in partnership with WHO, national and local governments, and health institutions. By bringing these actors together to generate collective impact on an ongoing basis, the initiative has reached the point where eradication is only one country away.[30]

Meanwhile, the Bill and Melinda Gates Foundation has undertaken a number of breakthrough initiatives for global health, one of which is a partnership with JICA to eradicate polio in Pakistan. According to an estimate from the Global Polio Eradication Initiative, JICA provided about 4.9 billion yen (approximately $65 million) in loans to the government of Pakistan in 2011–2013.[31] The government worked closely with the WHO, United Nations International Children's Emergency Fund (UNICEF), and Rotary International to immunize children against polio through oral vaccination. When Pakistan met the milestone of their 2011 National Emergency Plan for Polio Eradication successfully, the Gates Foundation decided to repay the cost of the program to JICA on behalf of the Pakistani government, declaring, "The aim of this mechanism is to support the government of Pakistan's commitment to polio eradication without imposing a financial burden."[32] It hopes to apply the same mechanism to other similar health initiatives. Bill Gates has a strong commitment to making the foundation a backbone organization for global health promotion. This pay for success approach was created on a top-down basis through almost two years of coordination with JICA. Grant foundations may have some advantages in making a long-term commitment to forming and sustaining a coalition backed by strong expertise and plentiful resources, but in both leprosy and polio eradication the real key to success was the application of collective impact to their initiatives.

For various players in both the public and private sectors to join a collective impact initiative, a backbone organization has to find the best equilibrium point for each player, that is, the point where the benefits of participation outweigh the associated transaction costs. In cases such as those described above involving Ajinomoto and the Nippon Foundation, these groups had strong organizational incentives to commit as backbone organizations. Public organizations require strong top-down policy mandates in order to commit to cooperation in the face of high transaction costs.

Technical challenges are another bottleneck that raise transaction costs for public funding. For nongovernmental and private partners, coordination with Japanese public funding sources can be time consuming. Some prospective partners, especially foreign organizations, give up on the idea of utilizing Japanese public funds in the face of complicated documentation procedures and bureaucratic supervision, which, from the standpoint of public officials, is mandated by taxpayers.

Although "siloed governmental structures and processes are counterproductive," according to Thaddeus Ferber and Erin White, public-sector accountability to taxpayers can in some cases "allow and incentivize partnerships to create each of the five conditions necessary to achieve collective impact."[33] There are moves to make government more collective-work-friendly, such as the White House Office of Management and Budget's reporting requirement reform: "They now allow private organizations that receive money from more than one agency to consolidate their report."[34] In Japan, JICA and other governmental agencies could serve as catalysts for more private-public partnerships. But here too, it will be necessary to increase flexibility and streamline the many rules and reporting requirements that currently exist. In order for the two countries to cooperate in development assistance, it will be essential for them to harmonize the requirements their governments impose for this sort of partnership by displaying greater flexibility.

To tap more private money and expertise for social change, public and nongovernmental organizations funding social change will have to nurture adaptive leadership to catalyze connections among prospective partners, which is discussed later.

The Issue of Funding

Concerning the issue of funding to make collective impact possible, Kania and Kramer observe that funders:

> must be willing to let grantees steer the work and have the patience to stay with an initiative for years, recognizing

that social change can come from the gradual improvement of an entire system over time, not just from a single breakthrough by an individual organization. This requires a fundamental change in how funders see their role, from funding organizations to leading a long-term process of social change. It is no longer enough to fund an innovative solution created by a single nonprofit or to build that organization's capacity. Instead, funders must help create and sustain the collective processes, measurement reporting systems, and community leadership that enable cross-sector coalitions to arise and thrive.[35]

This thinking matches the concept of patient capital advocated by Acumen, a nonprofit global venture fund.

How patient must private-sector social investment be? In a time of fiscal retrenchment for many advanced countries' governments, hopes are that social investment will take up some of the slack in outlays for social projects. In Britain, Prime Minister David Cameron has been promoting public-private partnerships (PPPs) and private finance initiatives (PFIs), using the slogan "Small Government, Big Society." Britain's PFIs have their roots in the privatization drive undertaken by former prime minister Margaret Thatcher. Her Japanese counterpart, former prime minister Yasuhiro Nakasone took similar moves, privatizing Japan's national railways and Nippon Telegraph and Telephone. However, spending by the Japanese government has continued to swell in the twenty-first century and there seems to be no consensus on the level of return to be expected from social investment.

Harvard Business School professor Michael Chu, who served as chief executive officer (CEO) of ACCION International, a nonprofit that was a global pioneer in the field of microfinance, notes the need to consider the actual effects of impact investing. Chu came up with a schematic representation of the desired outcome of impact investing, presenting business risk on the y-axis and ecosystem risk (a function of the coherence of the business) on the x-axis. According to Chu, success for a social enterprise represents movement from the upper right quadrant of his diagram (where business and ecosystem risk are high) to the lower left quadrant (where these risks are low). In other words, the goal is to move from a state of reliance on support from venture capital to one of being able to draw on commercial funding sources. Producing this sort of outcome is the "impact" of successful impact investing.[36]

Meanwhile, philanthropic funds and CSR outlays serve as sources of social enterprises regardless of their position on the ecosystem risk axis. This categorization makes it possible to establish a certain degree of order in framing the timing and roles of different types of support—government funds, CSR outlays, socially responsible investment (SRI), and others—in keeping with their source's respective objectives. This sort of funding traffic control may also facilitate the formulation of strategies for achieving collective impact.

However, in order to achieve sustainable, quality growth, it will ultimately be necessary to bring social enterprises into commercial markets. If social problems are resolved and people's incomes increase, this will lead to the growth of new markets for the corporations involved in collective impact initiatives. Hence, even if CSR activities are used for impact investment, they should also be undertaken with an eye to future business potential.

One good example is seen in the efforts of the American firm Procter & Gamble (P&G), which noted the future potential of the Asian market in the 1980s and started distributing sanitary napkins to female students in rural villages and elsewhere. The company also provided maternity education on a philanthropic basis to them as they matured. These female students have since grown up and become mothers, and their entire families are now the target for P&G's daily-use products. This company's success was based on the congruence between its CSR activities and its business strategy, and it has given it a strong lead over its Japanese competitors, which did not recognize the region's potential until after the twenty-first century.[37]

Another example is Japan's Benesse, a company in the education business, which in May 2013 established the Benesse Social Investment Fund with an investment quota of $15 million and a mandate to promote the spread of education in developing and low-income countries. The impact investment activities of this fund reportedly include investment in an Indian information and communications technology (ICT) educational enterprise. What made Benesse look overseas was the decline in Japan's population. Facing the continued shrinking of its domestic market, the company decided that the way for it to keep growing was by tapping the future potential of emerging countries with growing populations and rising middle classes. It has undertaken a marketing innovation of sorts: instead of moving to extend its own operations directly to emerging countries by matching its educational products to their particular needs, it is seeking to acquire know-how by working together with local education-related social enterprises and NGOs through this fund.

In Japan, meanwhile, non–cash-based, small-scale financing has picked up in response to the March 2011 Great East Japan Earthquake. One interesting example is the Securité Disaster Region Support Funds initiative launched in 2011 by Music Securities, a Japanese crowdfunding firm. The firm establishes funds for narrowly targeted recovery projects, soliciting participation in units of 10,800 yen (roughly $90). Half of the money is treated as a donation and the remaining half as an investment. One of the funds was targeted at Yagisawa Shoten, a 200-year-old soy sauce maker in Rikuzentakata, a city devastated by the post-quake tsunami. Yagisawa Shoten's factory and storehouse were destroyed, but traces of the precious cultures used in making the company's soy sauce were found in some of the broken barrels left behind by the receding waters, and the company's ninth-generation CEO was determined to rebuild. A sum of 150 million yen (about $1.3 million) was raised from 4,250 investors, and about four years after the disaster the company was able to resume production and sales. The scheme was distinctive in that it drew on the patience of investors and shared the returns with them in an unorthodox manner—not with stocks or cash dividends, but with bottles of the company's newly brewed soy sauce. Similar financing initiatives have provided funds to support many specific projects in the quake-struck region.

Developing Leaders: Capacity Building for Development Cooperation

The next issue for development cooperation is to develop leaders capable of turning an assemblage of actors with disparate talents and strengths into a coherent body for the promotion of social change. The United States is advanced in this respect as colleges and graduate schools offer many courses to train such leaders, and the qualities required for leadership in social innovation are a subject of lively discussion.

Jeffrey Kushner, a partner at Social Venture Partners Boston who became involved in venture philanthropy after 20 years of experience at hedge funds and other financial services firms, identifies the qualities required of grantees as sustainability, relevance, and leadership, noting that they must be "addressing a critical need in a novel and effective manner" and need to have a "credible, effective, and coachable leader."[38]

Meanwhile, Acumen and other social innovators addressing issues in developing countries cite qualities such as empathy, resilience, and commitment as keys traits of the leaders they seek. They provide intensive training in the United States before sending these leaders to work on social projects in developing countries. Here I would like to introduce the partnership between Acumen and my organization, the Tokyo Foundation.

Since 2009, we have been sending Japanese to participate in the Acumen Global Fellows Program in the United States to receive leadership training in both technical skills and skills relating to adaptability and self-reform. The areas covered include commitment to dealing with social issues, tolerance toward others and teamwork, basic knowledge of marketing and corporate finance, and the ability to communicate using precise, detailed content in English. For example, workshops held in rural Massachusetts and disadvantaged neighborhoods in New York City focus on such topics as adaptive leadership, storytelling, and empathy building. The program also includes liberal arts content, such as readings from Eastern and Western philosophers. The training aims to foster values such as generosity, accountability, humility, audacity, and integrity. Participants then go on to spend eight months in a developing country working at social ventures, where they gain experience in management for stability and scaling up of operations. There they soon realize how difficult it is to be empathetic with local people and the importance of social leadership education.

The focus in the United States is on creating superior leadership development programs that bring together diverse participants in small groups to learn and grow in friendly competition. The 10 Acumen fellows each year come from every continent, and their backgrounds are reflected in their leadership styles. Japanese participants are accustomed to having their abilities assessed with paper tests, but leadership training of this sort is something they often find more challenging. Even so, in every one of the past five years a Japanese woman has been among the 10 people selected to participate in this program out of a field of about 1,000 applicants from around the world. These women have gone on to work in various capacities in developing countries: leading the scaling-up of a private-sector ambulance service in India; joining with local farmers in a drive to increase rice yields in Ghana; and putting the management of a microfinance enterprise in Nigeria on a solid footing.

Japanese leaders generally get good marks for working from morning to night together with local staff members, for their egalitarian attitude, and for their diligence in arranging for the wheels to keep turning smoothly after their departure. This Japanese-style leadership has been noted frequently in JICA assistance projects in Asia. It is generally based on long-term participatory observation of the recipient countries. Some observers suggest that this approach has its roots in Japan's own experience as an aid recipient after World War II: the amount of aid was huge, but the results were mixed, and the social memory of this experience may in part explain why Japanese aid workers take time for observation and focus on working together with recipients. This sort of leadership can function effectively when Japan and the United States jointly provide social innovation services to local communities in Asia.

The women who have returned to Japan after completing their training overseas, having acquired precious leadership skills in the process, have, without exception, been unable to find positions in Japan where they can put their experience and skills to full use. In almost every case they have ended up returning to developing countries and resuming social enterprise work. Japanese society has experienced brain drain by being unable to add the know-how of these leaders to its store of capabilities. The story is much the same for those who serve in JICA's Japan Overseas Cooperation Volunteers (JOCV) program.

A major factor behind this phenomenon is the lack of occupational mobility among the government, business, and civil sectors in Japan—mobility that would allow people to take the experience they have gained in one sector and apply it in another. When young Japanese graduate from college or complete their graduate studies, the standard next step is for them to join a business or other organization. Job hopping is frowned on, and taking on more than one job at a time is strongly discouraged. Even today, the ideal is to serve a single master faithfully—to join an organization and stay with it—for one's entire career. Consequently, the skills that people acquire over the years tend to be specific to the organization they work for, and opportunities to achieve diverse capabilities are limited to members of top management. This applies to organizations of every type: business corporations, government agencies, and NGOs. The members of these sectors work in their respective worlds with their respective strengths, and there are few mechanisms to create a pool of human resources capable of leading cross-sector innovation.

Moves are afoot though to allow people to hold on to their employment status while accumulating outside experience within Japan or abroad, and to then use their new perspectives in promoting corporate and social reforms. One example is JICA's

Private-Sector Partnership Volunteer System, which helps companies develop human resources for their international business development and serves as a framework for support of local enterprises.

In Western countries, meanwhile, frameworks like Global Pro Bono and International Corporate Volunteers have spread. These allow employees of global corporations and other firms to spend time as volunteers in developing countries, where they apply their professional skills and leadership abilities to addressing social issues.[39] For global corporations that see the world as their market, personnel who can exert leadership with empathy are key resources for business development. Moreover, the experiences of volunteers in developing countries are said to help them serve as catalysts for innovation in their own organizations. These frameworks are also beginning to spread to Japan. At present, there is a social enterprise in Japan that is partnering with a group in the United States that acts as an intermediary for frameworks like Global Pro Bono in order to arrange for employees of Japanese companies to take part.

If Japanese ODA is to serve as a catalyst for mobilizing a wide range of resources, we should focus first on capacity building through the development of human resources capable of leading the development and implementation of initiatives in a manner that avoids increasing transaction costs. This should also promote the domestic and international mobility of Japanese personnel in the field of economic development, who have up to now been concentrated solely within JICA.

A good starting point for building the number of collective impact innovators in both Japan and the United States would be the establishment of joint adaptive leadership training programs between similar organizations, such as USAID and JICA, Keidanren and the Conference Board, a not-for-profit organization of US businesses and unions, and Japanese Government Pension Investment Fund and California Public Employees' Retirement System (CalPERS), which could then be expanded into cross-sector trainings (see Box 6.1).

BOX 6.1 CASE STUDY OF U.S.-JAPAN CROSS-SECTOR ALLIANCE FOR GIRLS' EDUCATION

On March 19, 2015, U.S. first lady Michelle Obama and her Japanese counterpart Akie Abe announced a pledge "to strengthen bilateral cooperation in helping girls around the world receive an education, especially in developing countries." The U.S. government will spend $250 million supporting girls' education in the 2015–2016 budget and the Japanese government will outlay 42 billion yen (approximately $35 million) or more under its official development assistance program during the next three years. According to the *Japan Times*, "Under the partnership, the Japan International Cooperation Agency . . . and the U.S. Peace Corps, both sending volunteers abroad, will formalize cooperation and 'focus in particular on advancing girls' education through cooperation on the ground in countries around the world.' "[1]

This is a good starting point for cross-sector cooperation among U.S. and Japanese aid agencies, companies, civil sectors, and local social entrepreneurs to create a collective impact on girls' education in Asia.

Both the U.S. and Japanese governments have policy incentives; the United States has already started the Let Girls Learn initiative under Michelle Obama, and women's empowerment is one of the key policies that Prime Minister Abe promotes. Women's empowerment is high on the agenda and the Asia Pacific is the priority region for the U.S.-Japan Development Cooperation Dialogue. Japan's new development cooperation charter aims "to mobilize a wider range of resources" and ODA "will serve as a catalyst for mobilizing a wide range of resources."[2]

There are several supporting reasons. First, girls' education will be a powerful drive in the push for inclusive growth in developing countries in Asia. But women's issues are deeply rooted in the norms, values, and culture of a society. For a

BOX 6.1 (continued)

society to adapt and change, broader social awareness is required, and the best way to boost the awareness of the many different strata of society is through a cross-sector approach.

Second, over 60 percent of Japanese corporate affiliates are located in Asia and hope to include lower- and middle-income populations in their value chains. Some educational companies have even established a social investment fund for education in Asia. As the supply chain extends, Japanese corporations will have to raise their awareness as responsible corporate citizens in developing countries.

Third, Japan has been developing women's education for hundreds of years, even when social norms did not allow girls to learn with support from Western girls' schools. This is evident in Japan's many schools for girls' and women's middle and higher education. In addition, increasing numbers of young Japanese professionals are entering the field of social innovation. This may provide an avenue for Japan's commitment to mobilize younger generations in traditional Asian societies.

Fourth, USAID and JICA desire cross-sector cooperation not because it is a top-down policy but because broader participation from the United States, Japan, and recipient countries will allow USAID and JICA to obtain further support from taxpayers, as well as people in the developing countries. Finally, U.S.-Japan cooperation on social issues may create a new form of shared soft power in Asia.

Transaction costs of partnering may be justified using the rationale above. However, there are some bottlenecks, such as how to create backbone organizations. One possibility is to use the 1.5 track framework, like the Tomodachi initiative, by establishing one common campaign identity and creating a backbone organization under its name. A philanthropic foundation with expertise in collaborative work, development in Asia, or education for the poor is desirable.

BOX 6.1 (continued)

The backbone organization needs a professional with multisector experience to play the role of a transmission gear in the middle of different actors with different stakes. Under this director, the backbone organization would need a fund manager to assemble public and private funding and donations. Private funds should be raised in such forms as social investment, cloud/group funding, or CSR outlays (including in-kind donation such as educational/daily materials and tools). After the March 2011 earthquake, information technology–based social finance gradually expanded and now represents a useful tool, especially among younger Japanese. Corporations that seek new markets in Asia, too, have to share fair membership fees so that they will be able to collect data and information through the collaborative work.

To empower this public-private partnership, aid experts from governments and international institutions, as well as local professionals with social enterprises operating in Asian countries, will play core roles in proposing a theory of change for cross-sector initiatives with clear benchmarks and exit strategies. Some technical improvements will also be required to decrease transaction costs, such as standardizing reporting formats.

USAID and JICA have long accumulated expertise with overseas volunteers. Involving the business community will give younger generations the opportunity to train leaders, which is the best way to invest in people. Under the new charter, the Japanese government is encouraging use of ODA money as a catalyst, so this sort of arrangement would be well-advised.

[1] Masaaki Kameda, "Michelle Obama, Akie Abe Pledge Bilateral Effort for Girls' Education," *Japan Times*, March 19, 2015.
[2] Ministry of Foreign Affairs of Japan, "Cabinet Decision on the Development Cooperation Charter," February 10, 2015.

CONCLUSION

I have considered the prospects for Japan-U.S. development cooperation in Asia and some of the issues that will need to be addressed to make it succeed. Japan and the United States have different types of soft power, and the strengths and weaknesses of the two countries' government, business, and civil sectors also differ. Pulling these disparate elements together in a partnership to promote inclusive growth in the region will not be a simple undertaking. If we hope to achieve this, the most urgent task at hand is developing the human resources capable of leading the process.

Through joint cross-sector efforts by Japan and the United States in the field of social innovation, we will be able to enhance inclusive growth in developing Asian economies, create a new format for U.S.-Japan cooperation in pursuit of collective impact, and deploy this cooperation as a form of shared soft power in Asia. We will need to examine the strengths and limitations of various actors in both countries—including aid institutions, companies, the civil sector, social enterprises, and social investors—and match their strengths and weaknesses appropriately. Where do we start? By putting together concrete projects for collective impact and fostering leaders capable of advancing such cross-sector endeavors—people who have empathy, respect diversity, and are able to exert adaptive leadership.

NOTES

1. Asian Development Bank, "Middle-Income Trap Holds Back Asia's Potential New Tiger Economies: 12 Things to Know," March 14, 2014. According to ADB president Takehiko Nakao, the middle-income trap may affect countries that have grown rapidly and are "no longer benefiting from low wage/low cost production but still cannot compete against countries producing higher value-added products." Takehiko Nakao, "Statement by ADB President Takehiko Nakao at the Japan-LAC Business Forum" (speech, Tokyo, Japan, April 24, 2014).

2. However, it should be noted that a fair share of private flows are remittances, which, because they flow directly to individuals living in the developing countries, usually do not contribute to societies as a whole.

3. Ministry of Foreign Affairs of Japan, *Japan's Official Development Assistance White Paper 2014: Japan's International Cooperation* (Tokyo: MFA, December 2015), 23.

4. Ministry of Foreign Affairs of Japan, "Cabinet Decision on the Development Cooperation Charter," February 10, 2015.

5. Ippeita Nishida, "'Hatten kyoryoku taiko' seifuanwo yomu—sono tokucho to kadai" [Reading Japan's Development Cooperation Charter—Features and Themes], Tokyo Foundation, November 13, 2014.

6. Tokyo Foundation, "Overview of CSR in Japan: Ideals, Intentions, and Realities at Advanced Companies," September 10, 2014.

7. Keidanren and 1% (One-Percent) Club, "Summary of the Survey on Corporate Philanthropic Activities in Fiscal 2013," October 14, 2014.

8. Toyo Keizai, *CRS Company Survey* (Tokyo: Toyo Keizai, Inc., 2015), 16 (in Japanese).

9. Ministry of Economy, Trade, and Industry, "Summary of the 43rd Basic Survey on Overseas Business Activities," July 2013, 2.

10. Takeda Pharmaceutical is a good example. For details, see Tokyo Foundation, "Overview of CSR in Japan."

11. Asia-Pacific Economic Cooperation, "Lima Declaration: A New Commitment to Asia-Pacific Development," November 23, 2008.

12. Richard Welford, "What's Hot for CSR in Asia in 2015?," CSR Asia, January 7, 2015.

13. Ministry of Foreign Affairs of Japan, "Opinion Poll on Japan in Seven ASEAN Countries," April 18, 2014.

14. Pew Research Center, "Global Opposition to U.S. Surveillance and Drones, but Limited Harm to America's Image," July 14, 2014.

15. White House, "Fact Sheet on United States–Japan Global Cooperation: Meeting Modern Challenges," December 3, 2013.

16. Ministry of Foreign Affairs of Japan, "Japan–United States of America Relations," February 10, 2015.

17. Ministry of Foreign Affairs of Japan, "Joint Press Release: The Second Japan-U.S. Development Dialogue," February 10, 2015.

18. In their book *Leadership on the Line*, Ronald A. Heifetz and Marty Linsky of the Harvard Kennedy School write, "People have problems for which they do . . . have the necessary know-how and procedures. We call these technical problems. But there is a whole host of problems that are not amenable to authoritative expertise or standard operating procedures. They cannot be solved by someone who provides answers from on high. We call these adaptive challenges because they require experiments, new discoveries, and adjustments from numerous places in the organization and community. Without learning new ways—changing values, attitudes, behaviors—people cannot make adaptive leap necessary to thrive in the new environment. The sustainability of change depends on having the people with the problem internalize the change itself." Ronald A. Heifetz and Marty Linsky, *Leadership on the Line: Staying Alive through the Dangers of Leading* (Cambridge, MA: Harvard Business School Press, 2002), 13.

19. John Kania and Mark Kramer, "Collective Impact," *Stanford Social Innovation Review* 9, no. 1 (2011): 36–41.

20. Ibid.

21. Ibid.

22. Ibid.

23. Ibid.

24. Ibid.

25. Fay Hanleybrown, John Kania, and Mark Kramer, "Channeling Change: Making Collective Impact Work," *Stanford Social Innovation Review* (January 2012).

26. The Hunger Project, "Global Theory of Change," April 7, 2011.

27. Lori Bartczak, "The Role of Grantmakers in Collective Impact," *Stanford Social Innovation Review*, supplement (Fall 2014): 8–10.

28. Ibid.

29. Ajinomoto Group, "The Ghana Nutrition Improvement Project," 2013.

30. Nippon Foundation, "Elimination of Leprosy," 2016.

31. Japan International Cooperation Agency, "The Japan International Cooperation Agency (JICA) and the Bill & Melinda Gates Foundation Announce Partnership on Polio Eradication" (press release, August 18, 2011).

32. Ibid.

33. Thaddeus Ferber and Erin White, "Making Public Policy Collective Impact Friendly," *Stanford Social Innovation Review*, supplement (Fall 2014): 22–23.

34. Ibid.

35. Kania and Kramer, "Collective Impact."

36. Michael Chu, "Case Study with Prof Michael Chu" (presentation, 16th Annual Social Enterprise Conference, Harvard Business School, Cambridge, MA, February 14, 2015).

37. Kazuki Moribe, "P&G kara Manabu Ajia no Chaneru Kouchiku" [Learning from P&G, Building Channels in Asia], *Nikkei*, November 17, 2014.

38. "Building Momentum: How to Achieve Scale, Sustainability and Social Impact" (workshop at 16th annual Social Enterprise Conference, Harvard Business School, Alston, MA, February 14, 2015).

39. Alice Korngold, "International Corporate Volunteering: Profitable for Multinational Corporations," *Huffington Post*, March 7, 2014.

INDEX

Italic page numbers refer to tables and figures.

ABOUT THE EDITORS AND AUTHORS

Michael J. Green is senior vice president for Asia and holds the Japan Chair at CSIS in Washington, D.C. He also holds the chair in modern and contemporary Japanese politics and foreign policy at the Edmund A. Walsh School of Foreign Service at Georgetown University in Washington, D.C.

Zack Cooper is a fellow with the Japan Chair at CSIS in Washington, D.C.

Akiko Fukushima is a professor in the School of Global Studies and Collaboration at Aoyama Gakuin University, Japan.

Akiko Imai is a professor at Showa Women's University in the Business Design Department and a public communications adviser for the Tokyo Foundation, Japan.

Jun Saito is a project professor at the Graduate School of Business and Commerce, Keio University; a senior fellow at the Japan Center for Economic Research (JCER); and a special adviser to the Cabinet Office, government of Japan.

Kazuya Sakamoto is a professor at Osaka University's Graduate School of Law and Politics in Japan.

Yoshihide Soeya is a professor of political science and international relations at the Faculty of Law of Keio University in Japan.

Yoko Takeda is chief economist at the Mitsubishi Research Institute in Tokyo, Japan.

ABOUT CSIS

For over 50 years, the Center for Strategic and International Studies (CSIS) has worked to develop solutions to the world's greatest policy challenges. Today, CSIS scholars are providing strategic insights and bipartisan policy solutions to help decisionmakers chart a course toward a better world.

CSIS is a nonprofit organization headquartered in Washington, D.C. The Center's 220 full-time staff and large network of affiliated scholars conduct research and analysis and develop policy initiatives that look into the future and anticipate change.

Founded at the height of the Cold War by David M. Abshire and Admiral Arleigh Burke, CSIS was dedicated to finding ways to sustain American prominence and prosperity as a force for good in the world. Since 1962, CSIS has become one of the world's preeminent international institutions focused on defense and security; regional stability; and transnational challenges ranging from energy and climate to global health and economic integration.

Thomas J. Pritzker was named chairman of the CSIS Board of Trustees in November 2015. Former U.S. deputy secretary of defense John J. Hamre has served as the Center's president and chief executive officer since 2000.

CSIS does not take specific policy positions; accordingly, all views expressed herein should be understood to be solely those of the authors.